An Accidental Life

Volume 4, 1980-1990:
Farewell to
Science Fiction

by Charles Platt

Copyright 2021 by Charles Platt
First edition, October 2021
ISBN: 9798500201829

Special thanks to
David Streitfeld,
Rudy Rucker,
and Gregory Benford.

Some of the text in this volume previously appeared in more prolix versions in *The Patchin Review, REM, Science Fiction Guide, The Magazine of Fantasy & Science Fiction, Thrust, Interzone, Cheap Truth,* and *My Love Affair with Harlan Ellison.*

Some names of former girlfriends have been changed, out of respect for the probable preferences of those involved. All events are described accurately, so far as I am aware, using contemporaneous notes and diary entries.

For Rudy and Sylvia

Foreword

For me, the 1980s were a carefree decade. I had failed so totally as a writer, a husband, and a parent in 1978, subsequent difficulties seemed trivial.

I met a variety of peculiar women through personal ads, owned a succession of impractical cars, relocated in Los Angeles for a while, and then regrouped in New York City. After failing to write an historical tetralogy that would have tripled my annual income, I created a humorous cat book, which did quite well in several foreign editions.

When I self-published a zine of gossip and polemical rants named *The Patchin Review*, this brought me into contact with many people in the science-fiction field, including the so-called cyberpunks, who coalesced but then dispersed.

Book publishing remained the center of my personal and professional life, but I also wrote mathematical-graphics software which I sold by mail order to universities, and I taught computer classes at a local college. This was more fun than it sounds.

Eventually I managed to write a serious novel that got good reviews, but after that I said farewell to science fiction.

Anxiety attacks and acute tendonitis were a serious problem near the end of the 1980s, but overall, the decade really was carefree, relatively speaking.

1980

Skepticism and Self-Esteem

I had delivered my book *Dream Makers*, containing twenty-nine profiles of people who wrote science fiction. Now that this obligation was fulfilled, I lay on my worn-out couch in my 100-year-old apartment and reflected on lessons learned.

The people I had profiled were writing science fiction successfully. Could I do that?

Two of their capabilities seemed a bit daunting:

1. Suspension of Disbelief. Usually we think of this as something that readers must do, but writers have to do it too, which I found difficult because so many ideas in science fiction are hard to believe. To take an extreme example, in one of Piers Anthony's books he wrote seriously about a giant orange telepathic talking spider. I felt too encumbered by my own skepticism to write anything like that.

2. Self-Worth. Novelists are so arrogant, they expect to be paid to describe characters and events that don't exist. I was doubtful that my science-fiction ideas were good enough to be worth money, and my doubts discouraged me from starting work on a novel, let alone finishing it. I was impeded by lack of literary self-esteem.

Fortunately I didn't have to address these issues right away, because I found a diversion that was much more interesting: Computer programming.

No More Gunk

Like so many addictions, it seemed harmless enough at the beginning. All I wanted was to free myself from the drudgery of using a typewriter.

I was sick of retyping whole pages just to add a couple of sentences, and exasperated by the ritual of using a tiny brush to paint over small typographical errors with white gunk. I had read about word processing, which seemed an obvious answer to my needs—but at the beginning of 1980, I couldn't find hardware that would do the job properly at a sane price.

If I was willing to pay an insane price, I could follow the example of Barry Longyear, a popular wordsmith who boasted that he had bought a Wang 2200 PCS-III. This was a dedicated office system selling for $6,500 in 1980 dollars (without a printer).

Then there was Jerry Pournelle, who owned a Compupro computer housed in a massive steel box. It had a separate keyboard, a separate monitor, and a couple of heavy-duty eight-inch floppy disk drives in another massive steel box, and probably cost as much as the Wang. Systems such as these wouldn't even fit on my desk, quite aside from being unaffordable.

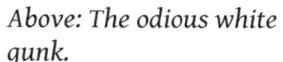

Above: The odious white gunk.

Far left: Early Wang word-processing console using a built-in cassette drive for text storage.

Near left: Wang 2200 PCS-III with dual eight-inch floppy drives.

Bottom left: An Wang, father of word processing.

Below: Compupro with dual eight-inch floppies boxed under the main unit.

So far as I could tell, no other writers, yet, were composing text on a screen. I would have to proceed on my quest alone, so I turned to the Yellow Pages, which referred me to a retail business in the East 50s. This turned out to be a small storefront where I found myself looking at a beige plastic box calling itself an apple][.

A sales person greeted me with an oddly beatific smile. "Hi! How are you, today?" he asked.

People in New York didn't normally talk or act this way, and I wondered if there was something wrong with him. Still, that was not my concern. "Can this computer do word processing?" I said.

"Sure!" He inserted a flexible black plastic square into a slot, and typed something on the keyboard. After a short wait, a little white rectangle winked into life in the top left corner of the screen. "Go ahead, type something!"

When I looked at the keyboard, I found that the quote marks, ampersand, parentheses, colon, and plus sign were all in odd places. Maybe I could get used to that, but some keys were missing entirely. There were no square brackets, and ironically this meant that the apple][wouldn't allow anyone to type its own name.

When I did start typing, I discovered that the text on the screen had colored fringes, making it hard to read. Also, it was all in capital letters. I searched for the Caps Lock key—and—there wasn't one. Then I held down the Shift key, but it didn't do anything. A suspicion dawned on me. "Does this computer display lowercase letters?"

"No." The sales person's smile persisted, undimmed. "You can toggle inverse video to distinguish caps from lowercase, and if you really need lowercase, the printer generates it." He pointed to a plastic box which called itself a silentype and was loaded with a roll of paper, the end of which protruded from a slot.

"That doesn't seem to be normal paper," I observed.

"It's *thermal* paper." He seemed to like that concept. "If you want a permanent print-out, you can make a Xerox."

"Oh." I turned back to the computer. "Well, what I really want is to see lowercase on the screen."

"It's not necessary."

He was really getting on my nerves. "Actually," I said, "I think it *is* necessary."

"No, you see, we use inverse video on the screen—"

As he looped back to the beginning, I realized that there really

Left: A screen shot. (In color, it looked much worse.)

Lower left: A 5.25-inch floppy disk in its square protective envelope.

Lower right: The keyboard where many symbols were in the wrong place, while some keys weren't there at all.

was something wrong with him. I couldn't understand it in 1980, but in retrospect the explanation is simple enough: He was infected with a kind of euphoric dementia that afflicts so many Apple apologists even today.

Computer historians tend to skip over the defects of the apple][when they wax sentimental over Jobs and Wozniak, the legendary visionaries of Los Altos. In fact Wozniak decided not to add lowercase letters because he was afraid of introducing errors when he recompiled the code by hand, and Jobs said the absence of lowercase was no big deal, because people wouldn't care. Apple then manufactured computers lacking a lowercase alphabet for five years.

All I knew was that someone was trying to sell me a product that didn't have basic features, would be difficult to use, and cost as much as a new motorcycle. If it couldn't display text legibly, was there anything else it could do that might make me want to buy it?

Of course! The sales person enumerated its attributes. It could run video games, and you could use it to store names and addresses, and phone numbers, or maybe some food recipes—

Page 9

The Hobby Shop

Evidently the Apple wouldn't satisfy my needs, so I went to the only other retailer selling personal computers in Manhattan at that time: Polk's Hobby Shop on Fifth Avenue. This seemed an unlikely source for what I wanted, but I went there anyway.

Inside, I found myself surrounded with displays of railroad trains and model aircraft, as one might expect in a hobby shop. "Where are the computers?" I asked a bored-looking female sales person.

"Basement," she said, without bothering to look up.

No vibrant positivism here! That was encouraging. I descended a flight of stairs to a low-ceilinged space which smelled of new industrial carpet, while the walls of lumpy old plaster had been covered with fresh white paint. Here I found an Atari 400, a Commodore PET, and a Texas Instruments TI 99/4 lined up on a home-made bench. None of them was switched on, so I walked over to a man in the far corner who was typing something on a cream-painted steel box that had a home-made appearance. A name plate identified it as a Challenger 1P, whatever that might be.

"Excuse me," I said. "I'd like to buy a computer.

"What do you want to use it for?" he asked.

"Well, I want to do word processing."

He turned and gave me an evaluating look. "That's an interesting coincidence," he said. "It so happens, I've written a word-processing program. In fact, I was just trying to find a bug in the code, here." He appeared to be around thirty, was wearing fashionable tinted eyeglasses, and was suntanned with a neat moustache.

"I thought you were a sales person," I said.

"No, I'm hoping this store will be selling copies of my program. What kind of writing do you do?"

I explained that I wrote books and magazine articles. We chatted for a while, and he introduced himself as Fred Beyer. Unlike the sales person in the Apple store, he sounded rational. In fact he seemed—well, normal.

"How about this," he said. "I can bring a computer over to your place, and then maybe you can test my program for me."

Well, why not? I told him where I lived, and he promised to be there that evening.

The Neighborhood

After winning a lengthy battle to secure a lease (described in *An Accidental Life Volume 3*), I had become permanently resident in a tiny one-bedroom apartment on Patchin Place, an idyllic little mews where squirrels scampered in the tall branches of ailanthus trees. The quaint old buildings looked delightful from the outside, even though plaster tended to fall off the walls on the inside.

Outside the gates which guarded this quaint enclave was an area in the West Village blessed with truly astonishing amenities. Within a three-minute walk I could count a large library, a barber shop, a shoe-repair store, a pharmacy, a bank, a coffee shop, a liquor store, an old-school grocery, and a little mom-and-pop restaurant run by a Hungarian couple who served home-cooked meat-and-two-veg dinners. Famous Ray's Pizza was nearby, and Barney's Hardware, and a corner news store which stocked periodicals from all over the world. There was a dry cleaner, two Chinese restaurants, an art supply store, and (a little farther away) a laundromat.

Today, as the median income among local residents in the West Village has risen, some of the amenities have been displaced by nail salons and fancy eateries. But Patchin Place is still there, and it remains unique.

Top: *The north side of Patchin Place viewed from the gates on West 10th Street.*

Bottom: *I lived Apartment 4 in house number 9.*

WP6502

Fred turned up at my apartment with another Challenger 1P, which he placed on my dining table. He put a generic cassette recorder beside it, then set a 9-inch monochrome monitor on top of it. The monitor looked like the sort of thing you would see hooked up to a camera in a convenience store, to discourage shoplifting.

He switched on the computer, and after a moment the monitor showed a prompt that looked like this:

D/C/W/M ?

Fred typed C, which he said meant Cassette, and he entered a couple more commands. He plugged in the cassette recorder and pressed its "play" key. The tape reels started turning, and after a while a message appeared on the screen: "Welcome to WP6502."

"What does that mean?" I asked.

"It's the name of my program. WP stands for word processing, and this computer is built around a 6502 processor." He made this sound as if it should have been fairly obvious.

I typed some text, and because it appeared on a monochrome monitor, there were no colored fringes. The letters were in uppercase and lowercase, and when I reached the end of the line, the incomplete word flipped down to the next line.

"That's called word-wrap," Fred said.

So, there was no need to press the Return key at the end of each line. Amazing! Then Fred showed me how to delete and edit text, and that was even more amazing.

He explained that the Challenger was made by a small company named Ohio Scientific, and it actually had a better specification than an apple II. The 1P model was really just for hobbyists, but a more expensive model named the 4P had 48K of RAM and came with a disk drive, which was more reliable than a cassette recorder.

"Do you have an instruction manual?" I asked.

He showed me some photocopied pages. "Actually," he said, "I was wondering if, maybe, you'd like to write a better version."

So that was why he was being so helpful. I didn't want to write a manual, but I needed an excuse to ask Fred a lot of questions, so I agreed that I might be able to help.

"I can't pay you," Fred went on. "But I may be able to get you a free computer."

Fred's Kitchen

The next day I visited Fred at a dilapidated four-floor tenement in Chinatown where the lobby smelled of boiled fish and old sweat. In his apartment on the top floor he showed me into the kitchen, where we sat on padded vinyl chairs at a Formica-topped table. The furniture was 1950s-style, with tubular aluminum legs.

Fred said that he'd reconsidered his situation, and maybe he didn't need new documentation for WP6502, because he was writing a new version, with a lot more features. Really he would like me to document that, and at the same time, because I was a writer, I might suggest some additional capabilities.

This sounded like more work, so I asked about the free computer.

"It shouldn't be a problem," Fred said. He had a friend named Hal Pollenz, who had been on the development team at Ohio Scientific. Hal could get me my Challenger 4P, including a monitor and a disk drive, normally selling for a total of about $2,000. Plus, of course, I would walk away with a free copy of the new version of WP6502, which was guaranteed to satisfy my needs because I would help to refine its specifications.

What a deal!

Okay, we got to work. First, Fred had to teach me some fundamentals. He drew a memory map for me, explained the boot sequence, and told me the difference between ROM and RAM.

Next he took me into a tiny room adjacent to the kitchen, where he was writing his software on yet another Challenger. The tools available in those days were appallingly primitive. There was no mouse, of course—that was still years in the future. Also, he could only view 24 lines of instructions at a time, and the display only scrolled upward. To find a section of his program, he had to type a command such as LS 5000-5100 to list that range of numbered lines. If he was lucky, he would see the op-codes that he was looking for; but if he was unlucky, he would have to type another LS command and try again. He had to be patient, because the lines of text drifted very slowly up the screen, like bubbles rising in a viscous liquid.

We started talking about the ideal look and feel of a word-processing program, and Fred was remarkably receptive to my suggestions. A control code to delete whole words instead of individual letters? Sure. Skip to the next page? Not a problem. Footnotes? Auto page numbering? Yes! He made notes of everything on a pad of paper.

Right: Connecting the 1P to a TV set or video monitor, and loading a program from the cassette recorder.

Below: The 1P came with a complete schematic. Here's a piece of it showing connections to its 6502 processor chip.

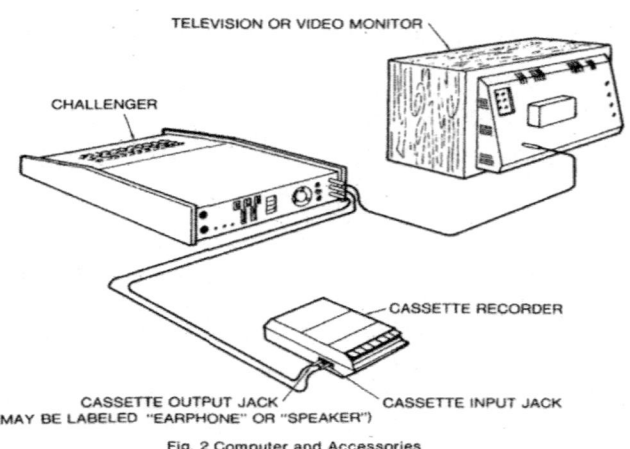

Fig. 2 Computer and Accessories

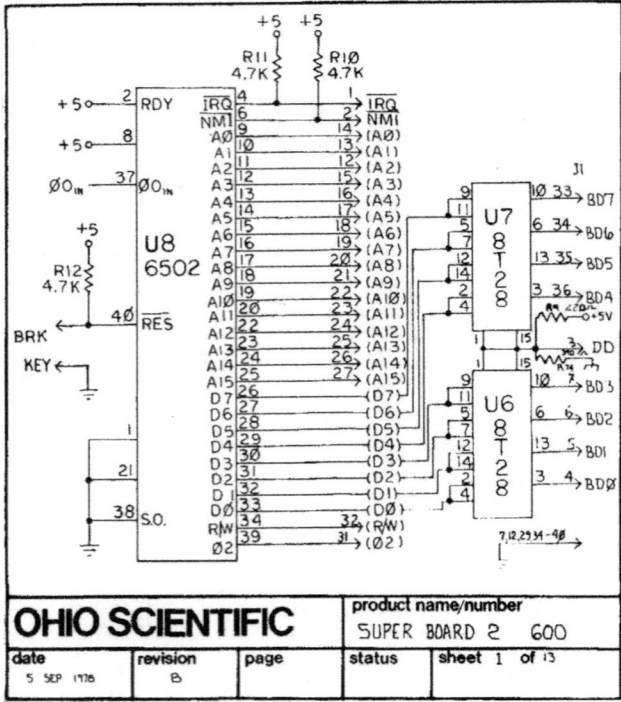

```
PLAYING BACK A PROGRAM
     The following steps show how to load the computer with a
program stored on cassette.
  1.  Check for correct cable connections between the recorder
      and computer.
  2.  Rewind the cassette so that the tape "leader" is visible
      on the take-up spool.
  3.  Turn on the computer and get into BASIC as indicated by
      the letters "OK" in the lower left corner of the screen.
  4.  Type in NEW <RETURN> .  This erases anything now stored in
      the computer.
  5.  Type LOAD.  Do not press <RETURN> .
  6.  Turn on the recorder to PLAY the tape.
  7.  As soon as the tape (dark brown) begins to wind onto the
      spool, press <RETURN>.
```

Finally he set me up in the kitchen with another Challenger running the upgraded version of WP6502 as he had written it so far. I started learning its features, while using it to write documentation for it and thinking of ways to improve it. Because it was still under development, it crashed a lot.

The Promiscuous Programmer

I returned to Fred's kitchen the next day, and the day after that. I grew to love visiting that old apartment, because an apprenticeship is always the ideal way to learn, and I was discovering a new technology that few people knew about yet. Bus width, clock speed, compilers, interpreters—it all seemed so *right*, somehow, as if I had always wanted to think like a computer, but had never known how.

I also learned about Fred. He had been a draft dodger in the 1960s and early 1970s, hiding in Canada, where he wrote software for a government department. Then he came to New York and met a young man named Joe Ming, who became his business partner.

C4P MEMORY

Decimal Location	Hexadecimal Location	Use
0000 – 0255	0000 – 00FF	6502 Page Zero
0256 – 0511	0100 – 01FF	6502 Stack (Page 1)
0512 – 8959	0200 – 22FF	Transient program area for user's language processor
8960 – 9819	2300 – 2658	I/O Handlers
9820 – 10826	265C – 2A4A	Floppy Drivers
10827 – 11896	2A4B – 2E78	Disk Operating System (DOS)
11897 – 12664	2E79 – 3178	Page 01/1 Swap Buffer
12665 – 12920	3179 – 3278	DOS Extensions
12921 – 12925	3279 – 327D	Source file header information
12926 TO END OF MEMORY	327E	Source File

Left: A memory map. Computers were a whole lot simpler in those days.

Below: The logo for Dwo Quong Fok Lok Sow was included in all of Fred's literature.

Joe was the son of Chinese immigrants who owned a noodle import business. Fred assured Joe that there was a huge opportunity for anyone who marketed the first word-processing program for 6502-based systems, so Joe put up a bit of capital, and they started their own software company. They named it Dwo Quong Fok Lok Sow.

"That's a somewhat unusual name," I said, diplomatically.

"After someone gets that name right," Fred said, sounding defensive but determined, "they never forget it."

That might be true, although the process of getting it right might take a while. "What does it mean?" I asked.

"Joe's family noodle company is named Fok Lok Sow. I think that means luck, prosperity, and a long life. And Dwo Quong means—something like—even more."

I realized that Fred's "normal" look might be a bit deceptive. Then I had a sudden insight. "Does this building belong to Joe?"

"Yes. He lets me live here."

The phrase "undercapitalized" came to mind. But of course Fred didn't need much capital to write assembly language: He just needed a computer and some floppy disks. Marketing the software might be more of a challenge, but I decided not to get into that.

His office and the kitchen both faced a crosstown street, but the noise of trucks and car horns was muted in our location on the top floor. Radiators in the apartment hissed and clicked with each burst of steam heat that came up from the basement, and the only other sound was the murmur of an FM radio beside Fred's desk. It was always tuned to WBLS, the local black station which played all-disco.

Hal Pollenz (left) and Fred Beyer (right), when visiting my apartment. Both became friends.

This seemed an odd choice, so I asked Fred why he liked it.

"It reminds me I won't be here writing code tonight," he said.

"Oh, you go out to discos?"

He hesitated. "You could say that."

I experienced another sudden insight. "Are you gay, Fred?"

He avoided my eyes. "Don't worry, it's not catching."

That seemed a very quaint thing to say. "Surely, you don't really think it would matter to me."

"Well, it might."

"No, it's interesting."

"Interesting!" In those unenlightened days, I think he had assumed that any heterosexual person must be homophobic.

During the next few days, as he saw that I really was nonjudgmental, he seemed to enjoy sharing the details of his gay life. HIV had not yet been identified, and the club scene was a smorgasbord of promiscuity. Fred was indulging himself in a fugue of hedonism

So far as I know, the Challenger 4P was the only computer ever manufactured with wooden sides.

for most of each night, and he told me some epic orgy stories.

He also had a rich fund of anecdotes about everyday mores in gay bars in the West Village. His favorite bar catered to a macho-gay clientele, and didn't allow any sissy behavior. A man at the door was designated as a cologne sniffer, and if you smelled of cologne, he wouldn't allow you in. Also, there was a dress code: You could only wear denim or leather. Fred had not been aware of that on his first visit, and had turned up in a shirt, which caused him to be refused entry. After thinking for a moment, he suggested that he could simply take off the shirt and come in bare-chested. The man at the door said that would be fine.

Within about a month, the new version of WP6502 was finished. Fred had been able to write it quickly because the display was in monospaced text with no graphical user interface. Even so, with features such as mailmerge, WP6502 was advanced for its time.

I completed the manual, which Fred printed on a borrowed daisywheel printer. I had drawn some cartoons to amuse him, and he added them, although I wasn't sure it was a good idea.

I was pleasantly surprised when Hal Pollenz showed up, bringing me my Challenger 4P. "It has wooden sides," I observed.

"Yes," Hal said. "Mike Cheiky—he's the founder of the company—thought it would be a neat idea. They're made of teak. If you want oiled teak, you'll have to oil it yourself. The supplier's contract didn't specify that, so they didn't bother."

Hal had a wild beard, dishevelled hair, and a happy grin. He

looked like a classic computer guy, in contrast to Fred, who was probably the only nerd in America who maintained his good looks at a tanning salon.

Hal showed me how to power up the 4P, and warned me that if I flipped the toggle switch on the disk drive while the system was running, a voltage spike from the switch could crash the computer. "You might want to solder a capacitor across that switch," he said.

Um, okay.

I left the building carrying my 4P. It seemed good pay for a few weeks in which I had learned so much about computers and human sexual behavior.

HELLO!

I set my Challenger 4P with its funny wooden sides on the dining table alongside a crudely photocopied instruction manual from Ohio Scientific. Now I could run Fred's word-processing program on the computer—but another possibility seemed interesting. I could write my own program.

Was I smart enough to do that? It sounded a bit technical, but the manual suggested that I could type an introductory example in the BASIC programming language, like this:

Two of my cartoons that Fred thought should be included in his WP6502 manual.

```
10 PRINT "HELLO! I'M YOUR NEW COMPUTER." <RETURN>
20 PRINT <RETURN>
30 END <RETURN>
```

The manual explained that I should not actually type the word RETURN and the pointy brackets. I should just press the Return key at the end of each line. I did that.

Then I typed RUN and pressed Return, and the computer obediently displayed the text that was enclosed in the quote marks. I sat staring at it, feeling a sense of unreality. This might not have been a meaningful event to most people, but it was overwhelming to me.

The United States had a singular history of making complicated products easy to use, such as automatic transmissions in cars, cameras that adjusted their own exposure, and phonographs that could lower their own stylus to the run-in groove of a long-playing record. And now, in front of me, was the apogee of this genius for simplification.

Entering hexadecimal codes on massive mainframes was no longer necessary. Here on my dining table was a computer that could understand commands derived from the English language. I foresaw a cascade of consequences that would literally change the world.

It would change me, too. I didn't realize it, yet, but I had become infected with my own version of the euphoric dementia that afflicted the sales person in the Apple store. I felt a sudden and fateful urge to write programs, even if they merely stored names and addresses, phone numbers, and food recipes.

Very Ethical

Meanwhile, my occupation as a writer had been running in the background. Late in 1979 I had delivered a novel to Jove Books titled *Love's Savage Embrace*, in a category known as "bodice rippers" because of the mistreatment commonly suffered by a typical female protagonist, until she was rescued by a handsome, wealthy man who would remain mindlessly devoted to her for the rest of her life.

My editor, Ed Breslin, liked the book and only wanted to change one scene. His assistant, Robin, would work with me on that.

I went to the offices of Jove to meet Robin, and discovered that she was tall and slender, like a model, with a chic haircut and high cheekbones. She was also smart and literate, and as we looked at each other, I experienced an intense desire to ask her out to lunch.

I repressed this impulse, because I had not yet reached the most important step in the process of writing a book: The completion payment. If I had an affair with Robin which ended badly, she might get mad at me, and then she could delay my payment in a moment of petulance. She seemed nice enough, but most women seem nice enough till an affair ends badly, and after that, you never know.

I spent a weekend doing the rewrite, and delivered it to Robin at Jove. She approved the revisions, and said she would contact me when the check was ready. This would take at least a month, because publishers never issue checks in less time than that. Meanwhile, I was starting to learn about computers in Fred's kitchen.

One morning in February, Robin called to say that she had the check and would put it in the mail.

"Actually," I said, "can I come to the office to pick it up?"

She hesitated. "I suppose so, if you like."

I arranged to be at her office at 11:45 that same day, and took the precaution of dressing in a jacket and tie, since she seemed style-conscious. It was a brown cashmere jacket and a red tie, which I thought was a nice combination.

"So, I think this concludes our professional dealings as writer and editor," I said, as I received the envelope from her. She wasn't really an editor, but I thought she might like it if I used the word.

"I think it does," she agreed.

"Good," I said, "because I've been waiting to ask you out to lunch without it seeming inappropriate."

"How ethical of you," she said. "All right, I'll get my coat."

I was almost 35, which was really too old for affairs with editorial assistants, but I figured I would keep asking them out until they started to say "no."

The Bank Robbery

I enjoyed Robin's company, and we began seeing each other a couple of times a week. She was intelligent, affectionate, and flirtatious, which was a potent combination, but she didn't know what to do about her career. Most of the books that Jove published were—well, a bit crappy. She said she didn't want to edit crappy books for the rest of her life, but she had no idea what else to do.

She complained about this frequently, always looking for advice, and I realized that my instincts had led me to yet another needy woman. This was okay in the short term, because needy women placated my insecurities. In the longer term I tended to become impatient with women who were excessively needy—but there was no point in worrying about that before it happened, because this time, maybe it wouldn't happen.

Within a couple of weeks she decided to quit from Jove, so I suggested that I could use some of my completion payment to take us on a trip to England. I was overdue to visit my parents—

"And we can visit my mother in Geneva!" she exclaimed. She had grown up in Switzerland, and spoke fluent French. We could fly to England, rent a car, take it across the Channel into France—

Uh-oh. "French people despise the British," I said.

"You're being silly."

No, I wasn't.

We rented a car in London, and since the Channel Tunnel did not exist yet, we took the car across to France on a hovercraft. This was a classic piece of funky British engineering: Ingenious, impractical, and unreliable. It couldn't deal with high waves, and its huge rubber skirt wore out and had to be replaced every year or so. It was also horribly noisy: We were issued earplugs during the trip.

Back in those days before the EU, any British car venturing into Europe had to have a GB sticker on the rear, identifying it as being from Great Britain. Inevitably, as we drove south on the autoroute, French drivers saw the sticker, honked at us, and made offensive gestures. "You see?" I said to Robin. *"You see?"*

When we stopped at a gas station, the attendant gave me my change in one-franc coins, one by one. When he stopped, I remained with my palm outstretched, looking at him, while he looked back at me until, finally, with a sneer, he surrendered the last coin.

"First episode of attempted short-changing," I reported to Robin.

A hovercraft, as they once were.

Still, the Gallic loathing for British people worked to my advantage when we went into a bank in Paris to change traveler's checks.

The man ahead of me was receiving friendly treatment from a female teller who smiled at him coquettishly and spoke fluent English. He had an American passport, and of course the French are infatuated with Americans, for whatever irrational reason.

As soon as he left and I took his place, the teller saw my British passport and her smile vanished. From that point on, she spoke only French. So what was her problem? Well, she was French. That was her problem.

I signed nine $100 traveler's checks and pushed them across the counter. The teller dumped them in a drawer and started counting out bills very rapidly, still speaking French, using their deranged vocabulary for numbers. Quatre-vingt-dix ou nonante? Soixante-dix ou septante? I didn't know what it all meant, and I didn't want to know, but I couldn't help noticing that the pile of bills was higher than I had expected. In fact, quite a lot higher.

After she pushed the money over to me, I went to Robin, who was sitting at a table in the corner of the bank, writing a post card. "I think we should leave now," I said to her.

"Just let me finish writing—"

"No, I mean, we have to leave *right now*."

The urgency in my low-pitched voice captured her attention. We hurried out, and I ducked into a doorway to count the money. There was more than twice as much as there should have been.

The teller had seen my British passport and my traveler's checks issued by Barclays, which was a British bank, so she assumed the checks were in pounds. In reality they had been issued by Barclays Bank of New York, but the dollar sign was easily missed by a woman who was distracted by her loathing for British people. And a pound was worth more than twice as much as a dollar in those days.

Robin's eyes widened. "Are you going to tell them what happened?"

I wondered about that. "That teller spoke English to the man

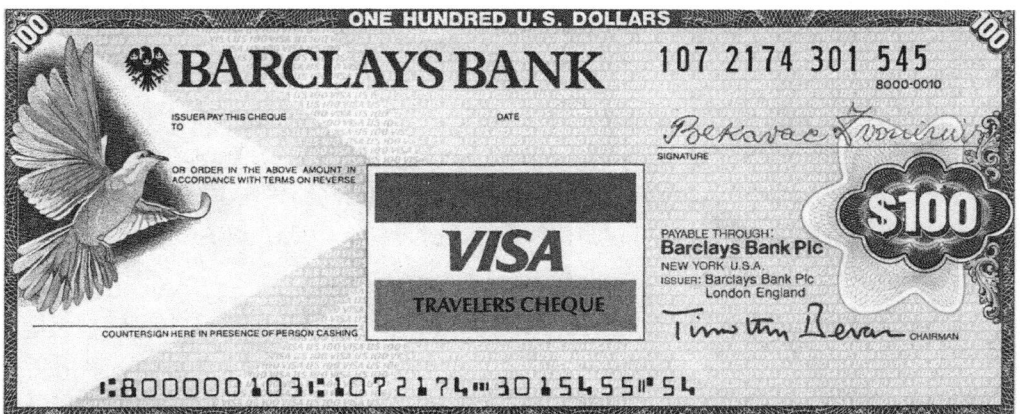

Suppose you saw this passport (below). How reflexively hostile to British people would you have to be, to miss seeing the dollar sign on a 1980s-vintage traveler's check (left)?

ahead of me," I said. "If she had spoken English to me, I would have understood all those numbers, and I would have stopped her."

"But she may lose her job," Robin said.

Ah, the "lose her job" argument. I had mixed feelings about that. If an employee is compulsively rude, doesn't pay attention to a simple but vital task, and makes a $900 error—maybe she's in the wrong job?

Of course, keeping the money would constitute theft. Or would it? The teller had given it to me. I wondered if that was a plausible rationalization.

Meanwhile, Robin was still staring at the cash. "What's my share?" she asked.

Her greed was so naked and undisguised, how could I disappoint her? I bought her a pair of fancy sandals, then spent the rest of the cash on our vacation. I was less scrupulous and more reckless then than now, especially when dealing with a French bank.

When we got back to the United States, a letter from Paris was already waiting from the manager of the bank. The letter asked me (in English) to remit the excess money that I had received.

I looked at it, wondering what to do. Then I picked up a red marker, wrote HA HA HA all over the manager's letter, and sent it back via air mail.

Nothing ever happened, but I never returned to France. I decided to quit while I was ahead.

```
1620 DATA TWELVE
1630 DATA WHAT IS A TOYWORT?,2
1640 DATA A petulant child
1650 DATA A shepherds purse
1660 DATA A carnivorous plant
1670 DATA None of the above
1679 '
1680 DATA THIRTEEN
1690 DATA WHICH ANIMAL HAS A TRUNK?,2
1700 DATA Aardvark
1710 DATA Elephant
1720 DATA Dolphin
1730 DATA Squirrel
1739 '
1740 DATA FOURTEEN
1750 DATA WHAT IS YOUR FAVORITE COLOR?,2
1760 DATA Red
1770 DATA Blue
1780 DATA Off-white
1790 DATA Ecru
1799 '
1800 DATA FIFTEEN
1810 DATA WHO WAS MOZART?,3
1820 DATA Politician
1830 DATA Opera Singer
1840 DATA Composer
1850 DATA Movie Director
1859 '
1860 DATA SIXTEEN
1870 DATA WHAT IS A SCULLION?,4
1880 DATA A grave-robber
1890 DATA A kind of onion
1900 DATA A kitchen storage area
1910 DATA A lowly servant
1919 '
1920 DATA SEVENTEEN
1930 DATA WHICH TOILET TISSUE IS SOFTEST?,1
1940 DATA White Cloud
1950 DATA Soft-Weve
1960 DATA ScotTissue
1970 DATA All much the same
```

General Knowledge

The first real computer program that I wrote was titled "General Knowledge Quiz." It was an entertainment, yet it riffed on the power relationship between people and computers.

Initially it asked the user, "Do you want to try the hard quiz or the easy quiz?" If the user chose "hard," the program answered, "Your arrogant attitude has been noted in your file." If the user chose "easy," the program answered, "Your reluctance to face a challenge has been noted in your file."

Really, of course, there was only one quiz. The program was just establishing its dominance over the person using it.

There were twenty multiple-choice questions, many of which were absurd, but they all had right and wrong answers—even "What is the sound of one hand clapping?"

Every visitor to Patchin Place was invited to take the quiz, and no one declined, because a desktop computer was such a novelty. Soon I discovered that the quiz uncovered personality traits which I had never known about.

The writer Edward Bryant, for instance, was widely thought of as a mild-mannered, easygoing fellow, but turned out to be highly competitive. When the quiz asked him "Which toilet paper is softest?" he went into my bathroom and checked my supply. When he was asked the number of cubic inches in a U.S. bushel, he asked me if there was a time limit, then sat and did the math.

The writer Harry Harrison was even more motivated. He scored 90%, which was almost impossible, but then nagged me to change his score to 100%. He became bad-tempered when I refused.

After "General Knowledge Quiz," I wrote programs of increasing ambition, including an AI routine which analyzed seemingly random binary choices made by the user and predicted, with better than 50% accuracy, which choice would come next. This was all a lot more interesting than writing books.

Love and Money

In May, my ex-wife Nancy called to tell me that her memoir about our marriage had just been published. I now had the fascinating experience of seeing her promoting the book on talk shows, where she described me weeping and eating Maalox tablets as I buckled under the threat of unfunded parental responsibility.

I watched one of these interviews while visiting my friends Chris and Janet Morris at their home in Cape Cod. Chris was a rock musician, while Janet was writing novels for Berkley Publishing. As the ten-minute interview ended, Chris turned to me with a funny expression. "You were married to her," he said, speaking very slowly to make sure he had it right.

"I was," I said.

Chris pondered it, then laughed and shook his head. He seemed to feel there must be some rational explanation, but it eluded him. In reality, of course, there was no rational explanation.

When I got back to New York, I called Nancy and congratulated her on the interview, although I wasn't sure it would sell any books.

"The reviews are coming in," she said. "They're not good."

Well, a lengthy session of handwringing about a doomed marriage would not be high on anyone's must-read list, especially since Nancy and myself had no celebrity status. I had hoped that if she made a lot of money from her confessional, I might not have to pay so much child support. Oh well.

Most of the $5,000 that I had received from Jove Books had now been spent, one way or another. The unfortunate error by the bank teller in Paris had been helpful, but not helpful enough. What should I do?

The challenges that discouraged me from writing science fiction remained unresolved, so I decided to write another erotic novel in the "Christina" series for Playboy Press. Actually, to be more precise, I would write an outline of it, so that I could get some advance money. Writing the actual book could wait until nearer to the delivery date. There was no point in rushing it.

I hammered out an outline for a new adventure featuring the sex-hungry heiress of Beverly Hills whom I found so perpetually unappetizing. I rode my bicycle up to Playboy Press, dropped the outline with them, and then hurried back home to learn more about computer programming.

Playland

Whenever I passed through Times Square, I struggled unsuccessfully to resist the lure of the Playland arcade. During the 1970s, it had been stocked with pinball machines, but they were now relegated to the back. Video games such as Space Invaders and Pac-Man had taken over.

The games I liked best were more primitive, with monochrome displays of character graphics. My favorite entailed chasing pedestrians with a car and mowing them down, at which point there would be a little screaming sound and a tomb stone would pop up.

Playland was a nightmarish place. It was dirty, full of cigarette smoke, and infested with teenagers who appeared to be dope dealers and gang members. It was also intolerably noisy, as all the machines were screaming and whooping at each other. I wished I could play the games in a more civilized environment, but then I realized: I knew enough, now, to write my games of my own.

Addictive Behavior

Robin found a new job at *Women's Wear Daily*, and while she worked there from nine to five each day I addressed the challenges of game design. In the evenings, sometimes we stayed at her apartment in the East Village, while other times we stayed at Patchin Place.

One morning Robin emerged from my bedroom around 8am and found me staring at the video monitor. She stopped and looked at me in surprise. "Did you get up early?" she asked.

"Um, no," I said. I had difficulty talking to her, because my head was full of code.

"Wait a minute. Have you been doing that *all night*?"

"Well, I—um—yes, I suppose I have."

"But you've never stayed up talking to *me* all night."

That statement seemed freighted with ominous overtones, but I was too preoccupied to deal with it. "Not the same thing at all," I muttered.

She went off to her office job while I continued working till the program was finished. Then I replayed her remark in my head, and wondered if I really could stay up all night talking to her. What would we talk about? I certainly wouldn't want to spend eight hours discussing her career options.

The conclusion was inescapable: My computer had become more interesting than my girlfriend.

We continued hanging out together, and eating meals together, and having sex together, but I think she could sense that a part of me was never quite there. A few days later she told me that she would stay on her own at her apartment that night. No special reason; she just felt like it.

Within a few days I concluded that she had started cheating on me, but when I hinted at this, she lied in an amazingly plausible manner. She looked me directly in the eye and maintained an expression of total innocence.

Eventually, however, the circumstantial evidence became irrefutable, at which point she reverted to a fallback position: The victim. "What did you expect me to do?" she complained. "You were ignoring me, because of that silly computer!"

This was true, so I apologized, but I still wished she hadn't cheated and lied about it.

There was a long silence. She seemed unhappy, and I felt unhappy. "I'm not sure how to deal with this," I said.

She looked thoughtful. "Maybe it would help if you spanked me."

What?

It made sense in a way, because it would be another form of male attention; but ultimately, nothing could distract me from my computer addiction. She could have been a Hollywood starlet, a nuclear physicist, an heiress with a family fortune, or all of these things combined, and it would have made no difference. Addiction makes everything in the outside world seem irrelevant, and I was addicted to writing code. In the end, I split up with Robin.

It took me a few more weeks to realize that my addiction was bad for my health. Each night, when I finally managed to go to sleep,

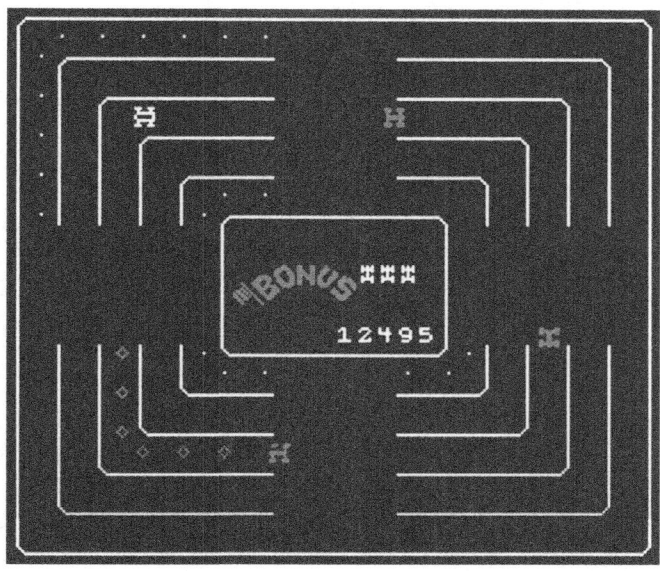

Some games in 1980 were still surprisingly primitive, yet could still be surprisingly addictive. This one was named Head-On. You had to avoid hitting cars that approached in the opposite direction. You can actually find complete videos on YouTube of people playing this game.

I dreamed in code. When I sat at the keyboard, I noticed that my hair had started to fall out. When I went shopping for groceries, I stumbled around like a zombie, thinking about binary sort algorithms and bit masking. Did I really want to be like that for the rest of my life?

I decided that I didn't, and so, in the end, I chose to moderate my behavior out of fear of the physical consequences.

Robin seemed pleasantly surprised when I went back to her and begged for another chance. We rekindled our romance—but from her point of view I was like a recovered alcoholic who still had a bottle of booze in the apartment. So long as the computer was on my desk, I could not be trusted.

She terminated the relationship a few weeks later.

The Writing On the Wall

Hal Pollenz opened a storefront at 26 East 20th Street to sell computers. This was a wonderful resource for me: I could bring in my latest game programs and watch Hal and Fred beta-testing them, and I could see new products which Hal was offering for sale.

Ohio Scientific was still an obscure brand, but was the first desktop manufacturer to offer a hard drive (for $6,000). When we did a directory listing, we saw a message something like this:

```
74,590,200 bytes free
```

The drive could hold almost 75 million bytes! That was equivalent to about 1,000 floppies of the density we had been using. A thousand! We stared at the screen in awe, trying to imagine what anyone would ever do with all those bytes. The programs that I was writing were generally 20K or less when saved in tokenized format, while the workspace in my Challenger 4P was 48K.

Here I am now, in the year 2021, writing this text, and I just did a directory listing of my current hard drive, which said:

```
595,647,901,696 bytes free
```

More than half a *trillion*. What can anyone ever do with all *those* bytes? Well, cute cat videos in HD could use a few.

Ohio Scientific now offered the Challenger III, which could serve up to sixteen terminals. Like all Ohio Scientific products, it was priced lower than its competitors, but computers in the early 1980s were all incompatible with each other, and any upstart manufacturer was confronted with a nasty little chicken-and-egg problem:

The Challenger III contained three processors (6502, Z80, and 8080) so that theoretically it could run a wide a range of software. It was capable of serving sixteen terminals on a network, which seemed amazing in 1980. Still, it was doomed.

No one wanted to buy a computer for which people were not writing software.

No one wanted to write software for a computer which people were not buying.

This problem would be fatal for Ohio Scientific. (The company was acquired in 1981, and the brand disappeared entirely in 1983.)

The apple][had attracted a nucleus of Bay Area fanboys who saw Steve Wozniak as one of their own, and couldn't resist writing software for it. Also, it had two big advantages:

Its name sounded nice, because everyone likes apples.

Its logo contained a rainbow, and people like rainbows even more than they like apples.

Actually the sequence of colors in the rainbow was wrong, which I found annoying, but no one else seemed to care.

The apple][contained a 6502 processor, but Fred didn't want to port his program to it, because the computer was so buggy. Various third-party boards now offered lowercase letters, but the boards were incompatible with each other. Some of them used the Escape key as a Shift key, because Apple had never wired the Shift key into the motherboard, but if the Escape key was used as a Shift key, a program couldn't use it as an Escape key anymore. It was a mess.

Bad Behavior

Science-fiction conventions in the 1980s were giddy events, fueled by the delusion that if struggling writers just got the formula right, they could become nouveau-riche bestsellers like Arthur C. Clarke and Isaac Asimov. The environment of a Hyatt or a Hilton encouraged this fantasy, as publishers rented suites and served free alcohol to anyone who had a halfway plausible excuse for being there. During a drunken weekend, we created our own reality.

People who took science fiction seriously, in those days, tended to be somewhat dysfunctional, so it was not entirely surprising when episodes of bad behavior occurred. Two such episodes marred the 1980 World Science Fiction Convention in Boston, both involving Susan Wood, a moody Canadian who taught creative-writing and had discovered William Gibson when he wrote his first story in one of her courses, titled "Fragments of a Hologram Rose."

When I met Susan at someone's room party, I thought we were getting along okay, until one of my opinions seemed to annoy her. Without warning, she grabbed the forefinger of my right hand and sank her teeth into it. Fortunately I managed to drag it out from between her incisors before she bit through to the bone, but there was some blood. Later the same night she threw a beer bottle at editor Terry Carr, who was widely regarded as a most easygoing and inoffensive person. The bottle opened a cut in his head requiring a quick trip to a local emergency room.

This was a bit extreme, even by convention standards—but only a bit. Bad behavior wasn't just confined to fans of the literature; many people in book publishing transgressed beyond everyday limits without fear of disapproval. One wealthy literary agent hosted room parties where there would be hookers and cocaine. One editor celebrated a promotion by dragging female associates into a closet for a group hug, and they didn't seem to care. When I expressed my literary displeasure for an editor's taste in fiction by pouring beer over her head, she laughed it off.

Decades later, in 2012, my LGBT daughter helped to put an end to all this when she played a role in banning a man from a regional convention, for the rest of his life, after he rested his hand on a woman's shoulder and said something flirtatious.

I wonder what the penalty would be, these days, for finger-biting, bottle-throwing, coke-snorting, hooker-fondling, beer-pouring, and closet-hugging. Public humiliation? Cancelation? Jail time?

Gate-Crashers

Since I had split up with Robin, I faced a situation that was depressingly familiar: My solitary life as a writer didn't bring me into contact with many women.

In 1979 I had discovered personal ads in *The New York Review of Books*, where females with an interest in literature also seemed to harbor a libidinous interest in men. Now, in 1980, I tried my luck again, and received a response from someone named Dina von Zweck.

We met at the Peacock Cafe on Greenwich Avenue. This was my default location for meeting advertisers, as it had a folksy West Village ambience, was quiet and never crowded, and was only half a block from my apartment. Minimizing my commute was important, because the success rate for meetings was so low. Also, the menu was cheap, consisting mostly of espresso and pastries.

A typical cover of The New York Review of Books *during 1980. Hard to imagine that personal ads from libidinous females would be found therein, although maybe a scholarly piece on "Sex and Sociobiology" provides a clue.*

Dina turned out to be older than she had made herself sound in the ad, and my unfortunate history with a molestational mother made me nervous about matronly women. Still, she was creative and fun to talk to. She wrote poetry, she wrote books, she had done some paintings, and she was Director of Publishing at CBS.

The absence of physical chemistry between us became obvious fairly quickly, but she said she would like to get together on a friendly basis, and had an unusual suggestion: I could join her and some friends who were professional gate-crashers.

Every Friday and Saturday they crashed political fund raisers, charitable functions, and art openings that Dina heard about through her contacts at CBS. While invitees were paying $500 or more per plate, she and her friends were eating for free.

The rules were simple. I had to:

Dress in a suit.
Be polite and charming.
Read text upside-down without squinting.

Page 31

The Guggenheim Museum in New York City, one of the most famous buildings by Frank Lloyd Wright.

The third requirement was necessary at functions where a list of attendees was usually placed on a table in front of some stiff-faced woman whose job was to keep out riff-raff. I had to smile ingratiatingly and say, "I'm awfully sorry, I seem to have left my invitation at home." Then I would identify myself using one of the names that I read upside-down from her list.

"Do you ever get caught?" I asked Dina.

"Never," she said. "The last thing they want to do is offend their guests, so even if you get a name wrong, they usually let you in. You just have to *look the part*."

A few days later I met Dina outside an upscale hotel in midtown, and found her flamboyantly dressed in a long green velvet dress and a wide-brimmed hat. She assessed my business suit a bit skeptically, but decided that it was good enough.

I had practiced the art of inverted name-reading before leaving my apartment, and when we went to the function room in the hotel, I managed it flawlessly. Soon I was sitting with my new friend among elegant people, ready for a four-course dinner.

I never figured out why she was so addicted to getting something for nothing. She was quite shameless about it. After the dinner, she went to a beautiful floral display and started plucking flowers out of it and poking them into her hat. A member of staff came hurrying over and asked her not to do that, as the flowers would be given to a hospital the next day, but Dina was unconcerned. "I'm sure they won't notice if a few are missing," she said.

A couple of weeks later, she invited me to an art opening at the Guggenheim Museum. This was a very exclusive event, restricted to patrons who donated at least $10,000 a year, but Dina didn't expect a problem. She wanted to see the new paintings by a very important artist, and would be getting there a bit early with some friends. I could arrive at any time and shouldn't need her help crashing the event, now that I had learned the drill.

Through another personal ad I had met a woman named Jennifer, who was a magazine journalist. She seemed a bit hyperactive and neurotic, but a lot of women writers in New York were like that, and it didn't bother me. I asked Dina if I could bring Jennifer along.

"Yes," said Dina, "so long as she—"

"Looks the part."

"Precisely."

I met Jennifer on the corner of East 89th Street and Fifth Avenue. She was nicely dressed for the occasion, but as we walked toward the museum I noticed that she smelled of wine and was a bit unsteady on her feet. "Are you—okay?" I asked.

"I'm fine," she said. "I just hope they have some decent champagne."

We penetrated security and found ourselves among the hyper-elegant crowd. I saw Dina and her friends and waved to them, but Dina looked at Jennifer with narrowed eyes. She seemed capable of detecting excessive alcohol use from twenty feet away.

"Let's go see the art," I told Jennifer.

"First I need a drink," she said.

I had a feeling, now, that something bad would happen. I didn't know what it would be, but it would be bad, and whatever it was, my best policy would be to leave the museum as soon as possible—although first, I did want to see the paintings.

While Jennifer went on her quest for alcohol, I hurried up a curving ramp to the exhibition. Here I discovered that the canvases were minimalist, abstract, and all solid black.

If you looked closely, you could see one or two rectangles in each canvas that were a slightly different shade of black. Some of the rectangles were larger than others, some of them were fractionally darker than others, but there were no other visible features.

Generous donations from the people around me had made this exhibition possible, and now they were confronted with the incomprehensible result. I saw a very elegant lady in her sixties, wearing a long black gown, squinting at one of the paintings with a bemused expression.

Scene of the scene: Looking down at the foyer of the Guggenheim where the traumatic incident occurred.

Page 33

"It matches your dress," I remarked to her.

She allowed herself a dignified smile. "Indeed it does," she said.

I returned to the lobby—at which point, Jennifer grabbed me. "Where were you?" she demanded. "You dumped me!"

"No, no," I said. "But the art is a bit dull, so maybe we should go home."

"I don't want to."

I studied her flushed face. She was much more drunk than I had realized. "Well, I want to go," I said. "You stay here, if you like."

"No." Her voice was loud, and some people turned to stare. Dina noticed, and did not look happy.

"Please don't do this," I said to Jennifer.

"You can't leave!"

I really don't like it when someone tells me that I can't leave. I started toward the exit.

She seized my arm. "No!" she shouted.

I couldn't believe this was happening, but it was happening, and I didn't know how to stop it from happening. My persuasiveness had failed, so I simply moved forward. Jennifer tightened her grip on my arm, trying to restrain me physically. Then she went limp, as if hoping that her body weight would anchor me; but she wasn't heavy enough, and her high heels started dragging across the floor.

A uniformed man beside the door stared at me in amazement. "Can you let us out, please?" I said to him. I didn't think I could push the door open at the same time as dragging Jennifer.

He opened the door, and I hauled her out to Fifth Avenue. Providentially, three taxis were waiting at the curb.

"I hate you!" Jennifer cried.

Yes, well, at this point, I wasn't too fond of her, either. I dragged her to a taxi, opened the door, and assisted her into the back seat. Then I slammed the door, hurried to the next taxi, and jumped in. "Tenth Street and Greenwich Avenue!" I cried.

My taxi pulled away from the curb, and the nightmare was over.

I never received any more invitations from Dina. Jennifer called me the next day and said that she didn't normally get drunk like that, and maybe we could go to the theater together, but I said it might not be a good idea. I picked up the latest issue of *The New York Review of Books* and started answering more ads.

Passive Aggression

As the weeks passed, there were more failed encounters through personal ads—far too many to recall at this point. They just went on and on.

Using *The New York Review of Books* wasn't really a sensible idea, but I became strangely addicted to meeting people who were a bit crazy. They were more interesting than sane people, and if all else failed, they were still able to talk about books.

One very intense woman in her thirties showed up to meet me at The Peacock Cafe dressed entirely in black, with her black hair pulled back severely. Her face was deathly pale, she had heavy mascara, and she used purple lipstick. I thought that she could be quite attractive if she could allow herself to apply less eye makeup and eat more food containing iron.

"What do you suppose the people in this restaurant are thinking?" she asked me, as we sat down.

I hesitated, wondering if this was a trick question. "Well," I said, "I don't really know."

She stared at me with unblinking intensity. "I think they're all thinking about sex."

"Oh. Really?"

She leaned forward, still staring at me. "Everyone thinks about sex, most of the time."

"Well, personally—"

"I'm sure you do. I certainly do."

Her stare was creepy, and her pale skin was vampiric. I escaped as

Recently I managed to find these photos taken of strangers in the Peacock Cafe during its halcyon days. The massive espresso machine occupied a position of importance, although it was of no interest to me, as I didn't drink coffee. Nor did I smoke cigarettes, although people could, back then. It was just a wonderful environment in which to meet and talk. Today, alas, it has become just another sushi restaurant.

quickly as possible, feeling relieved that she didn't know my home address.

Another advertiser told me she had just recovered from an undefined illness that had lasted for several years. "Now I'm eager to make up for lost time," she said.

"In what way?" I asked naively.

"I have my birth control with me in my purse," she said.

Instant sex made me nervous, but I felt I would be mean to refuse, bearing in mind her unhappy health history. Then it turned out that her real goal was to find a man whom she could serve as a slave. This sounded impractical, as I couldn't imagine how I would find enough tasks to keep her occupied while I was writing computer programs. I don't think she had considered the implications: Her demand for constant supervision would actually make the man a slave to her.

Another ad turned out to be from a woman who lived literally around the corner from me, on Milligan Place. She was somewhat overweight, but smart and entertaining, and I liked her face.

I was embarrassed, though, that I couldn't remember which ad I was answering. "I answered quite a few," I told her.

"Oh, you can figure it out," she said.

Well, could I? I re-read the classifieds the next day, and then called her. "It must be this one," I said. "Woman seeking kind man who will help me to lose twenty pounds."

"What?" she shouted. "You think I need to lose twenty pounds? You are the most passive-aggressive man I ever met!"

I wondered about that. I honestly didn't know if I was. Of course she really did need to lose twenty pounds—or a bit more—but if she was aware this, it could explain why she was so angry.

Meanwhile, I started writing computer games that were skill-based. The most ambitious one played the childhood game of "Boxes," which was difficult to develop, because the computer had to change its strategy if the player made a sacrifice in the expectation of doing better on the next turn.

I marketed my games through a small mail-order business that Fred and Hal had set up. Because of the declining fortunes of Ohio Scientific, I think I sold maybe twenty copies of each game, but I didn't care. The fascinating process of computer programming was an end in itself.

Review-Induced Rapture

In October, circumstances reminded me that I was still ostensibly a writer. Berkley published my book *Dream Makers*, and much to my surprise, it received the kind of reviews that authors dream of.

"Sharp, insightful, beautifully written essays," said *Publishers Weekly*.

"So vivid, you wish they would never end," said *Chicago Tribune*.

"There has never been a better book about science fiction," said *The Cleveland Press*.

"Pure genius," said *Heavy Metal* magazine.

"Platt held me spellbound for hours," said *Analog*. (This one made me a little squeamish, implying some kind of kinky physical restraints.)

Personally I didn't think my book was quite that good, and I suspected that the sales figures would be disappointing. Seriously, how many people would want to read about the personal lives of science-fiction writers? Three hundred, perhaps? Three hundred and fifty?

Still, the bad sales figures would take a while to come through, and in the meantime I might take advantage of a mental state that sometimes afflicts editors. I thought of it as *Review-Induced Rapture*.

Being a book editor is a thankless task, because there are always too many books competing for not enough readers. However, beneath the jaded, cynical shell of an editor may lurk a faint residue of idealism, fueling the hope that something may actually sell. Good reviews don't necessarily translate into sales, but *really glowing* reviews can spark a brief burst of excitement, which was the "rapture" I had in mind.

Victoria Schochet was the science-fiction editor at Berkley, so I placed a call to her and said how happy I was about the reviews. Was she happy too? Yes, she was really happy!

Excellent, we were both happy. In that case, how would she feel about a sequel? Some important writers had been omitted from the first volume because of insufficient space. In fact, Victoria could probably add some names herself.

Really I didn't want her to do that, but I thought she would be more likely to give me a contract if she could interfere with the content of the book. Sure enough, she was eager to add some names, because I had not included enough female writers in the first volume. What about Joanna Russ? Kit Reed? Andre Norton? Joan Vinge?

Oh—*them!*

I saw, now, that if I wanted a contract for Volume II, I would have to surrender to Victoria's demand for gender balance. "Excellent choices," I said.

"So ask your literary agent—"

"I have no agent at the moment."

"Oh." She sounded unhappy. I think she preferred not to negotiate directly with writers, because writers tend to whine and beg and plead poverty, and may become petulant when an editor is unwilling to humor their delusions about the worth of their work.

"I was thinking—" I went on.

"I suppose you want $15,000, something like that."

I had been planning to ask for $10,000, because that was the most I thought I could get, bearing in mind that the first volume had sold for a mere $6,500 advance. "Well—" I began.

"I can manage $12,500," Victoria said. "That's the limit."

I didn't need to negotiate with her, because she had done it for me. In fact Victoria was a rare and wonderful editor who would sometimes spend money on books as if she were buying shoes.

"All right," I said, "I could accept twelve-five."

When the sales figures for the first volume of *Dream Makers* did finally come in, they were even worse than I had feared. By this time, though, I had my contract for Volume II.

Review-Induced Rapture! If only it happened more often.

The Tetralogy

Ed Breslin, who had been my editor at Jove, moved to Warner Communications, where he became editor-in-chief of the book division. Ed was probably the nicest and kindest person I ever knew in the New York book business, and seemed concerned about my financial situation. I was concerned about it too, but not in a very proactive way. Ed was in a better position to do something about it than I was, and he had liked my bodice-ripper, so he called me to suggest something new: An American family saga beginning in the 1930s and culminating in the 1950s.

He described it as a "Best Years of Our Lives kind of thing," which puzzled me, because I had never heard of the movie. In fact, I didn't know it *was* a movie. I was generally ignorant about twentieth-century American history, because I was interested in the future, not the past. "I don't think I can do that," I said.

"I think you can," he said.

I wondered why he thought so. Maybe he sensed abilities in me of which I was unaware. It was conceivable, as I had difficulty judging my own work.

"It will be a series of four novels," Ed continued.

Four! I didn't have a very long attention span where writing was concerned. Even "Christina" novels seemed to eat up a lot of my time, and they only took ten days each. This was going to be a tetrology—no, a *tetralogy*. That was the word.

"I'm thinking of paying about $100,000," he said.

I felt stunned. I was accustomed to living on around $20,000 a year. In 2021 dollars, Ed was offering me about $335,000.

I now had a new agent, so I turned the negotiation over to him. Days passed, then weeks, and my new literary agent started making demands that I considered unreasonable. He kept asking for more money, and claimed—falsely—that the tetralogy wasn't really Ed's idea. Therefore, my agent felt entitled to take the project to another publisher if necessary. When I spoke briefly to Ed, he was concerned that the deal would collapse—which made me worried, although I was also worried about the consequences if it didn't collapse.

The books could keep me busy for months. In fact, longer: They could eat up a couple of *years*, because they would require me to do research, which was a very bad word in my personal lexicon. How was I supposed to lead my usual life? I wanted to be attending science-fiction conventions, visiting friends in England and California, programming my computer, answering personal ads, and maybe pursuing another episode of sequential monogamy if I got lucky.

However, when my agent finally finished wrangling, the total advance had increased to $135,000. I would receive just $15,000 initially, then more payments as I completed and delivered each volume.

I was even more stunned, now, by the largesse, and of course I was immensely grateful to Ed. As for my agent, he had spent so much time on the deal, he would be really pissed if I backed out. I felt I had no choice, so I thanked everyone and said "okay."

The next day, I woke up and thought, "What have I done?"

Ed Breslin, possibly the kindest man in New York book publishing. Alas, no good deed goes unpunished.

Of course, I knew what I had done, and now I had to cope with the consequences.

Maybe I should buy a car, drive out to the Midwest, and live there for a couple of months. I could get acquainted—somehow—with an all-American family of the type that I was supposed to portray. I could go to baseball games, and bake sales, and other things which I thought that people probably did out there. I could take a lot of photographs and use a tape recorder to capture colloquial American argot. That should work.

Meanwhile I went to The Strand bookstore and bought several remaindered books about the 1930s, as that was when the series was supposed to start. I had assumed that the period was quite miserable, but I discovered that it was even more miserable than I had imagined.

People were trying to recover from the great crash of 1929. They elected Roosevelt because they trusted him, but he treated them with patronizing contempt while seizing power far beyond the limits of his constitutional authority. He nationalized entire industries, and provoked the Japanese by blockading their country to prevent them from receiving oil. Then he put American citizens of Japanese ancestry into prison camps, and he sent young men into a European war that he had promised not to fight. In the words of H. L. Mencken, "his greatest fraud was his greatest glory, and sufficient excuse for all his other frauds." That seemed about right to me.

I didn't know what to do, so I decided to drown my troubles by spending some of my advance money before I received it. I threw a big party at a friend's industrial loft, attracting about 100 guests. We had disco dancing at high decibel levels, every conceivable kind of booze, and because the industrial building was empty at night, we took over the hallways in addition to the loft. I showed porno movies on an 8mm projector, which some people felt was a tacky thing to do, although I noticed they stuck around to watch.

The next day I woke up with a hangover, but I also saw a way to cope with my obligations. Here was my idea: I would create a little magazine of literary criticism about science-fiction book publishing. This would alleviate the drudgery of my new writing obligation, and keep me sane.

Of course, any magazine, no matter how modest in size and scope, tends to suck up all available time from the person running it. That's just the way magazines are.

But still—a tetralogy! I had to compensate somehow.

The Patchin Review

In December I went to California and stayed at the home of science-fiction writer Harlan Ellison, with whom I was friendly at this time.

When I told him about my magazine project, he became enthused. He thought it was just what the field needed, and asked me what the title would be.

"*The Patchin Review*," I said.

He gave me a puzzled stare.

I explained that all the obvious titles had been used. *Science Fiction Review, Science Fiction Chronicle, Science Fiction Monthly*. In any case, I didn't want to be "just another" science-fiction publication. I was going to define my own niche, and the magazine should have a unique identity. People would wonder what the title meant, and would have to buy the zine to find out. Plus, "Patchin" was an unusual word that seemed to stick in people's memories, while being easy to spell (unlike Dwo Quong Fok Lok Sow).

Ellison was persuaded, and said he wanted to write something for the first issue. "Something totally dynamite," he said. "Something that will really blow you away."

He seemed to like metaphors that involved explosions.

"Uh, that would be great," I said, although it might not be. His nonfiction was a bit unpredictable.

"Are you going to pay contributors?" he asked.

"Yes, I am. I'm going to print 1,000 copies, and I intend to sell all of them. No freebies. That way, I can pay contributors."

"How much?"

"A penny a word."

His face fell.

"Well," I said, "it's a startup, and I'm using my own money." I reached into my pocket and pulled out a $10 bill. "Here, this is an advance for your first thousand words."

"All right," he said, taking the money. "I'll do it. Because you're a friend."

Somehow that sounded ominous. I wasn't quite sure why—but I would find out, soon enough.

Harlan Ellison, probably taken in the 1980s.

1981

Get It While You Can

Omni magazine enjoyed a special status during the 1980s. It had a big circulation and was printed on fancy glossy paper in full color all the way through. It looked like a men's magazine—which was unsurprising, as it had been founded and financed by Bob Guccione after he made his fortune by publishing *Penthouse*.

Omni paid literally ten times as much as its competitors, yet for some strange reason, if your work appeared in it, no one noticed. The story died there as if it was interred in a neon-lit mausoleum.

Why should this be? I thought the answer was obvious. *Omni* had failed to follow the Pohl Insanity Rule, articulated by Frederik Pohl in his memoir, *The Way the Future Was:*

A magazine should reflect the insanity of its editor.

This may sound odd, but really the truth is obvious if you invert the statement. *A dull editor will create a dull magazine.*

Initially the fiction editor at *Omni* was Ben Bova, a charming man with impeccable credentials who was, I think, one of the dullest people I had ever met. Getting him to voice an opinion was difficult. Persuading him to say anything controversial was impossible.

Then in 1980 Bova was promoted to a general editorial role at *Omni*, at which point he replaced himself with Bob Sheckley. Bob was another charming man, and was a highly regarded writer, but he didn't seem very interested in being an editor. "I just like good stories," he said, with a shrug, when I asked him what his editorial policy was. Evidently the Pohl Insanity Rule was unknown to him.

He had been an exceptional short-story writer in the 1950s, although he told me he had a parasitical relationship with other writers back then. They did the hard work of developing ideas, at which point he came along and riffed on their scenarios for his own satirical purposes. He had a kind of court-jester role within science fiction.

A bohemian by nature, he traveled compulsively during the 1960s, was married a few times, indulged in recreational drugs, lived in Ibiza for several years, then London, and then returned to the West Village in New York City—where he started working for *Omni*.

His new-found income enabled him to rent a freshly renovated, high-ceilinged apartment near the Hudson River, with white walls, maple floors, and track lighting. He didn't buy much furniture, preferring to lie around on cushions on the floor. As he was averse to inconveniences such as washing dishes or putting clothes in closets, the place soon looked like a rich-hippie crash pad.

His philosophy seemed to be, "Get it while you can," and so long as *Omni* was feting him with its largesse, he did his best to get as much as he could. Bob especially enjoyed free meals, which *Omni* would provide if Bob invited a writer to accompany him. A writer such as myself could serve that purpose.

I had never even tried to sell a story to *Omni*, but I might try to sell a story one day, and in the meantime, I lived only a six-block walk from Bob's apartment. He could call me on the spur of the moment, and we'd be sitting down for a gourmet repast fifteen minutes later. I enjoyed his company, and I enjoyed the meals, so it was a pleasantly symbiotic relationship.

Some time in January, Bob mentioned that he had just emerged from a brief liaison with his new assistant, named Sally. He described her as having a magnetic sexuality, but she was twenty-two, he was fifty-three, and after a couple of dates she pointed out that he was older than her father. Bob was forced to recognize that their entanglement looked a bit insalubrious, especially as he had hired her to work for him. Their affair ended by mutual consent, although she continued as his assistant.

A thought had occurred to Bob: I was closer to Sally's age than he was. Maybe I should meet her?

What a kind man. I set aside my embarrassment about dating yet another editorial assistant, and found an excuse to visit the *Omni* offices.

A typical Omni cover, whimsically depicting butterflies on a piece of dead wood in space. Omni was not a science magazine, and was not a science-fiction magazine. It was a fictitious-science magazine.

Years later, in 1992, it would be useful to me when I wanted to run a contest offering free human cryopreservation as a prize to promote cryonics. Until then, I did not find Omni very interesting.

Page 43

Two Little Hitlers

Sally was petite and cute, and something about her did seem magnetic, although I couldn't figure out what it was. She didn't dress provocatively, and wasn't flirtatious. In fact, she seemed to view the world, and people in it, with indifference verging on scorn. Our initial dialogue, such as it was, went something like this:

"Where are you from?"

"Westchester."

"Oh, but you're living in Manhattan, now?"

"Yes."

"How do you like working here for Omni?"

"It's okay."

"Do you read science fiction?"

"Not much."

"Would you like to go out to lunch sometime?"

"All right."

A couple of days later, in a Chinese restaurant, she continued to behave as if conversation was an annoying imposition while I sat wondering why I was going through this. But as Bob had said, there was the magnetic thing, so I asked her out again, this time for an evening date. We ended up in my apartment, where I suggested that we could get into bed together. "All right," she said. Afterward she wandered off as if we had just been watching TV.

Her air of indifference was tantalizing. The subtext was something like, "I'll have sex with you, because I enjoy having sex, but I may not talk to you much, because I find most people boring." I saw this as an interesting challenge, although it became a bit too interesting when I discovered her weakness for promiscuity and drugs.

The first time I heard Steely Dan singing "Black Cow," it reminded me of Sally. A black cow was a drink made from Kahlua, Coca-Cola, and half-and-half, served in some East Village bars:

> In the corner of my eye
> I saw you in Rudy's, you were very high. . . .
> On the counter, by your keys,
> Was a book of numbers, and your remedies
> One one of these surely will screen out the sorrow
> But where are you tomorrow. . . .

I wondered if, maybe, somehow, I could become the one man whom Sally took seriously. As time passed and we continued to see each other, she did talk more, and allowed herself some displays of affection, but how serious were they? I could never be sure.

We did have some interests in common. She had broad reading tastes, and especially liked Anthony Burgess. We also liked the same music, particularly Elvis Costello. She told me that her favorite song of his was "Two Little Hitlers":

> Two little Hitlers will fight it out until
> One little Hitler does the other one's will.

She started spending most nights at my apartment, because it was convenient, or comfortable, and maybe she liked me, somewhat at least. One night around midnight, when I was waiting for her to arrive from whatever she had gotten into, I heard her trying to fit her key in the lock, after which I heard thumping noises.

I opened the door and found her lying on the floor at the top of the stairs. I had to drag her physically into the apartment. "Tell me," I said, speaking very slowly and clearly. "Which drugs?"

"Quaaludes," she mumbled. "And speed."

That was her favorite mix. Her pulse and respiration seemed close to normal, so I left her to sleep it off on the living-room carpet. I couldn't help her into the bed because it was a loft bed, elevated six feet, and I was unable to lift her up the ladder.

I learned that Sally had established a friendly relationship with Bob Sheckley's exwife Abby, who lived in Woodstock and was well connected among ex-hippie dope dealers. One morning when I walked downstairs around 11am to check my mail, I found an anonymous gray envelope in the mailbox addressed to Sally. It had a Woodstock postmark, no return address, and was about a quarter-inch thick. It crunched when I squeezed it.

I called her at *Omni*. "I've got this envelope for you here. I think maybe it's from Abby."

"Oh, yes, probably," she said.

Sally and myself at the polynesian restaurant in Westchester, near her parents' house. The bartender took the photograph.

"You know, I have a feeling that it might contain crystal meth."

No reply.

"It is, isn't it? You're using my address as a mail drop for narcotics."

"Don't *worry* about it, Charles," she said.

On weekends we sometimes visited her parents in Westchester. They were tort lawyers who sued corporations on behalf of victims such as a woman who got Krazy Glue in her eye.

"How is that the fault of Krazy Glue?" I asked Sally's mother. She gave me a vexed look and told Sally later that she thought I was very cold and heartless. She didn't approve of me at all, and I would overhear her in the kitchen telling Sally, "He's not right for you, you know," before we all sat down to eat lunch together.

In the evening Sally would borrow her parents' car to drive us to a local polynesian restaurant where the bartender played a game which might be called, "Let's get the caucasians really drunk." The drinks were the strongest I ever encountered. One Mai-Tai was enough to make me feel detached from reality, and after two, walking without bumping into things was a challenge. Sally always seemed very happy there.

I hosted a couple of parties with her, at one of which she shared her crystal meth with someone named Richard, who was dating a science-fiction editor whom I knew at that time. Richard ended up with heart palpitations and had to go to the emergency room at St. Vincent's Hospital, but Sally received the news philosophically. "I *told* him not to do too much," she said with a shrug.

Fortunately Richard was okay, and his experience didn't stop him from lusting after Sally. He tried to cover it up, but I could see it whenever he looked at her. "I really like her," he said. Well, I knew what that meant. Why should he be different from any other male person?

My biggest problem with Sally was that whenever I tried to do some writing, she became moody and petulant, and I sensed an unspoken threat along the lines, "I'll be out picking up men in bars if you keep doing this for long."

How was I going to deal with this dilemma? I had no idea, but Sally had become an addiction, so I kept putting off the day when I would actually start writing the tetralogy. As for driving into the heartland and getting acquainted with middle-American families—I put that on hold.

The Wrong Phoenix

My friend Robert Frenay asked me if I was interested in buying a 1967 Buick Gran Sport for $800. It was very similar to the legendary Pontiac GTO, being wildly overpowered, like all muscle cars from that period. I knew immediately that it would have slow steering, inadequate brakes, and marginal ability to go around corners, but that would just make it more exciting to drive. I had always wanted to own such a beast, and now, here was my chance!

I had known Robert since we did furniture moving together during the 1970s, and when he told me that the Gran Sport was a good buy, I trusted his judgment. The car was being sold by a childhood friend of his named Dave, who restored cars as a serious hobby and had been planning to pimp the Gran Sport, but ran out of money.

I rented a car and drove with Robert into upstate New York, where he had spent his youth. Soon I found myself in Dave's garage, assessing the Gran Sport, which turned out to be about 40 percent original paint, 40 percent primer, and 20 percent rust.

"It can all be fixed," Dave assured me.

Personally, I saw no need to fix it. The paint/primer/rust mix gave the car a badass look, like something a teenage criminal would use as the getaway vehicle from a 7-11 stickup.

"It only has 75,000 miles on it," Dave told me. "See, it was the last model before they introduced pollution controls." He grinned at the happy thought of a car unencumbered by a catalytic converter. "To find one like this in good condition, you really have to buy it in Arizona and drive it back."

"Where's this one from?" I asked.

"I bought it in Phoenix."

Phoenix! That sounded good.

"It does need a couple of things," Dave went on. "Like, a new exhaust system. But Meineke has a special right now, here in town. Flat rate, any vehicle, $49. But there is one other thing." He jacked up the car, and we crawled under it. "See, the brake line. I put it in, but it isn't, you know, the GM-authorized part. I think it's okay, but at some point, maybe you could think about replacing that."

I stayed overnight at Robert's parents' house, and the next day I gave Dave his $800. (He refused to negotiate.) Now came the interesting part: Driving the Gran Sport to Meineke. The old exhaust was literally dragging on the road, leaving a trail of sparks that caused a motorcycle cop to pull us over. When I explained our mission, he allowed us to continue but followed along behind. So, we reached the muffler shop with a police escort.

After the entire exhaust system was replaced, Robert stayed a few more days with his family while I started back to New York in the Gran Sport, although first I had to buy some little yellow plastic bottles of ether from an auto parts store, to raise 93-octane unleaded premium to the 100 octane required by the high-compression V8. The additive was costly, but I didn't care. With the pedal to the metal, the Gran Sport roared forward like a bull on steroids, burning rubber and slewing from side to side, just as I had imagined it.

My primary addiction was Sally, and my secondary addiction was computers, but the Gran Sport was now a close third.

Along the way back to the city, I detoured to visit Chris and Janet Morris in Cape Cod. When Chris saw the car, he acquired the same bemused expression as when he had seen my exwife talking about my failed marriage on TV. "You *bought* that?"

"It can all be fixed," I said.

Once again, I saw him looking for a rational explanation where none existed. This time, though, he might have a chance to intervene on my behalf. "There's a guy near here who specializes in body work," he said. "I'm going to call him. Don't go anywhere."

An hour later, the body-work expert was surveying my prize. "It's been stored for a while," I told him.

"What was it stored in?" he said. "Brine?"

Yes, he actually said that.

"No offense," he went on, "but this is beyond help. See the rust above the windshield, there? I think it's gone through in places. There's really no way to fix that. You see?"

Well, I did see, but I was like a teenager infatuated with a no-good biker chick. She might have a criminal record, bad teeth, and tattoos, but she was so hot, how could I care about the details?

I continued south along the New York State Thruway. As the sun set, I switched on the headlights, and discovered that the right-hand low-beam didn't work—but when I pulled over and kicked the fender, it came to life. So, that was not a significant concern.

My main problem was with teenage drivers who saw the Gran Sport as a challenge. One car overtook me, then slowed in front of me, and went slower, and slower, till I had to overtake him. I resumed chugging along at a cautious 65, mindful of the replaced

Seriously, does this look hot or WHAT? After I drove the Gran Sport to New York City, I photographed it on East 10th Street, near Fifth Avenue. The mottled patches on the body are primer, with some rust here and there. I don't recall why the rear-right wheel was generic. The missing trim strips were in the trunk.

My only camera in 1981 was a Polaroid SX-70, which is why the prints lack definition.

brake line that was not a GM-authorized part. The other vehicle overtook me again, and slowed in front of me again. This was a boy-racer ritual that I didn't understand. I overtook him again, and resumed my 65. For a third time he came up alongside me—and there was a sudden crack, like a rifle shot, from the passenger window.

The other car disappeared into the night while I pulled on to the shoulder in a state of shock. The window was spattered with beer where the driver had thrown a bottle at my car. Fortunately the window glass on the Gran Sport had been tougher than the bottle.

When I got back to Manhattan, Sally wrinkled her nose at the condition of the car, but she developed a sneaking affection for it as the days passed. When we took it cruising, if the right-hand headlamp flickered, she would get out and kick it for me.

Parking was a problem, but I mapped the alternate-side-of-the-street regulations in my neighborhood and learned that if I got there an hour early, I could sit in the car waiting in a spot until it became legal at 6pm. This was a major hassle, but I endured it because I was still in the grip of my obsession.

The rear bumper fell off the Gran Sport, so I stowed it in the trunk. Several pieces of chrome trim were already in there, having fallen off previously. Sometimes one of them would rattle around and poke out through a rust hole, and I would hear it scraping along the road. Stopping and pulling it back into the trunk became part of my ownership experience.

Finding a mechanic to work on my car was a challenge, as most mechanics in the New York area were not just crooked but incompetent. Eventually I got a referral to someone on Long Island.

I drove out there and was about a block from the garage, cruising along a suburban highway, when I saw a stop sign at an intersection up ahead. I pressed my foot on the brake pedal, which sank all the way to the floor without having any noticeable effect.

This was disconcerting, even though I had half expected it. Still, there was the emergency brake—that funny little pedal off to the left, connected with the drums at the rear by a steel cable. I stepped on it, and heard a distant twanging sound as the rusty cable separated. The little pedal now sank to the floor alongside the big pedal.

The stop sign was coming closer, and I wondered what to do.

I put the transmission into low, which helped. My speed diminished to around ten miles an hour, and then I steered so that the right front tire rubbed against the curb. I was relieved when the car finally stopped rolling just before I reached the intersection.

Now what? I didn't want the expense of calling for a tow truck, so maybe I would be okay without any brakes if I proceeded extremely carefully. Soon I saw the garage up ahead, and there was a sloping ramp leading up to a concrete apron, which was ideal for my purposes.

I adjusted my speed so that as I ascended the ramp, the Gran Sport lost speed and almost stopped. I opened the driver's door, jumped out, and arrested the car by restraining it physically. Then I ducked back in and threw the transmission into Park.

"A bit of brake trouble," I explained to the mechanic.

He didn't bother to lecture me. I think he could see in my eyes that I was too far gone.

When I went back to collect the car from him a few days later, he pointed out a few things that I had failed to notice. "You do realize," he said, "this car does not have air conditioning."

Oh. I hadn't thought about that. After all, this was the month of March. Could air conditioning be retrofitted? Yes, but the model was so old, there were no air vents. An aftermarket unit would cost a lot.

I had to have air conditioning, because I was still thinking of driving out to the Midwest during the summer, to research my unwritten tetralogy—assuming I could find enough bottles of ether to add to the gas tank along the way. I would also need a good supply of oil, as the car consumed about one quart every 150 miles—and transmission fluid, which was leaking from somewhere. The front wheel bearings were making a muted grinding noise which seemed to be getting louder, although that could be my imagination.

The mechanic had reattached the rear bumper and installed a new brake line, so I drove the car back to Manhattan to consider how to proceed with the list of necessary repairs and refurbishments. A few days later, Robert Frenay called. "How are you liking the car?" he asked.

"I love it," I said. "Except, it does seem to be surprisingly rusty, for a car that came from Arizona."

"It didn't come from Arizona," Robert said.

"What? But Dave said, Phoenix!"

"That's Phoenix, New York."

After the phone call, I consulted a map and discovered a town named Phoenix not far from where Dave lived. I liked Dave, and Robert was my friend, so I couldn't believe they had misled me intentionally. It must have been a misunderstanding.

Fortunately for me, the end came for the Gran Sport before I sank more money into it. I was motoring down the Bruckner Expressway with Sally, past rows of arsonized tenements in a derelict section of the South Bronx, when I heard a scraping noise from the rear.

"It's just another of those chrome strips poking through a rust hole," I assured her.

I stopped on the shoulder, got out, and was puzzled to see that even though the weather was dry, the highway was wet. Other vehicles were splashing through puddles on the road. Then I looked under the car and saw that the two steel straps which supported the gas tank had rusted through and separated. We had been dragging the tank behind us by its the fuel line, and the tank had ruptured. The road was now covered in 100-octane fuel.

"I think you should get out of the car," I said to Sally.

We retreated to a safe distance—at least, a distance that I hoped would be safe—and tried to hitch a ride. People driving past were unsympathetic at the sight of us sticking out our thumbs in one of the highest-crime neighborhoods in New York City. They jeered and cackled at us, and made rude gestures, but after about forty minutes someone picked us up and took us to the nearest subway station.

Back at my apartment, I called a towing company in the Bronx.

"You say it's on the Bruckner Expressway?" the guy asked. "Is it all there?"

That seemed an odd question. "Yes, of course it's all there," I said. "Except for the gas tank."

"How long ago?"

"Four hours, maybe."

The man laughed. "By the time I get to it, the wheels will be gone. And the battery, most likely. Forget about it."

As I hung up the phone, I felt a deep, sinking sadness. My car had been cruelly ravaged by salt and snow. It had spent its twilight years in Dave's garage, feeling unloved, until I'd brought it out of retirement, urging it to burn a little rubber for old time's sake. But now it had drunk its last sip of ether-laced gasoline.

I like to think that its spirit lives on in that special place where the seriously badass cars go. To whomever is the custodian up there, I would just like to say—kick its headlight one time for me.

The Grand Hotel in Brighton, as it used to be, before they added a tasteless glass enclosure on the ground floor.

The Grand Hotel

Sally and I were getting along okay—so far as I could tell—so I invited her to visit England with me.

Since I had abandoned London in 1970, my British friends had gotten used to me turning up with a new girlfriend every year or two. Each time, I could sense them thinking, "Who is it now?" and, "I wonder what happened to the last one."

Fortunately, they were discreet enough not to say what they were thinking.

This time around, I enjoyed seeing them confronted with Sally's weird mixture of magnetism and monosyllabic indifference. No one managed to get more than a few words out of her. What was her problem? Shyness? Hostility? Boredom?

My father had honed his ability to make conversation with almost any human being during his managerial years at Vauxhall Motors, but even he had to admit defeat. "She's quite a challenge," he said.

We decided to visit Brighton, where I thought it would be fun to stay at the Grand Hotel. I was disappointed when an apologetic woman at the front desk told me that no rooms were available, but then she looked at Sally standing beside me, and she picked up on the magnetic thing. "You know," she said, "we do have the honeymoon suite. Would that be—acceptable?"

John Shirley, some years after 1981.

The Silly Challenge

I really had to get to work on the tetralogy. First, though, I had to publish *The Patchin Review*.

I had been calling Harlan Ellison once in a while to remind him about his pledged contribution. He always made noises about delivering it, but everyone in book publishing knew that such noises from Ellison were meaningless.

Finally I received a call from him in which he read some text aloud to me over the phone. Now I believed that he really was writing it, and indeed, a week later I received a manuscript in the mail. Wonderful!

Or maybe not. It turned out to be a personal attack on a writer named John Shirley. Apparently John had written some letters to Ellison while drugged or drunk, making silly claims along the lines, "You're a phony radical. You're bullshit. I'm the real thing." Ellison decided to respond by challenging Shirley publicly to a "writing duel," as if Ellison was an aging literary gunfighter, ready to shoot it out with an upstart.

This was silly, but that was okay, as a silly challenge would still generate interest and sell copies of my magazine. The problem was that Ellison's text was also extremely offensive, describing John as a "gunsel." This slang from the 1940s usually describes a passive homosexual in a prison environment who hooks up with a thug in the hope of receiving protection against other thugs. Ellison wasn't using the term literally, but it was still a gratuitous slur.

I wasn't sure what to do, so I asked my friend Tom Disch for a second opinion. Disch was gay, and when he read the piece, he became angry. He telephoned Ellison and demanded that the word "gunsel" should be changed. After about half an hour of Tom scolding him, Ellison capitulated and retitled it "A Punk Is Not a Pistolero." Now it was not quite so offensive, although still just as silly.

I gave a copy of the piece to John, and offered him right of reply. A week or so later I mentioned this during a phone call to Ellison.

He was outraged. He absolutely refused to share my pages with John Shirley. "He can wait till the second issue," he said.

I wasn't so sure about that. I was happy to publish Ellison's text in any way that pleased him, but the other pages in my magazine were—well, they were *mine*. I tried to explain this concept to him as diplomatically as I could.

"No. Send it back," he snapped at me.

At this point I realized that from Ellison's point of view, if I was a friend, this meant I should do what he wanted.

For more than a decade, I had remained diplomatically silent during his notoriously obnoxious behavior. When he was abusive to servers in restaurants because the bread wasn't hot enough or the steak wasn't rare enough, I said nothing. If he became enraged by someone on the freeway who failed to use a turn signal or hogged the left lane, and he endangered their lives and ours by driving like James Dean on drugs, I said nothing.

Other incidents had been less trivial. One time, at night, when a car behind him dazzled him with its high-beams, Ellison forced the driver to pull over, then grabbed the baseball bat that he carried with him, stepped out, and smashed the other car's headlights. Another time, in a bookstore in Sherman Oaks, on a sunny afternoon, he demanded that his books should be removed from the science-fiction section and resituated under modern literature. The manager of the store refused, and an argument escalated into a grappling, physical fight. Writer Bruce Sterling happened to be visiting at the time, and stared in astonishment at the two men wrestling with each other. "Does this kind of thing happen often?" he asked.

Well—somewhat.

Ellison was a pugilistic prima-donna, and he made no secret of it. In speeches at science-fiction conventions and comics conventions, he entertained his audiences with stories of physical confrontations that often seemed to begin when he felt that someone showed insufficient respect for his writing. He claimed he had assaulted an executive at ABC Television named Adrian Samish for the sin of demanding a rewrite, and Samish had ended up with a broken pelvis. Ellison referred to him as "a failed homosexual."

He once said to an interviewer, "If I'm your friend, I'll go on broken glass, on hands and knees, to the center for the earth for you. If you're my enemy, you'll go to your grave with my teeth in your throat. I will not stop. I'm just like the Terminator—I can just keep coming. And I'll get you one way or another."

Below: A daisywheel of the type that generated the text in the magazine. The tip of each spoke was embossed with a character. The wheel would spin until the appropriate spoke was uppermost, at which point a solenoid struck the rear of the letter, hammering it through a carbon-film ribbon onto a sheet of paper. This sequence of events recurred at 30 characters per second, creating an aggravating drumming sound.

Right: The first issue. A friend complained that the first issue of any magazine cannot logically be described as "controversial." But actually, it was.

JULY 1981 NUMBER ONE TWO DOLLARS

The Patchin Review

the unique and controversial guide to science fiction

Featuring Harlan Ellison, Barry N. Malzberg

By defying his dictates, I realized that I was relocating myself from his "friends" list to his "enemies" list, and I might expect him to start gnawing my neck whenever he found time to fit me into his busy revenge schedule.

Of course I could have defused the situation by backing down and saying, "I'm terribly sorry, I'll do whatever you want!" but that was not my style. Instead, I reminded him that I had already paid him for his work. Surely, he remembered the $10 that I had given him? He had supplied his text in exchange for the money, and I had accepted it. He couldn't just ask for it back.

"I will seek an injunction against publication," he said, and hung up the phone.

I wondered if he meant it. Certainly he had a record of filing frivolous law suits. Well, I would just wait and see, but in the meantime, I was angry with him, and decided to vent it by inflicting the punishment that he would dislike the most: Public mockery. I didn't have time for it in the middle of 1981, but later in the year, I would.

Bitching and Snitching

The production process for *The Patchin Review* was less primitive than the paper-and-rubber-cement system that I had endured when working on *New Worlds* magazine in the 1960s, but only a bit less. I had bought a daisywheel printer which produced output comparable to that of a Selectric typewriter, and I wrote my own word-processing program to supply microspacing codes which the printer needed to create justified columns. Text could even run around illustrations, which was a radical concept in 1981. I also included halftones which were generated as veloxes by a small company I found in the Yellow Pages. This way, I could reproduce photographs of book covers and people in book publishing.

I printed my pages at 133% size on layout sheets, and took them to a little printing company named Xpedi that seemed to employ illegal immigrant Chinese labor and required me to pay the bill in advance. The company reduced the pages in a gallery camera and printed them on 8.5 x 11 paper, folded and saddle stitched.

Now for the interesting part. Could I sell 1,000 copies at $2 each?

In case contributors might get bored with lit-crit articles bitching about low literary standards, I added a unique ingredient: A gossip column. This had never been done before in science fiction, but now that some writers were making serious money, I felt they should expect the attention that celebrities would receive.

I wrote my column under the name Gabby Snitch, and placed it in the center pages. It opened with a report on the annual Nebula Awards banquet, which featured a keynote speaker who was so excruciatingly boring, many people gave up and walked out, including Frederik Pohl, who was normally a consummate diplomat. I quoted editor David Hartwell as saying, "Even Greg Benford's 73-year-old mother would have had to go out and smoke dope during that." David was the much-respected editor at Timescape Books, and was hugely influential. Was I quoting him accurately? Of course I was. But did he give permission to be quoted? Yes, I never quoted anyone without their permission.

Science-fiction writers and editors turned out to be a gossip columnist's dream. Lacking any experience or guidance in dealing with the media, they said anything that came into their heads. *Locus* magazine was too dignified to print stuff like that, but I didn't respect such pretensions of dignity, as *Locus* was always eager to reveal the amount of money that some second-rate fantasy writer had been paid for a derivative trilogy.

To show that Gabby Snitch was an equal-opportunity columnist, she described me throwing chocolate mousse at Sally during the awards banquet. I have no memory of that now, but if I wrote about it, I'm sure it happened, and it's safe to assume that Sally and I were drunk at the time. How else were we supposed to cope with an event like that?

Of course, the magazine had its serious side. My editorial in the first issue spelled it out very clearly:

> Many of the science-fiction writers I know are very impressive people whose world-views and belief in the future seem truly important. They are by nature innovators; and yet few of them ever have the time, money, or confidence to explore the most challenging themes, take risks, and stretch themselves as writers. They tend to play safe, because, they say, editors won't accept anything too unusual.
>
> Many of the editors I know are literate and imaginative people who claim that they really would like to publish innovative material. But they say they can't persuade their sales departments to push it into the bookstores, they doubt the bookstores will display it, and they doubt that the public will want to buy it. And so the editors become defeatist and the writers become cynical.

These were merely my opinions, but I substantiated them by including thumbnail reviews of science-fiction and fantasy titles being published each month. It was a major chore for me to read this deluge of mediocrity, but I was determined to document what was happening to the field, and it was not a pretty sight.

For example, regarding *Tactics of Mistake* by Gordon R. Dickson, I wrote: "1970 *Analog* serial, umpteenth in the Dorsai series. Cletus Grahame plays a complex game of strategy and death; but nerve, guts, and judiciously applied atrocities ensure that triumph is inevitable." I think that was a pretty accurate summary of the book.

The Steel of Raithskar by Randall Garrett and Vicki Ann Heydron was worse. I summarized it: "Blatantly reminiscent of E. R. Burroughs and A. E. van Vogt, our hero wakes up on a desert world as a master swordsman after his earthly body is hit by an (unexplained) fireball. Telepathically linked with his steed, a "giant war cat," he fights for freedom. Garrett can do better than this; evidently his wife cannot."

Vicki Ann Heydron was Garrett's wife, and Bantam Books seemed cynical when they published this collaboration to capitalize on the man's name. I felt that other reviewers should have owned up to this, but if they wouldn't, I would.

All I really wanted were three ingredients: Imaginative ideas, rational extrapolation, and storytelling without cliches. I didn't think that should be too much to ask.

The Patchin Review seemed to hit a nerve. During the next two years I would end up publishing articles and letters from Forrest Ackerman, Brian Aldiss, Piers Anthony, J. G. Ballard, Gregory Benford, Alfred Bester, Edward Bryant, Algis Budrys, John Clute, Arthur Byron Cover, Richard Curtis, Philip K. Dick, Thomas Disch, Harlan Ellison, Edward Ferman, Karl Hansen, David Hartwell, Sharon Jarvis, Ted Klein, Adele Leone, Pat LoBrutto, Richard Lupoff, Barry Malzberg, Shawna McCarthy, Michael Moorcock, Janet Morris, Henry Morrison, Frederik Pohl, Jerry Pournelle, Christopher Priest, Kit Reed, Joel Rosenberg, John Shirley, Robert Silverberg, John Sladek, Norman Spinrad, Alice Turner, Ian Watson, and F. Paul Wilson. Most of these people were writers; some were editors; a few were literary agents. It was a surprisingly diverse list for a self-published little magazine. Many of my contributors are dead now, but their names were noteworthy at the time.

As for Harlan Ellison, he never followed through on his law suit. But I would not forgive or forget.

All My Default

Mailing 1,000 copies of my little magazine was nontrivial, but once it was out of the way, I really, seriously had to do something about the tetralogy. The delivery date for the first book in the series was imminent, and no time remained in which to drive into the heartland.

I warned Sally that I might not be much fun for a couple of weeks, and sat down to formulate a plot. Then I wrote 6,000 words as a sample, and I delivered it to Ed Breslin, with much anxiety. Was it any good? I hoped it was. But it was so unlike my usual writing, I honestly didn't know.

And—maybe it wasn't any good. Ed said that my text lacked "passion and grandeur."

He was right. Passion and grandeur were two attributes that had not occurred to me when I assessed the misery of the 1930s.

Worse news followed. Ed had hired a new editorial assistant who took it upon himself to read my manuscript and write an evaluation, even though he had not been asked to do so. The assistant was sarcastic, sneering, and gratuitously nasty. He complained that the characters were stereotypes, the plot was obvious, and the settings were inauthentic. His memo was like the diatribe I had received from Damon Knight at the Milford conference in 1970, and it had the same effect. My confidence crumbled, and I decided he was right. I told Ed that I didn't know how to write the book.

In retrospect, maybe I was wrong about that. Outside of science fiction, I've written many different types of novels over the years. I think of myself as being a good mimic, and all forms of popular fiction tend to follow implicit rules that can be discerned fairly easily. Probably I could have salvaged the tetralogy if I had extricated myself from Sally long enough to study some novels that were similar to the ones I was supposed to write. Alas, I felt too distracted and dispirited to do that.

I subsided into self-blame. A contract is a promise, and I had no respect for anyone who would break a promise. Worse still, Ed was my friend, and he had tried to help me.

I had never defaulted on a contract before, and the consequences were nasty. Warner had paid out $15,000, of which my agent took 10%, leaving me with $13,500, which of course I had spent. Somehow I had to pay that back, *and* I had to pay an additional $1,500 on behalf of the agent, because he certainly wasn't going to forfeit his commission. I was the one who had defaulted, not him!

Well—I didn't have $15,000. I suggested to Ed that maybe Warner would accept a couple of old science-fiction novels of mine, which could be brought back into print: *Garbage World*, and *Planet of the Voles*.

Ed was not interested in my moldy old novels.

Well, then—I didn't know what to suggest.

Losing to Carl

Instead of keeping me sane, *The Patchin Review* had made me crazy. It had become yet another addiction, tempting me to waste countless hours instead of doing the necessary work to fulfill a contractual obligation to a publisher. That made no sense, and was self-destructive, but addictions are always self-destructive.

Part of my problem was, money wasn't a powerful motivator for me. I was happy with a bohemian lifestyle and mindset, and enjoyed my liberty. I had only one life to live—and so on, and so forth.

What if Warner had offered a truly huge amount for the tetralogy? Suppose the contract had been for $1 million—would I have sacrificed *The Patchin Review*? I honestly don't know. And in any case I still had to cope with Sally, who was another addiction. Add it all up, and I had a lot more reasons for not writing books than for writing them.

I sent a letter to my father, asking his advice about declaring bankruptcy. He replied that he didn't think it was a good idea. Well, okay, I would put it off for as long as I could, and in the meantime I went on a road trip with Sally to California. *Dream Makers* had been nominated for a Hugo award, and the awards would be given out at the World Science Fiction Convention in Denver. We could stop there, then continue to Los Angeles, where I had always wanted to stay at the Disneyland Hotel. After that, Sally would return to New York while I remained on the West Coast to do interviews for *Dream Makers Volume II*. I felt confident that I could write that, because it was nonfiction and could be completed in little pieces instead of the long-time immersion which serious novels require.

Also, I still had to write the "Christina" novel for which I had received an advance—but Playboy Press had not started nagging me about it yet, and if I was going to declare bankruptcy, I thought I should do that first.

I rented a little Toyota, and we drove west. I didn't win the non-fiction Hugo, because it went to Carl Sagan for his book *Cosmos*. Did Sagan actually write that book? Er—maybe. Did it relate to science fiction? Not much, but everyone had heard of it, and Sagan was popular because of his TV series. Awards are almost always popularity contests, and I was not very popular.

Our vacation was a lot of fun. In Las Vegas Sally persuaded me to break my usual rule of avoiding nonprescription mind-altering substances, and she dosed me with her favorite combo of Quaaludes and speed. We stayed up all night, and I realized why she liked the mix. "You see?" she said, as we finally stumbled to our hotel room at dawn in a deranged condition. "I was right. I knew you'd enjoy it."

Yes, of course she was right—so long as I didn't have to think about earning a living.

While we were on the West Coast, we visited the physicist and science-fiction writer Gregory Benford, his wife Joan, and their children Mark and Alyson. They lived in a lovely house in the hills overlooking Laguna Beach, which was a great opportunity for Sally to enjoy an activity that I couldn't begin to understand: Sunbathing punctuated by immersion in salt water. Well, if that was what she wanted, I would build sand castles with Mark and Alyson.

Sally was a lot more photogenic than I could ever be, so I'm including a few vacation pix without apology.

Left: Victor, Colorado, back in the days before it became touristy.

Right: The obligatory Vegas Strip photo, when we indulged in mind-altering chemicals. Alas, the wonderful Stardust sign isn't there anymore.

"I was hoping to talk to you about Victorian literature," Greg complained to me.

"I want to build sand castles," I told him.

"Really? That's what you're going to do?"

"For at least half an hour. Maybe longer."

"Why?"

"Because I like to build sand castles."

Greg became a friend, and our friendship has endured for more than forty years, for reasons I do not fully understand. He's much more serious than I am.

Sally went back to New York, while I remained in California and did interviews with Theodore Sturgeon, Jerry Pournelle, Larry Niven, Poul Anderson, and Jack Vance, in that order.

Sturgeon was living in a tiny cube-shaped basement room that had only one tiny window, about six inches above ground level. You could see people's feet as they walked past.

He greeted me warmly, gave me some room-temperature water in a cup without a handle, and told me that normally he was a nudist, but he had put on pants and a shirt for my visit. I was grateful for that. He showed me a picture of his girlfriend, who appeared to be half his age, or maybe one-third, and he studied it for quite a while, making me fear that he might start crooning over it. Then he started talking about himself, and he wouldn't stop.

I think I managed to ask four questions during a couple of hours.

He was obviously a very interesting man, and I had revered his book *More than Human* when I was a teenager, but he just would not, or could not, shut up. Like many loquacious people, he apologized for talking too much but then talked more.

Greg Benford in an author photo, and in a family photo with wife Joan and children Alyson and Mark.

Niven was just the opposite: Circumspect and self-contained. He referred to himself in the third person, saying things like, "That was good for Larry Niven," making me feel as if I were listening to an annual report summarizing profit and loss in The Niven Corporation. Encouraging him to be spontaneous was as impossible as encouraging Sturgeon to stop being spontaneous.

Anderson was even more circumspect. I think he really loathed giving interviews, and only consented to do so because Gregory Benford and his brother Jim persuaded him. I found him likeable, because he was obviously smart and sincere, but he hummed and hawed, hesitated, backed up, and did his best to avoid making any declarative statement of any kind whatsoever.

Jack Vance seemed to feel that he was witty and droll, and made it clear that interviewing him was a rare privilege. In fact, twice he suggested that he might abort the whole thing—which would not have bothered me too much.

I wondered how I was going to make readable profiles out of these experiences.

Pournelle, however, was wonderful. A couple of years previously he had threatened to "take my head off" in response to a book review in which I had foolishly and inaccurately referred to him as

Clockwise, from top left:

Theodore Sturgeon, from a painting by Musiriam.

Larry Niven, photographed quite a while after 1981.

Poul Anderson. I recall him looking like this when faced with the prospect of granting an interview.

Jack Vance.

"that boring old fascist." He had also threatened to sue me and attach my income for life—but this contentious legacy was now forgotten (almost). He was a southern gentleman at heart, and I think this meant that if I was a guest in his house, he would treat me with impeccable manners, so long as I was polite in return. I knew how to be polite, so we got along pretty well.

Unlike my other interviewees, he treated us both to alcohol, which was a very good idea. We drank several glasses of sherry during a period of about three hours in which he debated my half-baked liberal beliefs with a condescending smile that suggested pity on his part. He was an ex-communist, and knew the dogma of the left better than I did.

From Bob and Bucky

When I got back to New York, I found a letter from Warner Communications. They would cancel the contract for the tetralogy if I would write two erotic novels for a new series to compete with the "Christina" novels at Playboy Press.

I was amused by the idea that I would be competing with myself, but I wasn't happy about the financial terms. The $15,000 which they had already paid would be necessary and sufficient to cover two pieces of porn, and that would be all. No additional money. Take it or leave it. They wouldn't even allow me to own copyright.

I took it, because I had no choice.

In the meantime, I had a more pressing obligation: The second issue of *The Patchin Review*. Response to the first issue had been impressive, as unsolicited contributions had arrived from Brian Aldiss, Alfred Bester, Edward Bryant, Algis Budrys, Thomas M. Disch, and Janet E. Morris. I especially enjoyed the Aldiss piece, because it mocked my first issue. In fact Brian's article complained that my magazine was trashy. Wonderful! If I published this, it would make me seem arrogant. John W. Campbell had taught me the importance of editorial arrogance, which I regarded as being just as essential for a magazine as Pohl's Insanity Law.

I had to increase the number of pages from 36 to 56, which would cost money that I didn't really have, but I didn't care, because it filled my neurotic needs. Also, I felt that the zine served as a useful outlet for the angst that writers felt as they watched book publishing changing before their eyes. Not everyone agreed that my zine was useful, but that was okay, too. I really enjoyed the letter from Robert Silverberg which advised me to shut up and give up:

> Look, s-f is mass-market commercial entertainment, consumed largely by unhappy adolescents, many of whom are dummies looking for easy escape.... A bunch of us ... marched out there boldly circa 1966 and did what we could. Most of those books are now out of print, and the ones that survive survived because a few of us are good at the fancy dancing necessary to stay in print. But it was folly to go out there and be Prousts and Joyces and Manns and Kafkas in that particular arena. ... S-f is just a goddamn business; we are all entrepreneurs peddling our wares; fight the next revolution without me, okay?

Silverberg was right: The battle would be futile. But I would enjoy fighting it anyway.

I also enjoyed a letter to the editor from someone signing his name as "Bucky," postmarked Doylestown, Pennsylvania:

> Dear Mr. Patchin, thank you for your review which I liked v. much. I showed it to my friends in Jumpin' Joe's Saloon and they liked it v. much. A specially the sexy and drinking parts which they liked v. much. Also the fighting B cause we always thought writers who did writeing was all fairies.
>
> Tiger Leekhower says why can't you also show pictures of naked girls like they do in the other to (2) $ magazines. A specially the kind that shows all the front. We would like that v. much.
> V. trully yrs....

I have no doubt that Alfred Bester wrote that letter (in addition to a serious article that he wrote for me under his real name). He had a weekend retreat in Doylestown, in Bucks County, where he liked to hang out at a local redneck bar. I could imagine him sitting there chuckling over *The Patchin Review*, borrowing a pen and a sheet of paper from the bartender, and writing his letter to me with his customary glass of brandy at his elbow.

He had been my idol and role model when I was a teenager, and now he was sending a funny little anonymous note to my self-published zine. This was immensely valuable to me. Science fiction has always been the most egalitarian category of fiction.

LDV Limbo

In December I began my campaign to punish Harlan Ellison for threatening me with a frivolous law suit. Was this a waste of my time? Probably, but I would find it entertaining, and I thought it would be therapeutic for him.

His area of greatest vulnerability was *The Last Dangerous Visions*, an anthology of original science fiction. He had acquired more than 100 stories, but the publisher required him to write introductions to them, and somehow he never got around to it. He missed deadlines, he made excuses, he claimed he was doing the work (when he wasn't), he threw temper tantrums, and made threats when some authors got impatient and withdrew their stories. Somehow, this ridiculous situation had continued for *ten years.*

What was the big deal about writing the introductions? Ellison had no problem writing short stories, and he wrote them in peculiar circumstances such as at a science-fiction convention, or while

Always trying to lighten the mood of lit crit (in case anyone might mistake The Patchin Review *for* The New York Review of Science Fiction), *I wrote a column in the third issue under the byline "Cousin Clara," offering advice on the topic likely to be most important to male science-fiction fans: How to hook up with females at science-fiction conventions. Personally I knew almost nothing about this, so I turned to Ed Bryant for advice. He launched into a stream of helpful tips, such as the best costumes to wear to conceal obesity, and even suggested carrying a small furry animal that women would want to pet. I began to suspect that Ed had actually used some of his manipulative suggestions, but such questions were best left unasked.*

THE "TOTAL COSTUME" APPROACH CAN BE USED TO CONCEAL EVEN THE MOST MAJOR BLEMISHES....

sitting in a bookstore window, or during a radio broadcast. Surely, stunts of that type had to be more difficult than writing introductions, in which case I had to conclude that he hadn't written them simply because he didn't feel like writing them.

I tended to be a procrastinator myself, when faced with a writing chore that didn't appeal to me. I could understand the mindset. But—ten years! And there was a serious aspect: People were now dying while waiting for their stories to be published.

When I checked, I found that seven contributors were no longer alive. How many more would die while Ellison was making excuses and screwing around? It seemed to me, a simple actuarial calculation based on the birth dates of authors would provide an answer.

Birth dates were not readily available, but I had a mole who would feed them to me. Edward Bryant was supposedly a close friend of Harlan Ellison, but he could never resist a prank, and so, during his next visit to "Ellison Wonderland," Edward waited for his host to go to sleep, then raided the box of manuscripts under Ellison's desk. The birth dates were all in there.

After doing the math, I concluded that if Ellison procrastinated for another ten years (which I considered likely), another twenty contributors were likely to expire. I published this conclusion under the title "L.D.V./R.I.P." and waited for the repercussions.

I didn't have to wait long. Ellison called and told me in a gruff, deeply serious voice that I was in physical danger, maybe even mortal danger. He had friends who took him very seriously, and—

"What do you mean?" I interrupted. "Did you say, 'Charles Platt should have his legs broken,' and someone took you literally?"

"Um, something like that."

He urged me to leave town for a week and stay in a hotel till he could, somehow, call off the hit. He would pay my transportation costs and hotel bill. He begged me to take him seriously, because if I should be injured, he would never forgive himself.

I had witnessed many of his acting performances over the years, and this wasn't one of his best. I thanked him for his kind offer and said I preferred to go about my daily business.

Days passed. Nothing happened.

When he realized that I hadn't made a fool of myself by falling for his hoax, he couldn't admit that he had made the whole thing up, so he called again. "I just want you to know," he said, "I managed to get in touch with my friend, and it's safe, now."

Like so many ridiculous aspects of his life, this had a serious aspect. Even if a physical threat is indirect, it's still a threat, and when someone makes a threat in response to a factually accurate piece of text, I find this unacceptable. I felt angry with him all over again, and decided that I would mock him some more whenever possible.

Annual Report

I ended 1981 feeling surprisingly happy with my life. I lived in a crappy little apartment, but it was in one of the most desirable locations in New York City. I had found a peculiar niche in the world of science fiction, writing commentary and criticism. My girlfriend was troublesome, but I was still infatuated with her. I had lost money on the tetralogy, and still felt bad about it, but was thankful that I didn't have to write it. I had to do a few more interviews for *Dream Makers Volume II*, but that would be easy enough. I had to write two porno novels for Warner, but each of them would only take about a week. In due course, I really would deal with the "Christina" novel.

Of course, I wasn't making any progress as a writer in any particular direction, but somehow this didn't bother me.

1982

Becoming Cantwell

I visited Ed Breslin at his office to receive a briefing about the porn that would pay off my debt to Warner Communications. Ed told me that Howard Kaminsky, head of the book division, wanted each title to feature two sexy women who were twins, and because they looked identical, they would get into all kinds of naughty adventures—maybe a bit like Shakespeare's "Comedy of Errors," written around 1600.

Howard Kaminsky, at some publishing party. I never met him, which was okay with me.

I stared at Ed. "Are you serious?"

He sighed. "It seems a bit corny, but that's what Howard wants."

And, there was more. "Howard wants the first book to be titled *Double Delight*, and the second will be *Tease for Two*," Ed told me.

Those titles sounded like Gold Medal paperbacks of the 1950s. I wondered how Kaminsky had risen to such a formidable position of power in New York book publishing.

"Howard also came up with a house pseudonym for the books," Ed went on. "Aston Cantwell."

That sounded like a sly reference to my recent failure to write a tetralogy.

"You know," Ed said, "I was almost fired when you didn't come through with those historical novels."

"I'm very sorry, Ed."

"Don't worry about it." He was a remarkably forgiving man. "The sisters will be named Abigail van Pelt and Moira van Pelt."

"You're serious."

He nodded. "Just write the books, Charles."

"I will. What do the van Pelt sisters do for a living?"

"Who knows. Make something up. Just deliver the books, okay?"

Fashion Tips

In February I realized with amazement that my relationship with Sally had lasted for a whole year. Somehow the two little Hitlers had reached a kind of detente, mostly because my simple-minded obsession with her outweighed my exasperation over her drug use and promiscuity.

I still didn't understand her dealings with men, although maybe her older brother was something to do with it. She said he had been mean to her when they were growing up, although that might have been just a cover story.

He was nice enough to me when I met him at the wedding of a family friend. He showed me that my necktie would hang more neatly if I slipped the narrow end through the label in the underside of the wide end.

I asked him how he knew this.

"I read about it in a book called *Dress for Success*," he said.

A few days later, I bought a copy. It was full of valuable tips. It didn't advise me on how to deal with Sally, though.

Philip K. Dick

At the beginning of March, I received the terrible news that Philip K. Dick had died. My communications with him had begun in 1974, when I was a consulting editor to Avon Books and wanted them to buy paperback rights to his novel *Flow My Tears, the Policeman Said*. Robert Wyatt, a senior editor at Avon who seemed to derive pleasure by being arbitrary and obnoxious, refused my recommendation, stating that he didn't like the title of the book. This had been the deciding factor prompting me to quit from Avon, and the gesture seemed important to Phil at the time.

We remained in contact intermittently after that. In 1978 I wrote an introduction to the Gregg Press edition of his book *The Zap Gun*, and he called me to express his appreciation, which was meaningful to me. I returned the compliment soon afterward by telling him how much I enjoyed his novel *A Scanner Darkly*, and we talked about the book at some length. It remains, for me, the most unflinching and insightful description of wasted lives in the drug-addled subculture of the late 1960s.

Thus we were already on friendly terms when I visited him in

1979 to interview him for the first volume of *Dream Makers*. At that time very few people knew that Phil had been having mystical experiences, and he used my interview as his opportunity to go public.

Rationally, he knew that he sounded crazy, as he described his conversations with a tutelary spirit. Later he described this dissonance in his novel *Valis*, but when I interviewed him, he just presented me with the problem and said, in effect, "Here's what's going on inside my head. You figure it out."

Thanks a lot, Phil! Well, I did my best, and he seemed to like the way I handled it.

A year or so after that, when I visited him during a trip to California, *Valis* had just been published, and he was in a more sanguine mood. This time I suggested that we should go out to get something to eat, as I didn't really want a delivery of Chinese food in his apartment, with its dusty stacks of papers, a strong odor of cat litter, and a carpet that looked as if it had not been touched by a vacuum cleaner in a while.

My suggestion interrupted his sanguinity. He paced to and fro, debating where we should go. Then he took most of his money out of his wallet, in case we might be robbed. When we emerged from his apartment complex onto the sidewalk, he glanced behind him uneasily.

We ended up in a cheesy local bar-restaurant where two long-haired guys dressed in denim were holding acoustic guitars. This kind of thing is always an ominous sign for me, but for Phil, it turned out to be worse. "We're going to do an old favorite," one of guitarists said, as we were sitting down. "From Buffalo Springfield."

Phil looked dismayed as the musicians began singing:

> There's something happening here
> What it is ain't exactly clear

Page 71

And on to the climax:

> Paranoia strikes deep
> Into your life it will creep
> It starts when you're always afraid
> You step out of line
> The man come and take you away

"God, I really hate this song," Phil said.

If ever there was proof of his contention that each of us lives in a separate reality, here it was. In Phil's reality, he was paranoid because *he had good reason to be paranoid.* He couldn't even walk down the street to a cheap restaurant without something happening to freak him out.

Later, when we got back to his apartment, he added a surreal twist by telling me that he had just been elected by the local tenants' association to monitor the residential complex for criminal activity. "You mean you're like a rent-a-cop?" I asked.

"You better believe it," he said. "I'm the law around here." He gave me his mock-serious look, which was so serious, he could almost con you into thinking that he really was serious.

As we talked some more, he mentioned that he'd had a new religious revelation. According to his tutelary spirit, the core concepts of Christianity were all entirely true.

"Let me get this straight," I said. "You have been appointed to a very conventional position of authority. At the same time, your tutelary spirit has convinced you to embrace a very conventional religion. Is that a coincidence?"

This was one of the few times I ever found myself a step ahead of Phil. He was silent for a long moment, pondering the juxtaposition. "Well," he said finally, "whatever it is up there," he gestured heavenward, "it's certainly responsive to me."

Ah, yes, okay.

Then he went on, "You understand, I haven't had a chance to process this, yet."

Within a couple of weeks, he would conceive a framework in which the new revelation could be embedded, and his usual mix of solemn conviction, humor, and ironic detachment would protect him against probing questions from skeptics such as myself.

Alas, I never had a chance to talk to him again.

The Inappropriate Award

I was distraught about Phil's death, and so was Tom Disch, who had liked him a lot. Tom responded by telling me that he would create The Philip K. Dick Award for the best paperback original to be published each year. All of Phil's early work had been published as paperback originals, so the award seemed appropriate to Tom—although, not to me. Phil had always rejected the concept of "best," because it meant something different to each individual. An award would violate his own value system.

I became even more annoyed when Tom named Ursula Le Guin as one of the judges for the first year of the award. Phil had told me that Le Guin asked him to stop communicating with her about his tutelary spirit, because she thought he was crazy. She had cut him off. And now she would be judging an award named after him?

I protested to Tom that this was insufferable—but Tom never respected my opinion on anything to do with literature. At one point during our long and difficult friendship, he said to me: "You have to bear in mind, my incredible ego."

Tom Disch, in one of the many images he adopted for book-cover and publicity photographs over the years.

Denizens of Florida

During March, I went to interview several writers located in the inaccurately named "Sunshine State," which enjoys more annual rainfall than Oregon. Coincidentally, the Conference on the Fantastic in the Arts was being held in Boca Raton, so I decided to stop there first, even though a manicured Florida enclave populated by irascible retirees in gated communities did not seem an appetizing prospect.

Still, the event was harmless enough. Most of the attendees were English professors whose expenses were reimbursed by their educational institutions. In other words, it was an academic junket.

I was happy to find that Bob Sheckley was on the guest list. John Shirley's wife, Jay Rothbell, had left him and hooked up with Bob, who had quit his job at *Omni*. Jay and Bob were now driving around the United States in a scuzzy old car, staying overnight in camp grounds where they slept in a tent and ate MRE military rations. This seemed to be Bob's idea of a good time.

At the conference, I found the itinerant duo in a suite that had been assigned to Bob as an honored guest, although he and Jay had become so habituated to an itinerant life, they remade the bedroom as a camp site. A little propane stove had been brought in from their vehicle and was set up in the center of the floor where they could sit cross-legged on the plush carpet and heat their rations. They had also stretched some strings across the room on which hand-washed items of clothing had been hung up to dry.

I thought nostalgically of the days when Bob had enjoyed free gourmet meals in the West Village at *Omni*'s expense, but he expressed no regrets. He was charming, as always. Jay seemed to be putting up with his hobo predilections, and he was tolerating her tendency to be somewhat talkative.

After hanging out with them for a while and declining an offer of some rations, I walked down into the hotel and eyed the attendees.

Left: Joe Haldeman, in a relatively recent photograph.

Center: Andre Norton, probably in the 1980s.

Right: Keith Laumber, from a book jacket published in 1967.

Many of the women had the same eager look as the libidinous advertisers whom I had met through *The New York Review of Books*, but I was of no interest to them here, because I wasn't literary enough. I think they hoped to rub shoulders (and perhaps other body parts) with esteemed authors such as Brian Aldiss, who had somehow acquired the label of "Perpetual Special Guest." That was, literally, his title in the conference program. Brian always charmed the academics, none of whom seemed to realize that he was a college dropout.

After the conference, I went on a road trip to visit Piers Anthony, Joe Haldeman, Keith Laumer, and Andre Norton.

Joe and his wife Gay were embedded in the social world of science fiction, and had the friendly demeanor that is its most positive attribute. I had not always been so mellow myself, but I think they still saw me as a member of the fraternity, which seemed to mean that I was automatically welcome as a guest in their home. Their kindness was appreciated.

I was fascinated when Joe told me about his daily schedule. He only needed half as much sleep as most people. He would go to bed around midnight, get up at 4am, and write till 8am or 9am, when everyone else woke up. After that, he didn't need to work during the rest of the day. He was getting an extra four hours of conscious time, every day, for the rest of his life, and I felt overwhelmed with jealousy.

Andre Norton was difficult to deal with. I did my best to show the necessary respect, but probably she sensed that I had not read every word in her many books. Later, when I wrote my profile and mentioned that visiting her on a Florida back street reminded me of visiting my aunt when I was a kid, she took offense. She deleted my reference to her home being "warm," and she was annoyed when I mentioned that she served me some cookies. I always gave people the option to review their profiles, and she took advantage of this to delete or revise about thirty sentences altogether.

Piers Anthony lived in a backwoods location, in a rustic house that hadn't been completely finished, and even though he was now making a lot of money writing Xanth novels, he worked in a shed in the back yard. He talked as much as Theodore Sturgeon, but that was okay, because he was succinct, sardonic, and self-analytical in a way that I found fascinating. His eccentricities were also interesting, because he defended them so logically.

Visiting Keith Laumer was a singular experience. A few years previously he had suffered a stroke that left him partially paralyzed, although he insisted that it wasn't really a stroke at all, and was merely a psychological reaction to accumulated life traumas. While he received some kind of dubious therapy for this, he lived alone in a beautiful home that he had designed himself before he became disabled. For reasons that were never made clear, he had collected more than forty late-1960s Mercury Cougars that were strewn around the property, each of them numbered in spray paint. He insisted that he was going to restore all of them, just as he insisted that he would restore himself.

My visit became a surreal and somewhat threatening experience when he mentioned a character named Magnan who appeared in some of his novels, and I failed to catch the reference. He seized an ornamental saber and pounded it on the floor while screaming at me with inarticulate rage. Eventually he subsided into a refractory state, set down the saber, and asked me how I thought I would transcribe his screaming when I wrote the profile. He even suggested the spelling.

Later, when I wrote about Keith, I wasn't sure if I should mention his raving, but I took a chance and included everything. He had no problem with it, because he respected the truth when he saw it. He was a remarkable man.

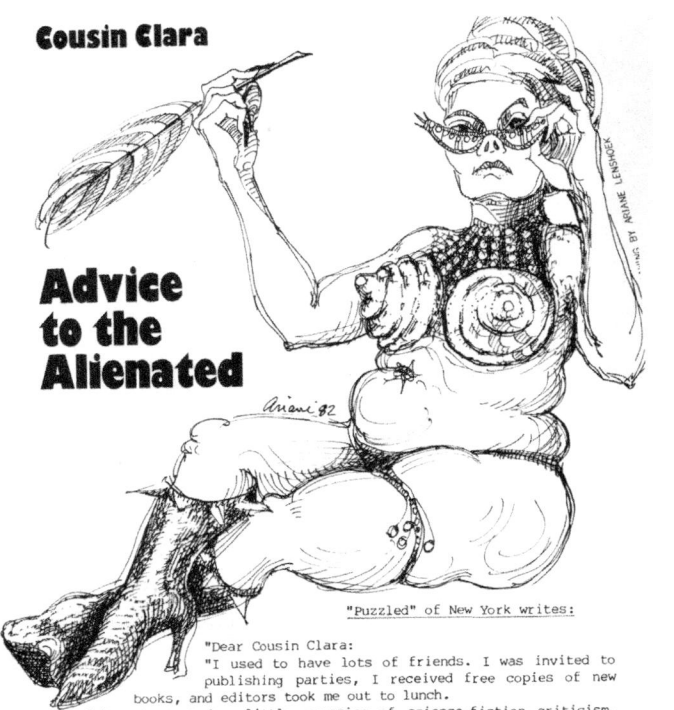

Cousin Clara

Advice to the Alienated

"Puzzled" of New York writes:

"Dear Cousin Clara:
"I used to have lots of friends. I was invited to publishing parties, I received free copies of new books, and editors took me out to lunch.
"Then I started a little magazine of science-fiction criticism. Suddenly, everyone has turned against me! Several of my oldest pals have stopped talking to me. One of them refused to stock my magazine in her bookstore, and another even threatened me with legal action!
"I tried to tell people that my magazine is just a bit of good-natured fun. No one believed me. So I wrote an editorial explaining that it's all done for very idealistic reasons, and has lofty aims. But this doesn't seem to have made any difference, either. What can I do?"

Oh, Puzzled, you silly, silly boy! Surely you don't imagine that distributing an evil little package of sneers, diatribes, and embar-

First Literary Elitist: "I SAY OLD CHAP, YOU'VE BEEN VILIFIED IN 'THE PATCHIN REVIEW'!"

Second Literary Elitist: "A FLY, SIR, MAY STING A STATELY HORSE, AND MAKE HIM WINCE; BUT ONE IS BUT AN INSECT, AND THE OTHER A HORSE STILL."

Incessant Whining

The fourth *Patchin Review* included some gratuitous backlash from F. Paul Wilson, who contributed a piece titled "Literary Darwinism" in which he mocked "those dour, tight-lipped, finger-wagging neo-Puritan biddies who moan constantly about Literary SF." That would include me and most of my readership, wouldn't it?

Paul scolded them—or, us—for our "incessant whining." This was fine by me, as I felt that publishing him would be like taking out an insurance policy. How could anyone attack *The Patchin Review* when the magazine kept attacking itself?

As counterpoint, David Hartwell contributed an article complaining that writers who used "rubber science" were exhibiting a "deadly laziness." He also said he had noth-

I had fun with cartoons in the fourth Patchin Review. Ariane Lenshoek created a perfect persona for my advice columnist, Cousin Clara. I dug up a Samuel Johnson quote in response to accusations of "literary elitism." And how better to illustrate F. Paul Wilson's diatribe, which was titled "Literary Darwinism"?

ing in common with a new generation of science-fiction readers who were ignorant of classics in the field. Hartwell was still very influential; to see him stating bluntly that he felt estranged from his own readers seemed odd and perhaps ominous, although I would not discover just how ominous until a year later.

King and Winter

My friend Douglas Winter had started to compile a book of interviews with horror writers titled *Faces of Fear*, as counterpoint to my book *Dream Makers*.

Stephen King agreed to do an interview for Douglas, at which point Douglas asked me if I would like to come along. Our idea was that if we talked to King for maybe three hours, half of the material could appear in *Faces of Fear* while the other half could go into *Dream Makers Volume II*.

Douglas had a day job as a high-level attorney for Covington and Burling, one of the most prestigious law firms in Washington, DC. He was much more disciplined and organized than I could ever be, and as an attorney, due diligence came naturally to him. On the night before our King interview, he handed me a thick stack of photocopies of previous interviews with King that he had tracked down and compiled.

I stared at it in dismay, wondering if there was anything left to ask that hadn't been asked already.

Then I went through the clippings and realized that the interviewers had been hopelessly unimaginative. This was my first exposure to the laziness and cluelessness of many journalists, which would make my life so easy in years to come, because they offered so little serious competition.

"What is the most important ingredient of horror?" was Douglas's opening question to King, and it elicited an interesting response. "Love" was his answer, because if a writer doesn't care about his characters, why should anyone else care what happens to them?

He turned out to be immensely likable, although touched with an undercurrent of melancholy. He was also very analytical about book publishing, more savvy than any other writer I met, and disarmingly candid.

He gave us a command performance.

I feel privileged to have known Alice Sheldon and her husband Ting. After I had gone through weeks of meticulous edits of her profile, she rewarded me by sending me a picture of herself with a kind of flirtatious yet sympathetic message, which I saw as symptomatic of her childhood training, always to please the people around her.

Alice and Ting

The last of my interviews for Dream Makers II was with Alice Sheldon, who wrote under the pseudonym James Tiptree Jr. I was unfamiliar with her work, because she only wrote short stories, and I preferred to read novels. Really, the only reason I went to interview her was that my editor, Victoria Schochet, demanded that I do so.

Alice was just as reluctant to talk to me as I was to talk to her, because she wasn't happy that her pseudonym had been uncovered a year or so previously. The scene was set for an awkward, unrevealing interaction—yet somehow a rapport developed, which must have surprised her as much as me.

Alice's life was remarkable. Her parents had been explorers who went in search of mountain gorillas for the American Museum of National History. In 1921, at the age of six, she was "the first white child ever seen by pygmy tribes," according to a contemporaneous account. With her parents, she literally walked across Africa.

Subsequently she worked in CIA with her husband, Huntington Sheldon, whom she referred to as "Ting." He had been Director of the Office of Current Intelligence, and had briefed John F. Kennedy on a daily basis in the years after the Bay of Pigs fiasco.

When she introduced me to Ting, I discovered that he had the manners of a British gentleman, partly as a result of attending a British boarding school. I knew how to play that role, and found myself spending hours talking to both of them. At some point, Alice asked if she could pay me to come back and interview him as many times as necessary, so that I could write his biography. He had never told anyone the details of his work at CIA.

I told her I would do it for the cost of a train fare, and I returned to their home in McLean, where I spent a lot of time interviewing him—or trying to. He was more comfortable gathering facts than disclosing them, and whenever I started my tape recorder, he became circumspect.

Alice sat listening to us from the next room, and finally became exasperated with his evasions, especially regarding his supervision of German prisoners at the end of World War II. "Why don't you tell Charles about the time you had Goering naked from the waist up, shoveling shit in the horse stables?" she said.

"Why, I remember nothing about that," he said, with an inscrutable smile. "And if such a thing had happened, it would have been a violation of the Geneva Convention."

At this point I think Alice realized that the task she had assigned to me was impossible, much to our mutual regret.

When I tried to write my profile of Alice, her work ethic kicked in. She was determined that the job should be done right, and so the phone calls began. We would talk for an hour or more each time.

I wrote a draft and sent it to her, at which point the correspondence began. She was meticulous and relentless, and I started to dread her detail editing, even while I admired it. Still, we ended up with something that made her happy, which was what I wanted.

After that, our communications became sporadic.

In 1987 I called her, just to make contact. She was not in a stable state, because Ting had lost the sight of both eyes. He was coping with the situation by listening to a lot of classical music, but he was somewhat deaf and had to turn the volume up high. Alice said she was going crazy with loud music filling the house all day, in addition to the chores of taking care of him.

She had always been preoccupied with death, and the situation was too much for her to deal with. Supposedly with Ting's consent, on May 19th, 1987 she shot him in the head with a revolver that they kept in the house. Then she shot herself.

Editorial Discretion

I delivered the two erotic novels to Ed Breslin at Warner, and I think he would have been happy if I had written a couple more, but as things turned out, this was not permitted.

Typically the female characters in my books manipulated and humiliated the men in a light-hearted manner, and in fact one of the naughty van Pelt twins was a professional dominatrix. Alas, to the female proofreaders and copyeditors at Warner, female empowerment was irrelevant. They seemed to feel that all porn written to titillate men exploited women, no matter who did what to whom, and they demanded that Warner should cease publishing such offensive trash.

The publisher capitulated, and the series was summarily cancelled.

Back in the 1950s, judges used to put people in prison for writing or publishing sexually explicit books. That was an appalling violation of free speech, but at least the a verdict could be appealed to a higher court—which was how laws against pornography were ultimately found unconstitutional.

Publishing companies, unlike judges, are not constrained by written statutes. They don't have to publish anything that they don't like, and a writer has no recourse. Editors also tend to influence each other, as New York publishing is a small community. White male writers couldn't get away with much in 1982, and they get away with even less today.

Women with Large Mouths

In October, I found myself invited to a party at Bob Guccione's mansion on the Upper East Side commemorating the four-year anniversary of *Omni*.

Science-fiction writers wandered around the four-story brownstone looking dowdy and confused, like indigents who had been admitted to a well-funded church for a turkey dinner. I had always known, in theory, that money could be made from smut, but I'd never realized quite how much. The basement of the brownstone was entirely filled with a swimming pool. The upper floors were paved in white marble and featured huge fireplaces, while original paintings were hung where one might expect to see prints. I recall "The Madonna of the Cherries," by Quinten Massys (1466-1530), and even a canvas by Hieronymus Bosch. Seriously! An original oil by Bosch! Heavy-set, watchful, craggy-faced men stood beside the art, wearing dark blue suits that showed bulges under their jackets where shoulder holsters might be.

Tall women with elaborately styled hair were wandering around, giving the guests fixed smiles. They all had large mouths and were wearing too much makeup, and I wondered who they were.

Isaac Asimov was standing holding a drink, wearing a promo button for his new novel, *Foundation's Edge*. "It's a real experience," he remarked, "to see a Penthouse Pet in the flesh."

Oh, *that's* who they were! Asimov was too dazed with lust to talk to me, so I left the party and went home.

Give Us Some Money

In August, a new computer was announced: The Commodore 64, a flimsy brown plastic box, barely bigger than a keyboard. It was priced at $499.

When Fred Beyer saw it, he realized he might still have a way to salvage his word-processing program, because the Commodore contained a 6502 processor, enabling him to port his code with minimal modifications. He could be the first vendor of word processing for a computer that would sell millions of units.

He only needed two things: A better business name than Dwo Quong Fok Lok Sow, and money.

He renamed his business Quick Brown Fox, which was a step in the right direction. For money, he went back to Joe Ming, and I sat in on a meeting between them in the kitchen where I had served my apprenticeship in computers just a couple of years ago.

Joe was charming, had impeccable manners, and was wearing a nicely tailored black suit. Fred explained to him that the Commodore 64 was the brainchild of Jack Tramiel, who had marketed the Commodore PET and then the VIC-20, after which he bought a chip factory so that he couldn't be held up to ransom by any semiconductor manufacturer. He knew how to do mail order, and without a doubt, he was going to start a price war. The computer had so much credibility, developers would start writing software immediately.

The Commodore 64 was the plastic box located at the front in this photograph, looking like a thick keyboard. That was the whole computer. The floppy disk drive, at right, was unnecessary if you bought software as firmware on cartridges. The drive didn't work properly, anyway; it often gave a mysterious flashing-red-light error when you tried to format a disk. The printer, at left, was dot-matrix, and you didn't need that either if you just wanted to play video games.

Advertising for home computers often showed a screen with a bar chart on it, as if the system would be used by sales managers, stock brokers, or science students. That was silly; the horrible touch of the keyboard, and the slowness of the system, made it unsuitable for serious use. But it was cheap!

The Commodore 64 would be sold as a games machine, but sooner or later the people who bought it would use it to print text on paper. They had to, didn't they? Word processing was fundamental. Everyone would need to do it.

Joe listened attentively to the presentation. "This shouldn't be difficult," he said, when Fred was done. "We'll have a fund-raising dinner in Chinatown and ask people to give us some money." He explained that his family was well connected with other Chinese-American families, and when one family saw a business opportunity, their standard procedure was to throw a dinner party where everyone would kick in some cash. After a year or two, everyone would share the profits.

Fred seemed doubtful. "You'll need a business plan," he said.

"Not necessary," said Joe. "Just give me some talking points. I'll be speaking in Chinese, you realize."

I asked Joe if I could attend the dinner. "Definitely," he said. "We'll have Hal there, too. It will look good to have more people."

"And it's really that simple?" I asked.

"Yes," he said, "it happens all the time."

Page 83

Love and Work

I started to have pain urinating, so I visited my friendly neighborhood MD, who diagnosed it as an infection easily cured with antibiotics. "But how did I catch it?" I asked.

He gave me a wry smile and shook his head. "There's only one way."

When I confronted Sally with the news, she went into her expressionless mode and said absolutely nothing.

This was very irritating. "Why aren't you talking to me?" I said.

"Because you're accusing me of cheating on you." She sounded deeply hurt by such a cruel implication.

I realized that my fascination with her insouciance was finally wearing thin. "Look," I said, "what do you really want?"

After a brief discussion, she delivered her non-negotiable demand: If we were going to continue as a couple, we would have to go out drinking and partying together at least four times per week.

That was incompatible with my need to earn a living, so Sally moved out and I got my life back. Even now, whenever I listen to Steely Dan singing "Black Cow," I think of her:

> Like a gangster on the run
> You will stagger homeward
> to your precious one
> I'm the one
> who must make everything right
> Talk it out till daylight
> I don't care anymore why you run around
> Break away
> Just when it seems so clear that it's over now
> Drink your big black cow
> And get out of here

The Fund-Raiser

In a utilitarian meeting room above a restaurant in Chinatown, Fred, Joe, and myself were the only people who didn't look Chinese. Everyone seemed to know everyone, and they were all being polite to each other, but in an uptight, businesslike manner. They were competitors, I realized, coming together strictly for the purpose of making more money. This made me nervous, because if they were as serious about money as they seemed to be, they might not react very well to losing some of it.

Food was served, and was quickly consumed. Even the process of eating was businesslike. I sat between Fred and Hal, feeling worried on Joe's behalf. But he seemed unconcerned.

At the end of the meal he stood up holding a Commodore 64 computer. He talked about it briefly, then gestured to Fred, Hal, and myself, and talked some more. After about fifteen minutes, he sat down, and people started getting out their check books.

"That's it?" I asked Joe.

"Yes," he said. "I told you it wouldn't be a problem."

Fred grinned, but it was a nervous grin.

A few days later, he used some of the money to rent a loft at 536 Broadway. The neighborhood was not yet fashionable, and the loft was a big, echoing, empty space containing just a few folding chairs and tables. Fred figured he would take a month or so to port his software, after which he would use the loft for warehousing the product and dealing with a flood of mail orders.

He asked me to drop in, because he had something for me. It turned out to be a Commodore 64, a disk drive, and a color monitor. I asked him if he wanted me to write new documentation for his program.

"No," he said, "I have something else in mind. I want you to write a typing tutor program."

Now that computers were penetrating so many areas of everyday life, a lot of first-time users were struggling to use keyboards. A couple of typing-tutor programs had been published, but they were unimaginative and boring.

"You can make it like a game program," Fred said, "since it's for the Commodore 64. We'll pay you royalties."

So, I had my first paying gig as a computer programmer. At least, I hoped it would be paying.

Behind the impressive facade of this fine old building at 536 Broadway, industrial lofts could be rented at bargain prices during the 1980s, before lower Broadway became fashionable. Fred Beyer's new company, Quick Brown Fox, was in there somewhere (I don't remember which floor).

Photo from Google Street View.

1983

Top: Missile Command.
Bottom: Keyboard Command.

Keyboard Command

I decided to model my typing tutor software on Missile Command, a nightmarish arcade game developed by Atari in which the player had to defend cities at the bottom of the screen by shooting down incoming aircraft, killer satellites, missiles, and smart bombs. No matter how fast you played, the attacking forces came in faster, and the game always ended with total nuclear annihilation.

My program would be a bit less apocalyptic. Letters of the alphabet would fall out of the sky, and to blow them up you had to type corresponding letters on the keyboard. A little man at the bottom of the screen would run for safety, and when he reached his refuge, you received points before the game advanced to the next level. A wider range of letters began to fall, there would be more of them, they would fall faster, and the man would run more slowly—but he could always reach his refuge if you typed fast enough.

Coding this game would have been relatively easy, except that the Commodore 64 had been rushed onto the market (like every computer in those days), and the manual was riddled with typographical errors. I had to spend hours just tracking down the incorrect values so that I could write code that didn't crash. Then I had to write utility programs that would minimize the drudgery of designing graphic objects.

After a month of this toil, I realized that I was now in a position to save other people from similar frustrations. I could put my knowledge into a book, perhaps titled *Graphics Guide to the Commodore 64*.

I had never tried to write something like that, and wasn't sure how to sell it, but I drafted a proposal and sent it to a California company named Sybex, which I chose at random because I liked their name. They responded immediately, offering a $4,000 advance and guaranteeing that they could move a bunch of copies.

This was how I started writing books that explained technical topics. It was more time-consuming than writing fiction, because I had to assemble a lot of information and make sure that it was correct. But I seemed to have an aptitude for it.

Larky

While writing the Graphics Guide, I had another idea. I could write a computer humor book.

Personal computers were now selling in huge numbers, even though the internet did not yet exist and the list of hypothetical applications was the same as when I had first encountered an apple][: You could play simple video games, and store names, addresses, and phone numbers, and maybe some food recipes—

I wondered if anyone had actually stored a single recipe during the past three years. I loved computers, but marketing them to people who didn't know what to do with them did not make much sense. Maybe I could satirize the whole thing.

I made the mistake of mentioning my idea while chatting to my ex-wife Nancy.

"What a coincidence," she said. "We were thinking of doing a humor book, too!"

By "we" she was referring to herself and her new husband, Bob, a computer scientist who worked at IBM. I didn't get along with Bob, perhaps because he was a ponderous, glowering control freak who was about as entertaining as a sinus infection. If he had a sense of humor, I had not been able to detect it, but Nancy insisted that he could be "quite larky" at times. "Just let me show you a sample of what we've been writing," she said.

Oh, all right. I visited her while Bob was at work, so he would not be hanging around, giving me moody looks.

Her pages were—odd. They were whimsical, but they didn't seem to be funny. In fact, I didn't quite understand them. "Look," I said. "I'll send out my portion and outline, and you send out yours, and we will go our separate ways."

Nancy wasn't so sure about that. "I'll have to ask Bob," she said.

The next day, she delivered his encyclical. "You have to wait for us to go first," she said. "Because we thought of it first."

This was a concept that I had not encountered before in book publishing. I couldn't think of any instance when one writer had tried to stop another writer from working on an idea that was similar but had been conceived separately. "What if you can't sell yours right away?" I asked.

Nancy was a very positive person, so she hadn't considered the possibility that her work might not sell.

"I don't want to wait," I went on, "while you submit your book to another publisher, and another, and another, until finally you find one who will buy it."

"Well, I'll have to ask Bob," she said.

The next day, Nancy said that according to Bob, if their book was turned down by a publisher, I could submit my book to that one publisher only. If their work was turned down by another publisher, I could submit mine there. Finally when a publisher bought their book, I would be allowed to submit my proposal to any publisher.

At this point, I was tempted to advise Nancy that Bob was even more of a preening dipshit than I had imagined, and I was unsympathetic toward his delusions of importance. I refrained, however, because there was another aspect to consider: Bob had taken over paying child support for my daughter.

This had happened about six months previously, when I was

struggling financially. I had complained to Nancy that she seemed to be using my child-support payments for little indulgencies such as a trip to Canada and the custom-fabrication of a beautiful new desk.

"I hate arguing about money," she told me, and since Bob was wealthy from an inheritance, she felt sure that he wouldn't mind the trivial amount required to support my daughter in the manor to which she had become accustomed.

Indeed, Bob went along with it, perhaps because he was still intoxicated by the novelty of cohabitation. But regardless of the reason for his generosity, I was pathetically grateful for it, and didn't want to disrupt the status-quo.

With this in mind, I reined in my annoyance regarding Bob's proprietary attitude toward book ideas. "When will you be ready to send out your book, or a piece of it?" I asked politely.

"Oh, a few months, I guess."

Months!

There were no humor books about computers, yet. The first book would grab the market share, and someone could be out there writing it at this very moment. Time was of the essence! We should be thinking in terms of weeks, not months!

"Well, we'll do our best," Nancy said. "But are you sure you don't want to collaborate with us?"

"Ahhh, maybe not this time," I said. "Just let me know how you proceed."

The most exasperating aspect was, I didn't necessarily believe that they had come up with their idea before mine. Who could say when the words "computer humor book" had entered their heads? Still—*child support*, I reminded myself.

I wrote a portion and outline of my book. Then I called my ex and asked how things were progressing at her end.

"We haven't had a lot of time to work on it," she said.

"Okay," I said, "I am going to send my proposal to John Douglas at Avon, who has published other books of mine. I will not send it to anyone else. I just want that one opportunity. You will have every other publisher in New York City available. Maybe that sounds fair?"

"I'm not sure," she said. "Let me talk to Bob."

I was unsurprised when she reported that Bob didn't think it was fair at all. If I wanted to submit my humor book to John at Avon, Bob said that I would have to wait until he and Nancy sent him their proposal first.

All right! All right! I gave Bob and Nancy a week to put together some pages for John. They actually managed to do this, after which I called John to see what he thought.

"I don't quite understand it," he said. "And it doesn't seem to be funny."

I rode my bicycle to the offices of Avon and delivered my proposal that same afternoon. John read it and said that he had some reservations about it, but at least he could understand it, so he would issue a contract.

When Bob heard about this, he was not "larky." He and Nancy felt that I had acted unethically by forcing them to submit their text before it was really ready. If only I could have been a bit more patient!

Throughout my entire life, probably going back to the age of three, people who lack any sense of urgency have told me to be "a bit more patient." What they really mean is, "Why can't you work slowly, like us?"

I don't know if Nancy and Bob ever finished writing their book. The irony was that my fears turned out to be groundless: No one else was writing a humor book about computers, and so far as I know, no one ever did. Moreover, the market for a computer-humor book turned out to be smaller than I had imagined.

Really, quite a bit smaller.

Disorganized and Irresponsible

Unexpectedly, a small company named Cinnamon Productions contacted me to buy a movie option for my book *Garbage World*. I had written it in 1967 as a quick little comedy featuring a bunch of deadbeats living in a garbage dump on an asteroid. I couldn't imagine how a production company had ever found this obscure dalliance, let alone why they would want to make a movie of it, but their phone number had a 212 area code, so I gave them a call.

I found myself talking to the owner, Joel Freedman. Was he really interested in my novel? Yes! In fact I should come on over and talk to him about it.

The offices were on Lower Broadway, near the loft that had been rented by Quick Brown Fox. When I stepped out of the elevator I was received by a cute, youthful receptionist who gave me a moist-eyed look as if she were greeting her long-lost uncle. "I just loved your book!" she gushed.

I wondered if she had actually read it. If she had, I wondered how it had instilled such a transcendent experience. I checked her face for any sign that she might be mocking me, but she seemed entirely serious.

Then Joel came out to meet me, and he was serious, too. He said he saw the book as a grim warning about the consequences for humanity if we failed to pursue a sustainable lifestyle and didn't recycle our trash.

Really?

Yes, really!

Joel walked me back to his office, and along the way we passed a ragged man sitting at a tiny desk, hunched over an old manual typewriter. He appeared to be around 60 and had a gray, dissipated face hidden by long greasy hair.

Joel paused to introduce me. "This is Terry," he said, beaming at the aging hippie as if he were an art object that had been acquired cheaply at an auction. "Terry, this is Charles. He's a writer, too!"

"Wait a minute," I said. "This is Terry Southern."

Joel looked at me in surprise. "Oh, you've heard of him?"

"Of course I've heard of him. The coauthor of *Candy*, wrote the screenplay for *The Magic Christian*, collaborated on *Dr. Strangelove*, wrote dialogue for Peter Sellers—"

Terry avoided my eyes. He radiated misery and self-loathing.

"He's fixing up a script for us," Joel said cheerfully.

I stared at Terry, imagining myself twenty years in the future, so desperate that I was willing to do a quick script-doctor gig in a loft on Lower Broadway for Cinnamon Productions, so that I could pay the rent and maybe buy some pharmaceutical products to ease the pain of human existence.

"I'm very pleased to meet you," I said.

Terry said nothing. I imagined him broadcasting a desperate telepathic message: *Just ignore me. Move along.*

Top: Soon to be a major motion picture. Seriously!

Bottom: Terry Southern in the early 1980s.

Nothing to see, here.

In Joel Freedman's office, I signed a contract giving Cinnamon Productions the exclusive renewable option, for $1,000, for one year, to buy motion-picture rights to my book. If they exercised the option and actually bought the rights, they would pay $12,500—which was a pittance, but I didn't care, because I knew that it wasn't going to happen.

Joel, however, didn't share my negative attitude. He said that he was going to raise the money to make the movie as soon as possible.

I wondered how he was going to create the environment of a garbage dump on an asteroid, with space ships landing and taking off, and an amphibious vehicle in a lake of wet mud, zapping a giant slug with a death ray—

Well, none of that was my concern. I took the check, deposited it in my bank account, and forgot the whole thing.

Barely a month later, I was reminded of it in the most traumatic way when I received a letter from the Scott Meredith Literary Agency, which had represented me in the late 1960s. They were sending me a check because Gale Tattershall had renewed his movie option on my novel *Garbage World*.

I felt a terrible dizzy, sinking sensation as I realized that I had sold two options on the same book to two different people.

Was it possible? I dragged out my *Garbage World* file. Sure enough, Tattershall had bought an option in the 1970s, and had been renewing it ever since. How could I have forgotten? I had been inconceivably disorganized and irresponsible. That was how.

I did vaguely remember receiving a check from the Meredith Agency once in a while, but never paid much attention to payments of this sort, as they usually related to old novels earning a few dollars from foreign rights. I would spend the money, and that was the end of it.

I called an editor friend who was more worldly than myself, and confessed my incompetence. What should I do? Should I confess? In which case, should I confess to Tattershall or Freedman? Tattershall might be a better bet, as he lived in England, and was less likely to be litigious.

"Don't worry about it," my friend said. "Neither of them will ever make the movie."

"But one of them might."

"No, they won't. It's *Garbage World!*"

Logic was on his side—but if one party merely found out about the other, the consequences were hard to imagine.

Now as I sit here writing this memoir of malfeasance, I will violate the Unity of Time as I fast-forward to the outcome.

On the first-year anniversary of Cinnamon Productions buying their option, I hoped they might not renew it. This would solve my problem—but, they did renew it. Joel Freedman said that raising the money to make the movie was turning out to be just a little more difficult than he had expected, but the book was more topical than ever, and he was just as serious as he had been before.

A month later, the anniversary for Gale Tattershall came up. I waited for the inevitable check from Scott Meredith, and—it didn't arrive.

I felt a glimmer of hope. I checked the original contract, and eventually the deadline passed. Tattershall had let his option lapse. Oh, joy!

Then I received a letter from him, forwarded to me from the Meredith agency. After all these years, somehow Gale had forgotten to renew. He was distraught. He said he had always been in love with my book. He had paid for the options out of his own money. He had even paid someone to write a script. He had scouted locations (where—maybe a municipal dump in Wales?) and he begged me please, please would I sell him another option!

Needless to say, this would be crossing the line separating incompetence from fraud. I wrote back to Tattershall, telling him that I was extremely sorry, but someone else had already optioned the book.

He sent me another letter, even more distraught. Who had bought the new option? Could he acquire it from them? He loved *Garbage World* so much! He really wanted to make the movie!

I felt sorry for him, if only because his judgment of literature was so poor. I also felt guilty, of course—so I called Joel Freedman. Would he, perhaps, be interested in letting go of his option? Someone else might be willing to pay him a premium for it. He could make a quick profit.

"Who wants it?" Joel sounded angry. "Some other production company?"

"Well, yes, I mean, er, maybe."

"Who are they?"

"Well, er, I can't really tell you." I thought quickly. "It would be unethical to give their name," I said.

"Then I'm going to exercise my option to buy the rights," Joel said. The idea of anyone else sniffing around his property seemed to be too much for him to bear. A few weeks later, I had a contract and $12,500.

I sent an apologetic letter to Tattershall. "The other party exercised their option and bought the movie rights," I told him.

I never heard from him again.

Decades later, I looked him up online and found a few references to him as a cinematographer for some BBC TV shows. So far as I could tell, he never produced or directed any movies.

As for Joel Freedman, he is still the lucky owner of *Garbage World*. When I searched online for him in 2021, I found that he was semi-retired in Westport, Connecticut, where he was teaching cello classes.

I also found a web site referencing various small productions that Joel was still involved in, although the details were a bit sketchy. I was surprised that his list didn't include *Garbage World*, since at this point it is surely more topical than ever.

When I Googled "Cinnamon Productions," I found a bakery cafe in California which went out of business during the covid pandemic of 2020.

The First Award

Tom Disch told me that he and his fellow judges had chosen Rudy Rucker's novel *Software* to win the first Philip K. Dick award. That seemed like a good choice to me, but Tom had a little problem. He didn't have an actual award.

Not even a plaque?

No, Tom hadn't thought of that, and didn't know where to buy such a thing. He wasn't very good at dealing with practical matters, and needed my help.

So: First of all, he had refused to listen to my complaint that the award was an insult to its namesake, and now he wanted me to organize it for him. I berated him briefly—but having vented my annoyance, I gave in.

I called Susan Allison at Ace books. She was a friend of mine, and she had published Rudy, so how could she refuse to scrape up some money for an award and a ceremony? I can't remember how much she pledged, but it wasn't quite enough to pay for the rental of a party space, so I called a few other editors and persuaded them to kick in some money. Then I found a loft which looked good enough for the event.

As for the actual award, I seem to remember that I generated a document using a template that I found at a stationery store.

The award party was fun, as the ambience of an industrial loft encouraged people to be informal. Rudy and his wife Sylvia drove in from their home in Lynchburg, Virginia, and Rudy was wearing a jacket and tie, which made him look impressively respectable.

Then he stood on a table to deliver a prepared speech, and the veil of conformity was cast aside. Sometimes, he suggested, "various authors are, as people, examples of the same higher-level archetype." He went on: "I'd like to think that, on some level, Phil and I are just different instances of the same Platonic form—call it the gonzo-philosopher-SF-writer form, if you like."

I liked that idea. A few people thought that Rudy was claiming to be the reincarnation of Philip K. Dick, but I saw no reason to set them straight. A bit of metaphysical speculation was a good way to honor Phil.

The Philip K. Dick Award is still being given each year. Originally its purpose was to keep his name alive, but the opposite has happened: He became so well known posthumously when his short stories were used as the basis of movies, his name now keeps the award alive.

Top: Rudy Rucker stands on a table to deliver his speech at the award ceremony.

Bottom: Sylvia Rucker.

Strategic Defense

In March, 1983 I was watching Ronald Reagan giving a speech on television where he announced the Strategic Defense Initiative, later known as SDI. He promoted a future in which we wouldn't have to live in fear of nuclear weapons anymore, because the United States would develop the capability to shoot them down.

As I listened to Reagan, I felt as if I were entering an alternate universe. I already knew about SDI, because it had been described to me by Jerry Pournelle in September, 1981 when I sat drinking sherry in his office. Jerry had established the Citizens' Advisory Council on Space Policy with Gregory Benford and Larry Niven, plus some astronauts and aerospace executives who could give it more credibility. The group had formulated the concept of SDI and recommended it to Reagan.

Jerry had an ulterior motive in all of this. He believed that the exploration of space was essential to the future of humanity, but NASA was mired in bureaucracy and showed no interest in sending human beings beyond low Earth orbit. From their point of view, it would be a big hassle without any benefits.

Where else could Jerry find the money to propel humanity toward the stars? Well, how about the Pentagon? If he could sell them a new idea for a weapon system, it might allow some subsequent spinoff for civilian applications.

This was the genesis of SDI. It was a unique and bizarre instance where a science-fiction writer influenced national defense. You can check the Citizens' Advisory Council on National Space Policy in Wikipedia; it's all there.

As things worked out, the biggest impact of SDI was to convince the USSR to give up on the arms race, at which point the cold war was over. We may thank Jerry Pournelle for that, partially at least.

The Community

Dream Makers and *The Patchin Review* had given me an identity in the science-fiction field. My life was now quite different from the way it had been in the 1970s, when I had known almost no one and felt that when I did meet people, they probably didn't like me, assuming they had any interest in me at all.

I now felt as if I had been an orphan waif who had been adopted into a kind of dysfunctional family on a trial basis. The community wasn't exactly a literary enclave, but I was in no position to be fussy.

In *The Science-Fiction Encyclopedia*, John Clute wrote a peculiar entry about me that ended like this: "Sf as a genre remains naggingly short of genuine iconoclasts: Platt has therefore been a *necessary* writer." I wasn't sure "necessary" was the ideal adjective, but it was better than being "unnecessary."

Next came the unintended consequence: I found myself writing reviews and commentary for other magazines. In fact, I think I wrote more about science fiction during the 1980s than anyone other than Clute himself. My reviews and opinions appeared in these publications, and probably some others that I have forgotten:

The Magazine of Fantasy & Science Fiction
The New York Review of Science Fiction
Washington Post Book World
Isaac Asimov's Magazine
Science Fiction Chronicle
Science Fiction Digest
Science Fiction Eye
Cheap Truth
Heavy Metal
Interzone
Nonstop
Thrust
Locus
Omni

None of them paid much (except for *Omni*), and some paid nothing at all. Still, writing nonfiction was easier than writing science fiction, and if I could be more "necessary" as a columnist than as a novelist, so be it.

Along the way, I made some friends among editors in New York book publishing. This was slightly unusual for a writer, because writers tend to have an adversarial relationship with editors. But I had been an editor myself on a modest level, so I felt sympatico with their role.

When I went to the writers-and-editors party organized by Science Fiction Writers of America every fall, it was the nearest thing I ever felt to being a bona-fide member of a social group, and their tolerance for my presence was quite remarkable, bearing in mind how many negative book reviews I had written in my unsalubrious little magazine.

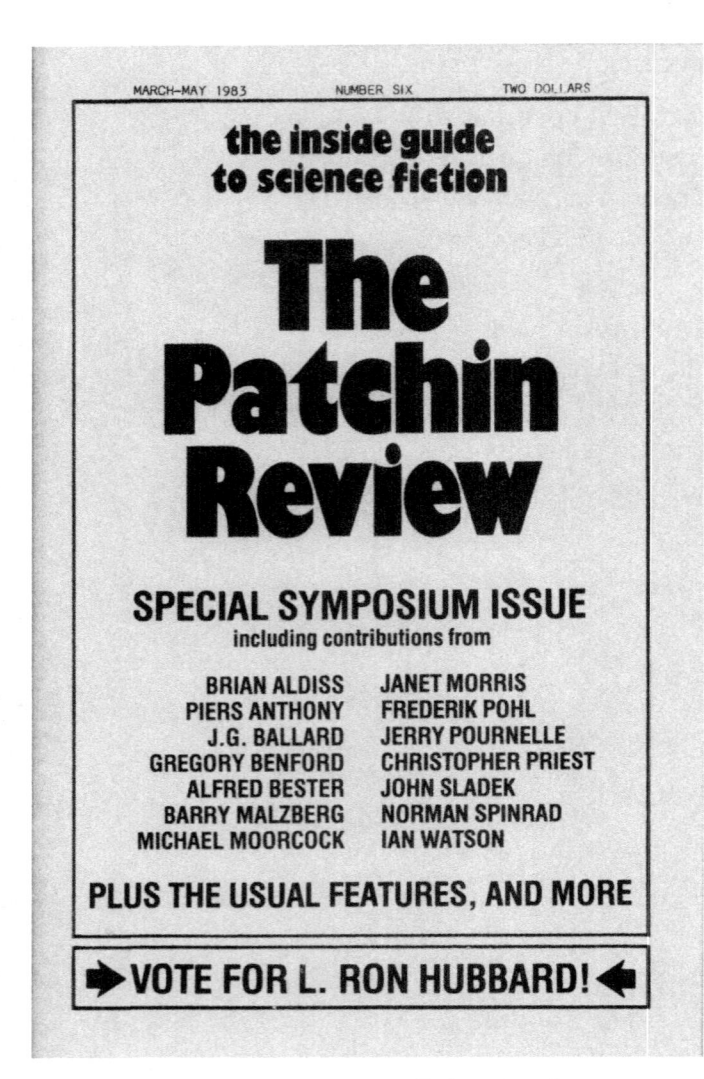

After this issue, there wasn't much left to say.

No Discernible Audience

If I had wanted to be part of a more refined group, Tom Disch made this possible when he obtained membership for me in the PEN American Center. This venerable organization had an impressive pedigree stretching back to 1922, and hosted gatherings for literary types whose typical work seemed to consist of slim volumes lamenting the tragedy of the human condition.

PEN members often had difficulty finding anyone to publish their books—or if they could get published, they complained that they weren't paid enough, and the publisher didn't print enough copies. This tiresome carping prompted PEN to sponsor a panel at which four editors did some role playing, acting out their conversations during a typical working day as they assessed books that they believed had no future.

The cynicism that I knew so well among my editor friends was flaunted for all to see during this exercise, and the message to PEN club members seemed to be along the lines, "This is *why* we won't publish your gloomy, pretentious books. Now, why don't you write something we can sell?"

When PEN circulated a transcript of the panel, I saw that it had relevance to science fiction, so I copied it and sent it to various writers and agents whom I knew. I invited them to reply, and their responses were compiled in the sixth issue of *The Patchin Review*.

Richard Curtis, a well-known literary agent, wrote in response to the PEN transcript: "My first reaction was shame. Although the transcript reads like a parody ... it could be a faithful recording of the dialogues that take place every day in the publishing business, dialogues in which I clearly recognize myself."

Richard was right. The editors' role-playing was accurate, and it was embarrassing—especially because, unlike him, they *didn't* have any shame. They seemed to enjoy mocking books that they didn't like.

J. G. Ballard picked up on this when he wondered about their motives for "going public" with their cynicism. "Perhaps," he wrote, "these publishers secretly admire their ruthless philistinism, their mastery of the ugliest sales conference jargon, the lack of the faintest glimmer of literate sensibility."

Norman Spinrad wrote: "... on a strictly *business* level, these people sound like the same sort of assholes who destroyed the American automobile industry." Norman didn't seem to worry that his scorn for the assholes might discourage them from publishing his own novels in the future.

Bruce and Nancy Sterling at their home in Texas, 1983.

But David Hartwell expressed the most disturbing sentiment, suggesting that "there is in my experience no discernible audience within the science fiction readership for high quality work not written by a familiar name."

Previously, Hartwell had said that he felt alienated from his readership. Now, he seemed to be saying that he was giving up. Just like that. In retrospect I think he must have known that Timescape Books was being axed, and he would soon be out of a job.

The sixth issue of *The Patchin Review* marked a kind of end point. My contributors had mapped the vicissitudes of science-fiction publishing, and the PEN symposium wrapped it up with devastating accuracy. There wasn't much left to say.

Cheap Truth in Texas

I didn't announce formally that I was ending *The Patchin Review*, but I made no secret of it to my friends. One of them was Bruce Sterling, whom I had met when he visited Los Angeles in 1979 and we watched Harlan Ellison trying to beat up a clerk in a bookstore, with inconclusive results.

Bruce was very serious about wanting to write plausible science fiction with a modern sensibility. He had published two novels that I admired, and a bunch of short stories. He was very ambitious and seemed convinced that some kind of new movement was happening, in which he could play a central role. If *The Patchin Review* wasn't going to stick around to promote it, he would do so himself.

He began to self-publish a broadsheet that he named *Cheap Truth*, modelled vaguely on Russian samizdat. *Good luck with that*, I thought to myself, assuming that Bruce would suffer the kind of disillusionment which usually afflicts serious, idealistic writers who try to do something radical for a large audience.

Intimations of Doom

Visiting a startup that has burned through its investment capital is like visiting a cancer patient. Everyone is still hoping for a miracle cure, but they know, in their hearts, the prognosis is terminal.

When I took a finished copy of my typing tutor program to the loft rented by Quick Brown Fox, I found three people sitting around, looking depressed: Fred Beyer, Joe Ming, and a woman they had hired to manage the office and fulfill mail orders.

The Commodore 64 was flooding the market, as everyone had expected. Fred had written the Commodore version of his word-processing program, and it had been reviewed in computer magazines, and burned into cartridges—but he was not selling many copies.

Maybe—just maybe—he had been wrong about Commodore users needing to do word processing. Maybe they were *only* interested in playing computer games.

In the big, echoing loft I saw stacks of unsold product, while the female employee was telling Joe that the company really needed a vacuum cleaner.

"I'd rather not spend the money on that right now," Joe said.

Not enough cash flow for a vacuum cleaner? Uh-oh.

Still, I demonstrated my software, and received some positive comments. Then I went out to get a sandwich with Fred, and he said he was thinking of leaving New York and going to Arizona.

"Why Arizona?" I asked.

"My parents live there."

Some very smart people were making a lot of money from the huge market for home computers, but for each success, there were many more who failed. Either they didn't raise enough money, or they misjudged consumer interest—or in Fred's case, both.

The Nightmare of Green

I completed my humor book about computers to Avon. It still had no competitors, and I was excited to think that it could dominate that niche in the market—although, as yet, such a niche did not actually exist. Somehow my book would have to create the niche, which might not be easy, especially because I didn't even have a title.

Wasn't a title rather fundamental? Didn't a writer normally come up with a title *before* he delivered a book?

Yes, but in this case a title was difficult, because in addition to being quirky, my book was ambivalent. It expressed affection for computers while mocking the practice of marketing them.

So, what would be an elevator sales pitch? "Unlike other books, this one tells the ridiculous truth about personal computers."

All right, I tried to make the best of the situation. I came up with *The Whole Truth Home Computer Handbook* as my title.

I had already proposed many alternatives to John Douglas, none of which were very good. I don't think he liked this one either, but time was running out, so he agreed to it.

Now, what should it look like? John asked Avon's design department to come up with something, and they created a cover that was mostly typographical. That was okay, but—it was green!

The great painter Robert Williams once created a painting titled "The Fear of Green." He wrote: "Green does horrify some artists. Portrait artists shun

Above: It would have looked so much better in red, or maybe yellow. Below: The great painter Robert Williams conveyed the horror I feel when faced with green art.

it, and gallery owners have, for years, cautioned their artists that green paintings don't seem to sell." Williams theorized that this "voodoo stigma" might be because green is an "indication of putrefaction and gangrene."

I thought he was right. I felt certain that green would be a fatal color, and I experienced a familiar feeling: Despite everyone's best efforts, my book was doomed. I told myself not to feel too bad about this, because after all, most books are doomed.

A blurry picture of J. G. Ballard in his living room, with his Forbidden Planet Award.

Yet Another Award

Mike Luckman, the owner of the big Forbidden Planet bookstore on Broadway and 13th Street, wanted to run a science-fiction convention to publicize his business, and he asked me to find some writers who would attend the event. He even said that he would pay me for my services.

The convention also served as an excuse for Forbidden Planet to give awards voted by customers at the store. I was quite surprised when J. G. Ballard won in the short-story category.

"I didn't know that there were so many Ballard fans patronizing Forbidden Planet," I said to Luckman's store manager, a cynical Brit named Rob Hingley.

"There aren't," Hingley said. He looked at me as if I were stupid. "I rigged the vote."

As the organizer of the convention, I asked myself if I had an ethical obligation to go public about the deception. In the end I decided not to, because a "Forbidden Planet Award" didn't mean much anyway.

The fact is, almost all awards, in my experience, are tainted in some way or other, at some time or other.

I took the trophy with me on my next visit to England, and gave it to Ballard. He was quite excited by it. "I don't think I've ever won an award before," he said.

Really, he still hadn't. But I didn't say anything.

Mania

In the UK, Christopher Priest, a fine writer who also served as my literary agent, sold my computer humor book to Malcolm Edwards at Gollancz. Malcolm didn't much care for my title, but in an editorial meeting someone suggested calling it *Micro-Mania*.

Hey, that was a great idea! Why hadn't I come up with something like that? Succinct, accurate, and fun—maybe Avon could use that title too?

No, it was too late.

Next Gollancz came up with a cover. They redrew a sketch I had done of an imaginary Pac-Man-style video game in which a little man tried to evade a screaming wife and children while he took money to buy computer equipment. I had created that cartoon, yet had failed to think of using it on the cover. It seemed so obvious, now. Maybe Avon could use it on their edition?

No, no, no. Too late.

Gollancz said that they wanted me to tour the UK, promoting the book. They would even pay my air fare from the United States. And their cover would not be green.

Most American writers don't have their own British agents. I was fortunate.

The British edition of my humorous computer book. The dominant color was blue.

Book World

At the world science fiction convention in Baltimore, someone told me I should meet Michael Dirda.

I found him sitting on the floor in the hallway, leaning against the wall, and staring at the other wall, apparently deep in thought, although later I learned that this was just his default manner. He looked studious but handsome, like Clark Kent in a Superman comic.

I sat on the floor beside him and learned that he was an editor at *Washington Post Book World*. He hade heard of me somehow—maybe through *The Patchin Review*. I felt intimidated by being in the company of someone who was a serious, professional critic, while I of course was merely dabbling in self-published polemical rants. Still,

Page 103

Michael said he was interested in publishing reviews of science fiction, and asked me if I would like to write some.

Naturally, I said "yes." But did he have any books in particular, which he wanted to see reviewed?

No, he would to leave that to me. There was just one condition: He wanted reviews that were reasonably positive, because other editors at *Book World* had an attitude along the lines, "We know science fiction is crap so what's the point of running reviews that say so?"

This presented me with an interesting challenge: To find recent science fiction that I could write about positively. I would have to give this some serious thought.

We talked for about an hour. Michael seemed a bit drunk, and I was concerned that he might not remember asking me to write for him. But, he did, and a few weeks later I managed to submit some reasonably positive reviews. I then continued to review books for him occasionally during the next ten years. He was intimidatingly erudite, but was somehow willing to overlook my literary ignorance.

During the rest of the 1980s Michael would visit me when he came to New York City for literary events. He slept on my couch, claiming that he enjoyed imagining that he was leading a bohemian lifestyle. Conversely, when I went to Washington DC I would visit him and his wife Marian, and I would sleep in their guest room while imagining that I had a fulltime job and a family.

Eventually Michael won a Pulitzer Prize for literary criticism, but he never bragged about it. Even now, he seems willing to overlook my literary ignorance. I think of him as my famous literary friend.

Rudy in Lynchburg

Ed Ferman said he would publish a profile of Rudy Rucker in *Fantasy and Science Fiction* magazine, so I went to visit Rudy where he was living in Lynchburg, Virginia.

I found him in a big old wooden house with his lovely wife Sylvia, who was talented in English and art. I wondered why I never seemed to end up with a woman such as her, so well equipped with common sense, which was the attribute that I lacked most. Maybe someone like Sylvia simply wouldn't put up with someone like me—but on the other hand, she put up with Rudy, so how did that work? Decades later, I still don't have an answer to that question.

Rudy drove me across town to a little office where he did his writing. As we cruised along Main Street, he stared through the windshield with a blank expression. "My God," he said, "what am I doing here?"

I think this was one of those moments when a person suddenly perceives an environment as it must look to a visitor. Of course I knew why Rudy had moved to Lynchburg: He had needed a teaching job, and didn't have many options.

His little office was full of memorabilia, wacky art, and junk. He showed me a military-surplus inertial gyroscope, and remarked that according to Ernst Mach, it only worked because of the presence of stars in the universe. This was because of "Mach's Principle," as Einstein had called it. Theoretically, rotation and inertia and angular momentum are a function of mass and velocity, but velocity can only be measured relative to other objects. Therefore, if there was only one object in the universe, it wouldn't have these properties.

Any conversation with Rudy tends to stray into such areas, which is why I always enjoy talking to him. He is almost exactly my age, and has been irresponsible at times, like me, although in a slightly different style. Both of us tend to be suspicious of groups and ready to reject them before they have a chance to reject us, which of course tends to be a self-fulfilling prophecy.

After I interviewed him, he managed to escape from Lynchburg and moved to the Bay Area, where he found a nice job teaching computer programming. "Looks like I will be teaching assembly language," he told me during a phone call.

"But you don't know assembly language."

"Well, that's true. But how hard can it be?"

Fortunately for Rudy, he was able to sit in on another professor's class in assembly language before he taught his own class later each day, and everything worked out well.

Millions of Minions

I visited a store that was selling the Commodore 64, and looked at some of the games that had been developed for it. They ran much faster than mine, and the graphics were more complex and realistic. "Maniac Mansion," published by LucasFilm, featured multiple interiors, scrolling backgrounds, animated figures, a complex story, and a variety of sound effects. How had someone done all that so quickly? Well, "someone" had not done it. The game had been created by a team of seven people.

Just three years previously, programming had been a solitary occupation. Now, software was being cranked out by gangs of minions in cubicles. What a nightmarish concept! I felt glad that I didn't have to program computers, because I could write books about them instead.

Soon I would discover that I could teach people to use them, too.

Volume II

The second volume of *Dream Makers* was published by Berkley. I don't think it received the kind of adulatory reviews that the first book had received, but at least no one complained that it wasn't as good as the first book. I think this is the most important consideration for volume II of anything.

Back to the Classroom

In the late summer of 1983 I was walking down Fifth Avenue when I saw a sign in a window announcing the imminent opening of The Computer Instruction Center, a new department of The New School for Social Research.

During the 1970s, I had stopped teaching creative writing at The New School because I didn't like having to be in the same place at the same time every week for twelve weeks. I missed the reliable income, though, so I walked into the new facility and met the head of it, who told me that each introductory computer class would last for four weeks, and he needed instructors.

Well, I should be able to manage that.

There was the issue of credentials—but I had written a game program for the Commodore 64, and had tested an IBM-PC in Hal Pollenz's computer store. Maybe that would be good enough.

I ended up teaching computer classes for the next fifteen years, in MS-DOS, advanced MS-DOS, batch files, BASIC programming, introductory Photoshop, Advanced Photoshop, introductory Adobe

Top: The animated graphics of Maniac Mansion were sophisticated by 1983 standards.

Bottom: Volume II appeared in trade-paperback format, as Berkley now realized that the first volume should never have been published in a mass-market edition.

Illustrator, advanced Adobe Illustrator, and other topics that I invented, such as "The Computer Survival Course" which told people how to recover from disasters such as erasing files by accident.

I enjoyed teaching these classes because my effectiveness was measurable. At the end of a course, students either knew how to use a computer, or they didn't. By comparison, when I had taught creative writing, I could never tell if anyone learned anything.

One person in my programming class who didn't learn much was John Ferraro, the son of Geraldine Ferraro, the New York congress person who became democrat nominee for vice-president in 1984. He wrote a "Political Quiz" that was so huge and poorly structured, it had the unique result of generating an "out of memory" message, which I had thought was impossible. If his mother was as insanely motivated and as clueless as he was, it would explain a lot about American politics.

One evening I was on Sixth Avenue, drawing money from my bank's cash machine, when a beautiful, chic, expensively dressed woman stared at me in surprise. "Mr. Platt!" she exclaimed.

I was wearing a ragged T-shirt, and my hair hadn't been trimmed in a couple of months. I stared at her, wondering how on earth she knew who I was.

"I took one of your classes," she said. "I had such a fear of computers. And now I'm going to be working for IBM in Zurich."

I congratulated her, and since I had been her instructor, I wondered why I wasn't working for IBM in Zurich.

I was too lazy to shave every day. That was one reason. There were more, but I didn't bother to go down the mental list.

Attitude of Entitlement

Sophie Moorcock, the daughter of Hilary Bailey and Michael Moorcock, came to New York and lived for a while in the apartment above mine, which was sublet by two old ladies in New Jersey. She shared it with Harlan Ellison's ex-girlfriend, Jane MacKenzie.

They wanted to do something for Halloween, which took possession of the West Village each year like a noir mardi-gras, so I went to a theatrical costume company on Times Square, where I rented a police uniform. Now I would find out how it felt to walk the streets as a cop. Of course, impersonating a police officer is a serious offense, but if I were challenged by a real cop I would just say, "Hey, lighten up, it's Halloween!"

As things worked out, none of the real police patrolling the streets during Halloween showed any interest me, and I roamed unchallenged.

I had expected my uniform to trigger a respectful attitude from conventional middle-aged citizens, but their behavior went far beyond anything I had imagined. They were so deferential, they were almost groveling as they asked me if I could be so kind as to pause in my duties and supply them with directions to the nearest subway station.

Halloween in New York City, 1983. Left to right: Jane MacKenzie, Sophie Moorcock, and myself.

I soon realized why police have such an attitude of entitlement: People give it to them.

The leather shoes that I had rented with the costume were uncomfortable, so I stopped at a pharmacy to buy some Dr. Scholl pads. Several people were waiting in line to pay for items, but as soon as the store manager saw me, he opened a new register and beckoned me forward.

"It's okay, I don't mind waiting," I said.

"No, no." He was insistent. "I'll check you out." Then when he saw that I was only making a small purchase, he refused to accept money for it.

Everyone should have the opportunity to impersonate law enforcement for a day. It was a sobering experience.

White Trash and a Yellow Camaro

Playboy Press wanted to know why I hadn't written my "Christina" novel. The reason, of course, was that I didn't want to write it, but I made a vague excuse about other commitments. They were unimpressed and told me I had been allowed all the procrastination time that I was going to get.

I felt bad about this, because they always allowed very fair contractual terms, and the first two books that I had written had even earned royalties. Really, it was past time for me to honor this commitment, so I got down to work and delivered the book.

In due course I received my completion payment, making me wonder what I should spend it on. Well, how about another car?

The Buick Gran Sport had been a nightmare of rust, but perhaps if I approached the challenge of car ownership in a more circumspect manner, I could find one that was fun to drive while being reasonably practical. How about a Camaro like the one that I had rented with Norman Spinrad and his girlfriend Terry, when we drove out to Death Valley together in 1970?

This time I would buy a vehicle that had been maintained in Phoenix, Arizona, not Phoenix, New York. Fred Beyer had followed through on his plan to move to Arizona, and when I called him, he said he was renting a house in Phoenix containing a guest room with a mattress on the floor. I was welcome to use it, if I wasn't too fussy, but he warned me that he was living with a male person. Once again, I had to go through the ritual of reassuring Fred that his gayness didn't bother me.

When I made my trip to Phoenix, I found him in good spirits despite the total, humiliating collapse of his ambitions to get rich by writing word-processing software. He told me that Joe Ming was in big trouble with his Chinese investors for losing all their money, but Fred had left all that behind and was now thinking of starting a new career as a realtor. In the meantime he was living happily with Ray, a sweet-natured young man who seemed insecure and dependent, like a male equivalent of the women I tended to end up with.

The house was terminal. Fraying carpet was brown with ingrained dirt, doors didn't close properly, and there were a couple of broken windows patched with cardboard. The place was furnished with decrepit chairs that Fred and Ray had found in the street, but I have always enjoyed a fin-de-cicle environment where I don't have to worry about messing anything up. Also there were two cats—named Tom and Jerry, although one turned out to be female—and I'm always happy when cats are around.

After a sound night's sleep on the promised mattress, I walked to a 7-11 located one block away. Just inside its entrance I found an arcade game console running Q*Bert, so I played that for a while before picking up a copy of Auto and Truck Trader magazine. I bought a carton of milk, a box of Kellogg's Special K, and a street map of Phoenix.

Back at Fred's house, he and Ray were still asleep. I pulled a chipped cereal bowl out of a drainer stacked with mismatched dishes, and went looking for a spoon. When I opened a drawer, it was full of old car tools, but I finally found a plastic teaspoon in an empty cat-food can.

I ate breakfast while sitting on cracked concrete steps outside the front door. Even in December, the Phoenix weather was warm. I leafed through the magazine and circled ads that looked promising, then went inside to make phone calls. Around noon, Fred and Ray emerged and said they were ready to help me to buy a car.

Fred was using a mint 1970 Olds Cutlass that he had borrowed from his parents, and after I paid for some gas, we went looking for addresses that I had circled on the map.

As we cruised through low-rent areas, I was surprised to see pickup trucks with bodies that were jacked up six or twelve inches above the wheels. "They're called high-riders," Fred explained. "It's a white-trash thing, to distinguish them from low-riders, in which the springs are lowered."

"Only Mexicans drive low-riders," Ray said.

"Who does the conversions?" I asked.

"They do it themselves. Like that." We were passing a guy working on his truck in the driveway outside a suburban home. A can of Bud Light stood on the hood of the truck under the mid-day sun.

Our first stop was at a house which was boarded up and seemed to have been abandoned. A broken-down motor home was parked in the driveway, with a Chevy Nova beside it. As an emaciated long-haired man in his twenties emerged from the motor home, I wondered if the missing home owner knew that the vehicle was here. Probably not, but it was none of my business.

The skinny hippie showed us the Chevy while his unappetizing wife sat holding a baby on her lap and staring at us with dull eyes. The man explained that he needed cash so that he and his wife could move. "I don't want my kid to grow up around Mexicans," he said.

The Chevy seemed in good shape, but wasn't my ideal ride, so we said we would bear it in mind while we moved along.

We visited a man who said he was a barber, and was assisting his son to sell a formerly white Camaro that had been resprayed canary yellow. The son seemed to need his father to help him negotiate the sale, as he had a slack-jawed expression and seemed retarded. His girlfriend had an elaborate hairstyle which I guessed the barber had created for her. She watched me skeptically while chewing gum. All three of these Phoenix residents had puffy pink flesh from a diet that I guessed might be high in carbohydrates.

They wanted $2,200, which was an acceptable price, but I offered $1,900 firm. I had the actual cash in my pocket, which clinched the deal. We went to a title transfer office, and an hour later I had my Camaro. I wasn't happy about the color, but I figured I could learn to like it.

Lap-Dance Horror

Fred and Ray insisted on taking me out somewhere to celebrate, and selected The Bourbon Street Circus, where a $2 cover charge paid for an amateur topless contest starting at 9pm. The huge, echoing interior was full of white-trash males drinking and shouting above loud country music.

Fred and Ray and my new old Camaro, outside their house in Phoenix, Arizona.

We sat sipping draft beer from disposable plastic cups, and I was wondering how I could tactfully ask to leave when a half-naked woman stopped in front of me and started undulating, giving me a red-lipstick grin. To my horror, she edged forward and squatted on my knees, facing me. Her cheeks were heavily layered with makeup, and her nose was inches from mine. Still grinning, she writhed for a couple of minutes that felt more like half an hour.

Finally there was a break in the music, at which point she stood up and walked away.

"What was *that?*" I asked Fred.

"It was a lap dance."

I had never heard of such a thing.

"Did you enjoy it?" Fred asked.

Suddenly I realized. "You paid for it!"

"Yes. I thought you'd like it."

Briefly I considered trying to explain my ambivalence regarding casual physicality with strangers—but this wasn't the best place to have a discussion of that sort. "What I would really like," I said, "is to go to a gay bar."

Roadside attractions on the drive back to New York City.

Top: I really miss totally cheesy motels like this. And yes, I did stay there. How could I resist?

Bottom: Paisano Pete, "The World's Largest Road Runner," in Fort Stockton, Texas. It wasn't really very large, but I suppose it didn't have to be.

Fred and Ray looked stunned, but I said I was curious about it, which was true, and I would never feel brave enough to do it on my own.

They took me to a bar that was known for its extravagant decor. The front half of a genuine semi truck was embedded in one wall, as if it had just smashed its way in from the parking lot. The rest of the bar was finished in raw planks, creating a backwoods-cabin ambience that was macho in a gay way. Muscular guys in leather and denim were strutting around, eyeing each other speculatively. A deck was open to the benign Phoenix evening air, and was under surveillance from video cameras connected with monitors above the bar. "This is great," said Fred, watching men on the screens. "You can cruise, here, without even getting off your bar stool."

The next day, I said goodbye to Fred and Ray and drove east in my new/old Camaro. I enjoyed being on the road again, but then the doubts began. Soon I would be struggling with the hassle of parking a car on the street in Manhattan, and moving it every day to conform with parking regulations. And if I took the risk of losing my parking spot by driving out of town, where would I go? I couldn't think of any interesting places within easy reach of the city, especially at the beginning of the winter.

Owning the car turned out to be just as big a hassle as I had expected, but I was glad that I'd been able to see Fred in Phoenix. In fact it was the last time I ever did see him, because a year or two later, Hal called to tell me that Fred had died of a heart attack. Hal theorized that it might have been induced by using capsules of amyl nitrate, popular as "poppers" in the gay world.

I still miss Fred. He was kind, generous, and a wonderful friend. He was also very good at what he did, but I don't think he could have adapted to the regime of writing software as a minion sitting in a corporate cubicle. He was fated to be left behind by the computer revolution. Maybe he really should have been a realtor.

Two Plus Two

New York publishers had seen small California companies such as Sybex making handsome profits by selling large, overpriced computer books, so they did what they always tended to do. They jumped on the bandwagon.

I guessed that market saturation could not be far away, leaving barely enough time for an opportunist such as myself to take advantage of the situation. I came up with two new proposals for computer books before the year was over.

Avon advanced me $7,500 for a book of entertaining little educational programs titled *More From Your Micro*. Then I sold a book titled *Basic Without Math* to Warner. This second book had a dubious concept: I would teach the BASIC programming language to people even if they had trouble adding 2+2. But why would anyone who was innumerate want to learn computer programming? Well, probably they wouldn't. But—they might!

All I could say in its favor was that the concept was unique and had never been used before (for obvious reasons). Nine publishers turned it down, but Warner was the tenth, and I got lucky because a naive young editor decided that he could corner the market among readers who wanted to program computers but were intimidated by mathematics.

I sold British rights to Virgin Books in the UK. The Virgin edition eventually appeared, and did not do well. The Warner edition never did appear, because they abandoned it when they discovered, to their surprise, that there were too many computer books.

The British edition of the world's most misconceived computer book.

Festivities

After selling four books during 1983, I enjoyed the unusual experience of having money in the bank. Sophie and Jane were still visiting, and they used my tiny kitchen to cook meals for guests such as Tom Disch and his companion Charlie Naylor. These were happy times for me, as I didn't like to cook but I enjoyed having guests.

Meanwhile I had resumed answering personal ads, one of which turned out to be from an editor at *Newsweek*. She sounded nice on

Dinner at Patchin Place with Sophie Moorcock, Tom Disch, Charles Naylor, and Jane MacKenzie.

the phone, so when she invited me to a big Christmas party, I took a chance without screening her initially at The Peacock Cafe.

I found that her ad had been somewhat deceptive. She seemed about fifteen years older than myself, and had just had a face lift. In fact, black dots along the edges of her jaw showed where sutures had been removed. This creeped me out, so I tried not to look at them—but I had to look at her at least some of the time when she was talking to me, and then I noticed the little black dots, which creeped me out all over again.

I had arrived at the party by bicycle, and was still holding my gloves while trying to decide how to deal with this appalling situation. "Let me take those for you, dear," she said. She plucked the gloves out of my hands and put them in her purse with an air of finality. I wondered what Sigmund Freud would have made of that, but decided it was best not to think about it.

"Here," she said, "I want to introduce you to a very interesting man. He's the former UN ambassador for Iran."

This was all so nightmarish, I could barely speak. Finally I told her that I had to leave because I wasn't feeling well—which was true, at this point. When I asked her to return my gloves, her jaw clenched and her eyes narrowed, and I thought she might actually refuse. Grudgingly, she surrendered them to me, and I fled.

1984

The Rolling Boulder

One misjudgment leads to another—at least, that's what seems to happen in my life. Writing my typing-tutor program for Quick Brown Fox had been an error of judgment, and so after their business failed, I made a new deal that was even worse.

My friend Hal told me that a man named Tom Kemnitz had dropped in at the computer store on 20th Street, just to get acquainted. Tom ran a little publishing business named Trillium Press which specialized in books for gifted children, and he was diversifying into software. Hal suggested to him that he might be interested in publishing *Keyboard Command*.

When I met Tom, he was a smart and charming man with a great sense of humor and a disarming talent for false modesty. I was so naive, I didn't realize (yet) that a person who seemed so kind and decent might actually lack certain scruples.

In the course of our conversation, he remarked that running a small publishing company often made him feel like Harrison Ford at the beginning of *Raiders of the Lost Ark*, when a giant boulder is rolling after him, and he has to keep running to avoid getting squashed. I wondered what this odd comparison really meant, but had to wait a couple of years to find out.

When I showed Tom *Keyboard Command*, he liked it. Most schools still used apple II computers, but they might start buying the Commodore 64, because it was so cheap, and Tom was willing to take a chance on marketing my program to them. He would go out on a limb for me, because he admired my program *so very much*.

Like any writer, I am vulnerable to flattery.

"All right," I said, "let's give it a try."

Tom said he regarded a written agreement as a formality. His contract was only one page long; he had found the text somewhere. He wasn't big on legalities. He trusted a handshake more.

The modest package created by Trillium Press for my typing tutor software.

That was nice, although I did read the contract, at which point I was somewhat shocked to discover that Trillium Press would own my copyright.

When I mentioned this, Tom seemed puzzled. Wasn't it a standard provision? How could he sell my work if he didn't own it? He seemed a bit naive on this subject.

Well—my software would only have a limited lifespan anyway, as some other computer would displace the Commodore 64 soon enough. I decided to sign his contract, but I did need a clause reverting rights to me in the event of Trillium Press declaring bankruptcy.

Now, Tom was astonished. He had never heard of such a thing. In fact, he seemed a bit hurt. Surely, there was no need for something so unpleasant.

I mentioned that during my many years as a writer, a total of four publishers of my work had gone bankrupt. Maybe this was because I had made the mistake of selling my work to sleazy deadbeat companies, but still—it could happen.

Tom couldn't take it seriously. He let the matter drop for a few days, then called me and asked if I had signed the contract yet. No, I said; I was waiting for the bankruptcy clause. He let it drop for a few more days, then called again and told me how much he was looking forward to selling copies of my program, because we both needed the money.

"I still need the bankruptcy clause," I said.

He showed a hint of irritation. My attitude was jeopardizing our friendship; but in the end, he was willing to add the clause, because he admired my work *so very much.*

I recompiled the software to include the fateful words, "Copyright 1984 by Trilliam Press," and delivered the disk—at which point, Tom lost it.

I made him a new one, and was told that someone named Danny had to test it. Danny had other things to do, and didn't test it.

Tom said he would test it himself—but didn't get around to it.

Finally a copy-protected version had to be made, but wasn't

made. Then it was made, but didn't work and had to be remade.

Then the plastic boxes for the disks had to be delivered, but they weren't delivered.

The delays continued for months. In fact, an entire year passed before copies of my software became available.

During that year, Tom tried to make up for it by inviting me to dinner at his apartment on several occasions. During one of these very pleasant social events, Tom started asking me to write a book for him. He had such a limited budget, he could offer no money in advance, but he begged for my help because I was the only person he knew who had the necessary knowledge and talent.

Looking back, I don't quite understand why I agreed to do it. Was it really just the flattery? I think it was more because I liked Tom, and he needed my help, and I don't like to say "no" to people when they are nice to me and need help.

I spent a couple of months writing a book titled *Artificial Intelligence in Action*. Tom liked it. In fact, he said he would be deeply proud to publish it. Those words still echo inside my head: "Deeply proud." That was really what he said. And he knew an artist who would illustrate it. (Later I discovered she received $6 per drawing.)

Meanwhile I started to receive royalty statements for *Keyboard Command*. At least, they seemed to be royalty statements, but most of a page would be blank, and somewhere near the bottom would be a single digit such as a 3 or a 7. Was this a problem with his bookkeeping software? Or had my work really sold only 3 copies—or 7? When I queried Tom about this, he was apologetic, vague, but optimistic. The royalty statements were a mess, he knew that, but they would be fixed, and sales would improve.

The royalty statements were never fixed, and sales did not improve. *Keyboard Command* never broke into double digits in any quarterly period. Then he published my book, and I couldn't find out if it had sold any copies at all.

I nagged him, gently at first, and then vigorously. The dinner invitations stopped. He became unresponsive. He moved out of Manhattan to a farm somewhere. Then I received an unexpected form-letter notifying me that Trillium Press had gone out of business.

How prescient I had been, demanding the bankruptcy clause! I sent a letter requesting reversion of rights, at which point Tom's wife wrote back explaining that the sentence which Tom had added didn't mean exactly what I thought it meant, and I would not be getting my rights back.

I reiterated my demand more emphatically, which elicited a one-line handwritten response from Tom: "Stop being mad at us and come visit us!" He was still willing to be friends even though I was cruelly unsympathetic regarding his financial difficulties.

I like to learn from bad experiences, so I thought a lot about Tom's strange mix of flattery, incompetence, and evasiveness. Here's a theory that I came up with. It is, of course, only a theory:

I think he wanted to acquire as many properties as possible, without paying anything for any of them, and with no clear idea of how he could sell them. He just hoped that something, somehow, might make some money—and if it didn't, he'd hold onto it anyway, because one day, it might.

He wasn't naive about contracts. He was determined to own everything outright, so that he could do whatever he wanted with it, for as long as he liked. Even when his business was going bankrupt, this principle still applied.

As for the "friendship" thing, he never actually said he was my friend. He just seemed friendly.

Probably he realized fairly quickly that schools were not going to buy the Commodore 64, so he had little interest in publishing *Keyboard Command*, and he put it off as long as possible, hoping I would write a book for him. Then he lost interest in that—but I might still be foolish enough to create something new that he could try to sell. So, yes, "Come visit! Let's hang out together!"

In the end, I became just another person in Tom's life, nagging him, leaving phone messages, and trying to get paid. This was the meaning of the rolling boulder: It was us. We all went rolling after him while he kept running as far ahead of us as possible.

Really, it was a valuable experience for me. In exchange for a few months of work, I learned to say "no," even when a charming and wonderful man begs me to help him because he admires my work *so very much*.

Gernsback at the FBI

A neighbor at Patchin Place told me he had received a phone call from the FBI, who wanted to know if Mr. Platt was a generally law-abiding citizen. My neighbor said that he assured the FBI agents I was a person of high integrity—but what the hell was going on?

I wondered if this had anything to do with the extra wire I had run down to the basement to power my air conditioner. Or what about the cash I had netted from the bank in Paris? It seemed unlikely, but why else would the FBI be asking questions about me?

The next day, I myself received a call from an FBI agent. He asked to drop in for a little chat. No charges were being filed—no, no, nothing like that. It was just a friendly chat.

I didn't think the FBI were ever friendly to anyone, but I agreed they could visit me, because I didn't think they would react well if I told them, "Leave me alone, I don't like people in law enforcement."

Two agents came to my humble apartment, wearing gray suits and white shirts as if they were actors playing G-men in a movie. They were thirtyish, polite, and totally humorless. They wanted to know about a computer conference in the Soviet Union, where my name had been on the list of attendees.

Oh, that! I explained that I had been invited to it because Tom Kemnitz of Trillium Press had listed me somewhere as a programmer of software for gifted children; but when I discovered that I would have to pay my air fare to the conference, I had opted out of it. I could prove this, and I was sorry to have wasted their time.

They seemed to believe my explanation, yet they were not ready to leave. They explained that the Russians often ran conferences of this type. Typically a conniving Russian would make friends with a young, naive, and trusting American computer expert such as myself. The Russian would then visit the United States and get together socially. Vodka would be consumed, and a naive American—such as myself—might speak a little too freely about computer secrets.

The FBI liked to intervene early, to stop such indiscretions before they had a chance to start. Therefore, they asked me to let them know if anyone else in the USSR contacted me for any reason.

Oh, okay. I would be happy to do that.

The agents glanced at each other. Then the senior agent gave me a steady stare. "How do you feel about communism?" he asked.

"I hate communism!" I exclaimed. I told him I had grown up in

England under the postwar socialist regime that had inspired Orwell to write *1984,* and I had come to the United States because I believed in individual liberty and the free market.

They exchanged another glance. I could almost hear them thinking: *Maybe he really means it.*

"You could get yourself invited to more conferences," the senior agent said. "You could be—what we call—an asset. Just make some notes for us about people's names, the work they do, the questions they ask you. That kind of thing."

That sounded easy enough. I wondered if there was any money in it, although after my speech full of patriotic fervor, I didn't want to seem as if I were motivated by crass financial considerations.

"So let us know what develops." The agent handed me his business card. "But when you call the office, you need a code word to identify yourself, so that we know it's you."

I thought for a moment. "How about, 'Gernsback'?" I spelled it out for him, and he wrote it on a little pad and paper.

"What does it mean?" the agent asked.

"Oh, er, nothing really." I decided not to say that Hugo Gernsback was the publisher of the world's first science-fiction magazine.

"Okay." He put away the pad and paper. "Now I need to take a photograph of you."

I wondered if this was getting a little out of hand. Still, patriotism, and all that. I let him take the picture.

He and his partner shook hands with me, and they left.

I called my friend Janet, who had friends in government agencies with three-letter acronyms. She knew about stuff like this, so I told her what had happened.

"Jesus Christ, they want you to be a spy!" she exclaimed.

"Well—not really."

"Yes, really! When they described you as an asset, that's what it means. If you go to Russia and anyone finds out you're working for the FBI, you'll be thrown in jail!"

Well, in that case, maybe there were limits to my patriotism, after all. I decided not to get myself invited to any other Russian computer conferences.

My secret ID must be still on file, though. If you want a little entertainment, just call the FBI and say the secret word.

They Don't Understand

I received a call from Alfred Bester, who had very bad news: His wife Rollie was dying of terminal cancer. He knew that I had a car, and asked if I could please drive him from Manhattan to his farm house in Pennsylvania. He was leaving his apartment on Madison Avenue and did not plan to return.

I was happy to perform this duty, although I wondered what I could possibly say or do to help him. Then, during the car journey, he talked a lot, and I realized that I might be useful simply by sitting and listening.

After we crossed the state line into Pennsylvania, we passed through a small town where Alfie directed me to stop at a bar on a back street. Inside, the bartender recognized him immediately and served a snifter of brandy without being asked. The time was around 3pm, and the shadowy interior was empty of people.

Alfie downed the brandy, and one more, before he was ready to continue.

An hour later we reached his farm house, which I had never seen before. It had been built in the 1800s and was beautiful. I tried to imagine the weekends when he and Rollie must have entertained friends from New York, and I wondered what had happened to all those friends. The house was empty, and Alfie was alone.

He invited me to stay the night, and made me dinner in a kitchen where I saw a professional-looking gas stove and at least a dozen copper-bottomed pans hanging from the ceiling. I found myself remembering a witty little story that he had written for *Analog* magazine in 1977 titled "Mastering the Art of Space Cooking," about the challenges facing a gourmet chef in a weightless environment. I felt sad thinking of the stories he had written, always so clever and expressing his individuality. I didn't think he would be writing any more stories like that, ever again.

After dinner he said he wanted to take me to his local bar, although he warned me to expect some redneck racism. Derogatory comments about black people were part of the package.

"Did you ever mention to them that you're Jewish?" I asked.

He looked chagrined. "We will not say a *word* about that."

The bar was a shack where draft beers cost seventy-five cents and the bartender placed a bottle of brandy beside Alfie without being asked. The customers were the Pennsylvania equivalent of good old boys, and they spent most of their time complaining about their wives, who seemed to be waiting at home, taking care of the kids. They treated Alfie as a "character," a wealthy celebrity from the big city who nevertheless knew how to talk dirty and drink like a man.

Around midnight, most of the regulars were barely able to stand. They were playing selections on the jukebox that were unlisted: Obscene songs about nymphomaniacs who were only good for one thing, or frigid women who got what was coming to them. Over by the ten-pin-bowling machine, an argument had been going on for fifteen minutes concerning whose turn it was to play, and it was starting to get unpleasant.

Around midnight we went back to Alfie's house, and he turned in, taking another bottle with him. I sat by the embers of a fire in the living room, reading a play that he was writing based on his short story "Fondly Fahrenheit." It was a solid piece of work, but I couldn't imagine how he would ever get it produced.

Around 2am he reappeared and seemed to want to talk. He said he knew that the play would be far too expensive to stage, because of the number of characters, but he just felt like writing it.

"They don't appreciate us, you know," he said abruptly. He picked up a poker and jabbed it into the embers of the fire. "They just—don't—understand."

He said he knew, beyond any doubt, that *Golem 100* was his best book, but readers couldn't grasp this. He felt disappointed and unwilling to write anything more. It was the first time I had ever heard him complain about the reception to his fiction, and I felt embarrassed, as if I were listening to one of the men back at the bar complaining about his wife. I have always felt that it is the duty of a writer to understand his readers, not the other way around.

The next day, I asked him about an unpublished novel titled *Tender Loving Rape*. In 1972, when I had started working as a consultant for Avon Books, the manuscript had been left for me by my predecessor, George Ernsberger, as a piece of unfinished business. At that time I encouraged Avon to publish it, but they refused, and I didn't know what had happened to it after that. It was a suspense novel set in the New York worlds of advertising and television which Alfie knew so well, and it also included a sensitive depiction of a scientist torn between love and work.

Alfie said I should forget about the novel, because it was a lost cause, but I pointed out that a small press might be interested.

"You're wasting your time," he said.

I persisted. I felt sure that the manuscript had to be in his house somewhere.

Finally, under duress, he went into his study, and we found it in a box at the bottom of some book shelves. "Take it," he said. "Do whatever you want with it."

I said that it might be hard to sell under that title. I thought for a moment. "How about if we call it *Tender Loving Rage*?"

"Sure, you can do that."

I promised to let him know if I found a way to publish it.

"Don't bother," he said.

I wondered why he had lost interest in it. Then I drove back to New York, and re-read it the book—and concluded that he had conceived it as bestseller material. He had thought of it as a ticket to recognition outside of the science-fiction field, but it had failed so completely, a small-press edition would just add insult to injury.

In the years that followed, I called him in Pennsylvania occasionally to see how he was doing. For a while, he seemed okay; he said he was keeping busy with gardening. "Aren't you lonely out there?" I asked.

"Oh, not at all," he said. "I talk to the plants. I talk to the bees."

He was still drinking heavily, and a couple of months later he developed a bleeding ulcer, causing him to be admitted to an emergency room after losing a lot of blood.

Then he went back to the farm house where local friends apparently took care of him, including his bartender. Probably I should have gone out to Pennsylvania to see him again—but by that time, I had sold my car. That was my excuse.

Eventually he was admitted to a nursing home, where he died in September, 1987. I was told that the cause of death was listed as malnutrition, perhaps because, like many elderly people who lose interest in life, he also lost interest in eating.

He was a brilliant writer, certainly the greatest influence on me when I was reading science fiction, but his best work was written in conjunction with one influential editor: Horace Gold of *Galaxy* magazine. When Alfie was thinking about writing *The Demolished Man*, it was Gold who suggested a telepathic society that would seem to prevent the protagonist from committing a perfect murder.

After Gold died, Alfie never found such a partnership again.

Adventures in Data Transfer

In March of 1984, IBM introduced their PCjr. It was against my principles to spend money on computer hardware, but I saw no escape from migrating to IBM's operating system, so I capitulated.

Now came the hard part. I had to get the data out of my Challenger 4P, in its funky steel box with wooden sides, and into the PCjr. Floppy disks created by the Challenger were unreadable by any other computer, so I had to use some other method. This was not a simple matter in those days, before modems and the internet.

A serial cable should do the job, except that the pin functions were not standardized. I had to visit a company named Cables and Chips, in an old warehouse building near the Manhattan Bridge, where a large hairy bearded person said he could make a cable for me in about a week.

Next I had to write a program on the 4P to send data through the cable at an appropriate transfer rate, and I had to write a program for the PCjr to wait for the incoming data using the same protocol. Even this wasn't the end of the story, because the 4P applied a voltage to one pin which wasn't quite what the PCjr expected. Fortunately Hal Pollenz was familiar with the problem, and told me how to solder a resistor between the misbehaving pin and ground. I had to go shopping on Canal Street to buy the resistor, which I think cost around 25 cents.

This is the kind of stuff we had to deal with, in those days. But, in the end, I did manage to migrate all my text files to PC-DOS, and I have them still, almost thirty years later. Patterns of computer data are like patterns of life, to me, and I have never accepted the inevitability of death.

Below: In my young day, we had to make our own cables.

Bottom: The IBM PCjr was an unpretentious little box containing one floppy drive and a couple of ports for game cartridges.

Janie

I had burned out on crazy people whom I met through ads in *The New York Review of Books*. So, now what? Well, there was an obvious alternative: *The Village Voice*.

I loathed the *Voice*, as it was infested with left-leaning female staff who imposed dogma-driven mandates and arbitrary prohibitions. They had a "code of ethics" for personal ads—they wouldn't allow the word "young," for instance, for reasons which remained inscrutable. Still, they had a huge circulation, so I started to advertise.

To my surprise, I met a smart, attractive woman of about my own age who didn't seem to be crazy. As I sat down opposite her in The Peacock Cafe, we said hello, and then she started laughing. "Now what do we do?" she said.

"Well, we get acquainted," I said.

"Okay," she said.

Janie sitting in her kitchen in Hoboken, New Jersey.

Her name was Janie, and she was an abstract painter living just across the Hudson River in Hoboken, New Jersey. She had a cat, which I thought was a good sign. Her father owned a lucrative retail clothing store in Connecticut, and I got the impression that he was supporting her, although that was not entirely clear. She had been feeling lonely and depressed, and her therapist suggested she should answer some personal ads, so here she was.

I started seeing Janie quite often, and we got along well. I was cautious, though, after making so many dumb decisions over the years. I came up with a question that I thought was an ingenious way to uncover any personality issues:

"Tell me, if I met some of your ex-boyfriends, how would they describe you?"

Janie laughed. "They'd say that I'm moody, and difficult, and I don't compromise, and I can be a real bitch."

"Wow," I said. "I guess they didn't know you very well, did they?"

Actually, of course, they knew her a lot better than I did. But this would not be apparent until later.

Less than Human

I ran across a couple of chapters of an unfinished science-fiction novel that I had written with my friend Gwyneth Cravens around 1972. It was a humorous dystopia set in a devolved New York where indigents were camping out in corporate offices and aging hippies had established a commune in the Chrysler Building. Clearly this was not a very serious piece of work, so maybe—just maybe—I could overcome my inhibitions about writing science fiction, and finish it.

At the back of my mind, I was still thinking of Bob Sheckley's court-jester role in the 1950s. I didn't have his deft sardonic touch, but I hoped that my love of the absurd could compensate.

When I asked Gwyneth if she had any interest in working on the book with me, she politely declined. She was now writing serious novels and selling them to Knopf, and I don't think she wanted to risk devaluing her brand. She said if I wanted to finish it, I was welcome to do so, and she wouldn't even need any payment for the small amount she had written more than a decade previously. As for her name, I should not put it on the cover.

Well, then, what name *should* I put on the cover? I didn't have a good track record, so maybe I should start over with a new name, and a good choice might be to combine the names of two of the world's most famous science-fiction writers. I could be Robert Clarke, and my book would be shelved next to Arthur C. Clarke in bookstores, which could be helpful.

I titled the book *Less than Human*, as a reference to Theodore Surgeon's classic book *More than Human*, and pitched it to John Douglas at Avon. John was amused, but said he had learned from bitter experience not to pay much money for ideas that amused him. He offered $2,000.

A pittance! I argued for days until, finally, he increased the amount to $2,500. Oh, all right. I wrote the book for fun, trying not to think about the hopelessly inadequate compensation.

The British edition was published under my own name. The cover art was meticulously accurate.

Gossip

The annual World Science Fiction Convention was not a happy event for me, as I had hoped that *Dream Makers Volume II* might win the nonfiction Hugo Award. My chances should have been good, as there wasn't much competition—but a man named Donald Tuck got it.

Donald who? Apparently he had written Volume III of a so-called science-fiction encyclopedia, but when I asked around, no one had ever seen it. Still, Tuck seemed to be a popular guy who had a lot of friends, and was adept at self-promotion. I was not so popular and didn't have so many friends, which depressed me, but was my own fault. In fact at the Worldcon I found a way to make myself even less popular.

Andrew Porter had asked me if I would revive Gabby Snitch to write a gossip column for *Science Fiction Chronicle*, a little zine that he published. The gossip column was guaranteed to piss people off, and it certainly wouldn't pay me any money, but it should be fun, shouldn't it? So, I accepted his kind invitation.

Word about the column circulated ahead of me, so I found myself running into people who wanted me to write about them for their own peculiar purposes.

First I met Harry Harrison's wife Joan, who ranted to me for fifteen minutes about Bob Sheckley, who had stayed in the Harrison residence while they were away for four months in Ireland. Joan complained that Bob "didn't change the bed linen once. I had to disinfect and repaint the bedroom and burn the mattresses." She demanded that I publish the name of the guilty party, to shame him, but (because Bob was still alive at that time) I declined.

Next there was Ellen Datlow, asking me to describe her as "the queen of punk science fiction," in a way that suggested she might actually be serious.

Then there was David Hartwell, who wanted me to report that he won the "most handsome editor award" in a poll.

I ran into Fred Harris, the tireless promoter of L. Ron Hubbard's science-fiction novels, who tried to entertain me by wearing joke spectacles that seemed to make his eyes bug out. "Just the thing for those Scientology auditing sessions," I said, "where you have to stare at each other without blinking."

"Ha ha," said Fred.

I went to a bidding party for a planned 1987 British worldcon, but the room smelled as if someone had been sick in it—and indeed, this turned out to be the case. I overheard the guest who had rented the room trying to bribe hotel staff to clean up the mess and say nothing about it.

This reminded me of a Norwescon that I had attended once in Seattle, where fantasy fans staged a ritual sacrifice in their hotel room. They killed a couple of guinea pigs, then flushed the corpses down the toilet. Unfortunately the guinea-pig heads got stuck and the toilet overflowed with blood, making a horrible mess. A member of the hotel staff there told me about this event in some detail.

Add it all up, and science-fiction conventions were still full of bad behavior. It was always entertaining, so how could I resist reporting it?

The award ceremony at the worldcon was in an arena sometimes used for sporting events, with a PA system that made master-of-ceremonies Jerry Pournelle sound like a game announcer talking through a CB radio with repeat echo. Dim slides flickered on a giant screen, showing personalities from previous worldcons, and just when everyone imagined that the agony could not be prolonged any further, Harlan Ellison appeared on stage to make a "special tribute" to an obscure, retired editor named Larry Shaw.

What did this have to do with Hugo awards? Nothing! But Shaw had bought Ellison's first story back in 1956, which of course was an event of great significance to Ellison, although slightly less important to everyone else.

He lectured the audience, at some length, on Shaw's career and his unique attributes as a person, then asked him to come up on stage to accept a plaque of some kind—at which point the audience discovered with dismay that the poor man had throat cancer and could barely speak. I have always been squeamish about public displays of personal grief, and found Ellison's grandstanding in terrible taste. When I wrote about it for *Science Fiction Chronicle*, I said so.

When Ellison read my column, he called Andrew Porter and yelled at him for having published it. "I'm going to come to New York and take you out," Ellison said, according to Andrew.

"What do you think that means?" Andrew asked me.

"Well," I said, "I doubt he's offering to buy you lunch at your favorite sushi restaurant on Columbus Avenue."

Personally I received no threats, but he would exact punishment upon me in his inimitable fashion in due course.

Self-Promotion

I went to the UK and appeared on talk shows to promote my book *Micro-Mania*. When I was placed opposite an author or authority who delivered the usual gung-ho nonsense, I asked them what, exactly, people were supposed to do with computers. The answer was no surprise: Games, and maybe storing names, addresses, and phone numbers, and some food recipes....

I got a short spot on Radio One at lunch time where I managed to mention the title of my book three times in five minutes, but the BBC quickly edited the recording so that only one mention remained. This was impressive, as they were still using quarter-inch tape, and their cuts must have been done with a razor blade on an editing block.

Most exciting to me was an evening radio show with Brian Mathew. I had grown up listening to his weekly program titled Saturday Club, which was the only enlightened source of new music on the BBC during the 1960s. Mathew had been a music guru in those days. He had known the Beatles personally.

I told him what an influence he had been on me, but he didn't want to hear it. Then I realized why: Twenty years previously, he'd been chatting with John, Paul, George, and Ringo, whereas now here he was, interviewing Charles Platt. I think he just wanted to go home and go to sleep.

When I got back to the United States, the publicist at Avon arranged for me to make a five-minute self-promotional videotape for the David Letterman show. This seemed like a great opportunity, so I tried to be as entertaining as possible—but Letterman's people were not interested, and later I realized why: He was the one who told jokes on his shows. Non-famous guests like me had to be humorless and slightly eccentric, so that Letterman could make fun of them. The last thing he wanted was to be upstaged.

Overall I think the concept of my book was better suited to the UK, where satire has a stronger tradition. The bottom line, though, was that the US edition had a weak title . . . and it was green.

Top: David Langford (seated left) who anglicized the British edition of my book, and Malcolm Edwards (seated right) who was my editor at Gollancz.

Lower: Brian Mathew in the BBC studio.

1985

No More Snitching

Andrew Porter had hoped that my gossip column in *Science Fiction Chronicle* would generate some buzz and sell more copies of his dull little zine. It did generate the buzz, but some of his readers were so offended, they cancelled their subscriptions. I apologized to Andy, and commiserated with him, although secretly I felt proud of my achievement. After all, none of his other contributors had ever offended readers so successfully. "Give me one more chance," I said.

Foolishly, he agreed that I could write about the annual Lunacon.

A year previously, it had been held at a Sheraton in New Jersey, but they had banned the event after a notorious "Emergency Stairwell Fornication Episode." Now in 1985 Lunacon would be at the La Guardia Sheraton, which was so disreputable, even a Motel 6 would have looked classy by comparison.

On the Saturday night, the hotel hosted a low-budget disco which attracted gum-chewing Long Island teen trash with hot-combed hair and tight pants. In the lobby I saw them nudging each other and snickering as they stepped over a plump Star Trek fan who was lying face-down on the tiled floor with his face inches away from a greenish puddle of his own vomit. Hotel staff were aware of the problem, but couldn't decide what to do about it.

Upstairs, I found a toga party where science-fictionoids in rumpled bedsheets had taken over the entire fifth floor, "releasing rank odors until the whole floor stank of stale sweat," as Gabby Snitch reported it. I fled to the convention party suite, where I ran into a book packager named Bill McCay who knew nothing about science fiction but had come to Lunacon to see if there were business opportunities. "As I understand it," he said, "science fiction is a substitute for sex in teenage boys, and fantasy serves the same function for teenage girls. This event confirms it. It also proves that black is a very bad choice as a slimming color."

Few writers were present, but I saw Somtow Sucharitkul, who

had spent his childhood in Thai royalty before relocating in the United States and writing science fiction under the pseudonym S. P. Somtow. He insisted on giving me graphic details of his recent circumcision, and asked for them to be published. "It was the most disgusting thing that ever happened to me," he claimed, laughing happily. Normally I enjoyed Somtow's noblesse-oblige attitude, which made him feel entitled to talk about anything with anyone, but in this case it ventured too far into gross blood-soaked detail even for my tastes (although of course I reported it anyway).

Out in the parking lot, three cars were burglarized and someone backed a 4x4 into the rear fender of my 1972 Camaro, leaving a large dent. The La Guardia Sheraton was really the lowest point in the history of Lunacon, and naturally I described it in unflinching detail. To his credit, Andy published my column without any edits, but it did induce more people to cancel their subscriptions.

After this, Gabby Snitch was forced into retirement, although I still fantasize about bringing her back one day. Gossip would be different now, since humorless women seem to have acquired such dominance in the field, but I'm sure a resourceful and courageous columnist could find something to reveal, so long as he was unconcerned about being deplatformed, banned, cancelled, or subjected to other punishment.

The lobby of the La Guardia Sheraton. This recent photo suggests that the place has been fixed up a bit since 1985, but you can still get a sense of the Lunacon if you imagine a large male science-fiction fan lying face-down on the floor near the front desk.

Necromancer

William Gibson's book *Neuromancer* was packaged as science fiction, but I think he knew, really, it was a near-future suspense novel in which the technology was a bit sketchy—especially when Bill described hackers "jacking in to cyberspace" by inserting plugs into sockets in their necks. How exactly did that interface work, Bill? Wisely, he didn't get into questions of that sort. He once told me that his book was like a brightly colored dragon in a street festival in Chinatown: Its goal was to distract you from the guys underneath using rods and levers to move it around.

I always enjoyed talking to him at science-fiction events, but

The man and the work. Actually I think he still had long hair when he wrote Neuromancer, but photographs from that hairy period are rare.

there was something a bit elusive about him. At one point I told him that I had added up his timeline of published work, after which I subtracted the total from his current age, and found a five-year period in which no one knew what he had been doing. He gave me a sly smile. "You are the only person," he said, "who has ever made that calculation." The *only* person? Why is it that journalists never ask the most obvious questions? All I can say is, if Bill ever writes about those five years, it will be memorable.

When I first read *Neuromancer*, I was a bit overwhelmed by his talent. After I got over my jealousy, I wrote a review of the book for *The Washington Post*. Then I called Bill to tell him that I had described him as "the Alfred Bester of the 1980s."

He paused thoughtfully. "I was hoping someone might say that."

Perhaps that sounds arrogant, but he simply had a shrewd assessment of his own talent.

Neuromancer won the Philip K. Dick Award, and Bill was tipped off that it would receive the Nebula Award in May. He flew in from Canada to accept it.

For some reason Frederik Pohl was tasked with handing out the trophy, even though he seemed to know little or nothing about the nominees. He stood in front of the audience, struggling to read from a piece of paper. "And the winner," he said, squinting, "is William Gibson—" squinting some more "—for Necromancer."

Any other writer might have been annoyed with Pohl for getting the title wrong at this very special moment, but Bill had an air of ironic detachment that seemed bullet-proof. "I am really honored," he said, with his sly smile, "to receive this award for . . . Necromancer."

A brilliant writer, a genuinely nice man, always poised, never pretentious—he was a role model for ambitious writers of the mid-1980s, but none of them quite succeeded in emulating him.

From Larry, Who's Dead

After the Nebula Awards, I was looking forward to the usual party where I could get some free drinks while trading cynical quips with depressed editors, but it was not to be. Jerry Pournelle intercepted me in the hotel lobby. "Harlan's upstairs," he told me in a confidential tone. "He's come here to hit you."

At this point I could have turned around and gone home, but I had never been in a physical fight, and I wanted to see how it would feel. If the pugilistic prima-donna became unduly aggressive, I decided that I wouldn't try to defend myself. Like a Quaker pacifist, I would sit down and wait for him to stop.

As soon as I entered the hotel suite where the party was taking place, Ellison marched up to me and hooked his fingers in my collar so that I couldn't back away. He then delivered his prepared quip: "This one's from Larry Shaw, motherfucker. Who's dead."

My first thought was that he'd had months in which to prepare his punch line (so to speak), but the syntax was terrible. Well, he never did believe in doing rewrites.

My second thought was, "Uh-oh, here it comes! The legendary Ellison punch!"

His fist grazed my jaw.

That was it? I felt ashamed of myself for ever believing his endless boasts about hitting people. Still, he seemed ready to do it again, so I grabbed his wrist in case he might try harder the second time. He struggled, but my biceps had been exercised regularly by carrying my bicycle up and down the stairs at 9 Patchin Place, while his only exercise came from playing games of pool and, on rare occasions, using a typewriter.

"I'm going to sit down now," I said, and dragged him down with me. We sat on the floor, still glaring at each other. Finally, I let go of his wrist, he got up, and he walked away. Subsequently, of course, he would embroider the event in heroic terms—"I made Platt kneel and bump his head on the floor, to beg me to stop hitting him, after which he ran away"—but he didn't start telling that version until years later.

Writer Donald Kingsbury had been standing beside me during the confrontation, and said he found it entertaining. Editor Ed Ferman also witnessed it, but as a quiet and civilized gentleman from Connecticut, he made a quick exit and retreated to his hotel room. Frederik Pohl came over to me and said he would testify in any suit

REM:1

A surprising number of people wrote letters lamenting the loss of The Patchin Review. This intermittent pamphlet is a diminished-expectations substitute, published and partly written by Charles Platt, 9 Patchin Place, New York, NY 10011 on an approximately quarterly schedule. To subscribe, send four 22-cent stamps or four international reply coupons per issue, for as many issues as you want. Copies are mailed first class within the USA and Canada, by air mail overseas. Initial readership consists of about 100 one-time Patchin Review subscribers and persons in the publishing trade. Short written contributions (expressing any viewpoint) are welcome; pseudonyms optional; payment nil. In the profoundly meaningful world of BASIC computer programming, REM denotes a piece of inessential commentary that is ignored while a program is running. It serves merely as an attempt to explain what is (or was) supposed to be happening.

---

that I brought for damages, which was nice of him, except that there were no damages.

When I studied my jaw in a mirror the next day, there wasn't even a bruise. Still, a friend urged me to call a law firm that specialized in suits against celebrities.

I got through to a nice young paralegal who extended his sympathy regarding the frightening and traumatic experience that I had endured. After getting that out of the way, he segued into practicalities. Was there any blood? Did I fall over? Had I been knocked unconscious? Could it have *appeared* as if I were knocked unconscious?

I told him that none of these things had happened, and I began to feel apologetic for taking his time.

He wasn't willing to give up, though. He still had one last question: Was the person who hit me famous?

"Not really," I said. "A writer named Harlan Ellison."

There was a thoughtful pause. "I think I read something by him in a literature class that I took at college. Look, the partners in our law firm will be lunching with some gentlemen of the press next week. We can see if Ellison is sufficiently well-known to interest them."

I was amused that the law firm would check with journalists before deciding whether to file a suit.

He never called back, though, so I contacted him again, ten days later. Now it was his turn to sound apologetic. "I'm very sorry," he said, "Mr. Ellison just isn't famous enough for our purposes."

Not famous enough! That quote was too good not to be shared, so I decided to continue publishing some sort of little zine, merely to report the phone call and tweak Harlan Ellison. Really, that was the only reason for it.

I titled it *REM*, which is a reserved word in some programming languages: An abbreviation for "remark," meaning a comment line which explains what is going on, but is often ignored.

That seemed a good metaphor for commentary about book publishing.

Cyberpunk!

"Punk SF," as Ellen Datlow had called it, was now vaguely recognizable as a new growth in science fiction, with its roots in *Neuromancer*. But didn't a new movement need a better name?

It ended up being packaged as "cyberpunk," a label promoted by Gardner Dozois. This appellation stuck, as silly labels often do. Some people hoped that it presaged a grand revival of the serious intentions and rigorous processes of "old-school science fiction," but I had lived through a previous idealistic movement in science fiction, and I had my doubts.

Rent Collector

I was still seeing Janie, who was still living in Hoboken. I got tired of riding the train out there, and we wanted to live and work together in Manhattan, but because of the market effects of rent stabilization law, we couldn't afford to move.

The law was despised by landlords, so they were disinclined to build new rental accommodation, and the lack of apartments naturally drove up their value. If I stayed where I was, my rent remained controlled, but if I moved to a new place, it would be at market price, which was about five times as expensive per square foot.

There was another option: I could rent an office. Commercial real estate was not subject to rent-stabilization regulations, so landlords preferred it, and therefore, commercial space was plentiful, and the supply drove the price down. The unregulated space was actually cheaper than the rent-stabilized space.

Through a classified ad, I found a woman named Caroline who had a long lease on more than 20,000 square feet in an old garment factory building at 594 Broadway, just below Houston Street. She had subdivided it and sublet all the new, fashionable offices at a profit, keeping the best space for herself: Room 1208, containing about 500 square feet with a clear view all the way across rooftops to Brooklyn. Now she wanted to move to a farm house outside of Manhattan, so she needed someone to supervise the twelfth floor and collect rents in her absence. If I would do that, I could use room 1208 indefinitely for $400 a month. What a deal!

Caroline had a British background, and found my accent reassuring. We reached an agreement on the spot. This turned out to be the beginning of a friendship that would continue for decades.

My office at 594 Broadway, room 1208. Behind my shoulder is the daisywheel printer that generated The Patchin Review. *Behind my head is a 747 Akai open-reel tape deck. On the desk is a PCjr with a monochrome monitor on top of it and a Princeton Graphics RGB monitor beside it (before the era of flat screens). On the top shelf at far left are plastic boxes of floppy disks (before hard drives became affordable).*

Page 136

A Magical Place

Room 1208 had a 12-foot ceiling and old hardwood floors, with huge casement windows facing east. Because 594 Broadway was a commercial building, it was pretty much empty after 6pm, and I could crank my stereo. It was a fantastic place in which to work.

On Sundays I would listen to WFMU, a college station in New Jersey, where a deejay who called himself The Hound played classic R&B. Black music from the 1950s was hard to find, but somehow The Hound had it all. Eddie Cleanhead Vinson! Joe Turner! Johnny Otis! Amos Milburn!

Imagine my surprise when I was collecting rent from the tenants at the beginning of the month and discovered a brooding, moody guy all dressed in black, using a small office next to mine. He turned out to be—yes—The Hound. Then I discovered that another office was rented by a company selling vinyl records and music CDs via mail order, especially 1950s R&B. They didn't know that The Hound was just down the hall, and The Hound didn't know that they were there. Something about the neighborhood on Broadway just south of Canal Street was attracting people who shared a natural affinity.

Another small space was rented by a man named Glenn Branca. He turned out to be a modern composer, influenced by Philip Glass. When I collected his rent check I saw behind him a Mac with composing software on it. We talked a bit, and he gave me some CDs of his music. A few months later, he participated in a concert in a midtown auditorium where David Byrne was the star attraction. Glenn got tickets for me.

In another space was an upstart video production company that was making TV commercials. Just across the hall from them was a woman named Christina Whited who claimed to be able to channel the spirits of dead people.

There was something very special about lower Broadway in the mid-1980s, shortly before it became a fashionable location for tech startups, when the Internet changed the world.

NASFiC

Neuromancer now seemed likely to win the Hugo Award as well as the other prizes, but the world convention would be in Australia. Fortunately, there was a second-rate substitute for cheapskates like me. It was NASFiC, the North American Science Fiction Convention, which would be in Austin, Texas. Bruce Sterling lived there, and he offered to let me sleep on his couch.

Now that cyberpunk fiction had a name, Bruce had positioned himself as the most visible and assertive promoter of it. I guessed that the small coterie of cyberpunks would gather there, and since I was an aging radical from the 1960s, I should have elder-statesman status, shouldn't I?

Bruce and Nancy lived in an apartment in an old wooden house on a little back street. The stairs were on the outside of their building, making me feel as if I were in an old W. C. Fields movie. The apartment had a leftover hippie ambience, which seemed appropriate, as Austin itself felt like an acid flashback. Long-haired people were selling tie-dyed T-shirts off tables in the city park, as if no one had told them that the Summer of Love ended fifteen years previously.

Bruce was a fun host, because he liked to bombard guests with reading material. "Look at this!" he exclaimed, brandishing the August-dated *Scientific American*. "Did you ever see anything like this?"

The "Mathematical Recreations" column featured color reproductions of something called the Mandelbrot Set. They were fractals generated by assigning colors to the output of a little recursive formula involving a complex number. Vaguely I remembered that a complex number would consist of a normal number coupled with an imaginary number, such as the square-root of minus-1.

"You think you could program that into my computer?" Bruce asked. He knew that I had wasted a lot of time teaching myself programming before I wasted more time writing computer books.

I wondered how software could represent an imaginary number. After all, byte values are not imaginary. On the other hand, the pictures in the magazine proved that someone had figured out how to do it, so (as my friend Rudy would say) how hard could it be?

I went to his computer, which was an Atari 800. I had never used one before. "Do you have a manual for Atari BASIC?" I asked.

Bruce presented it to me. Damn! Now I had no excuse to avoid this challenge.

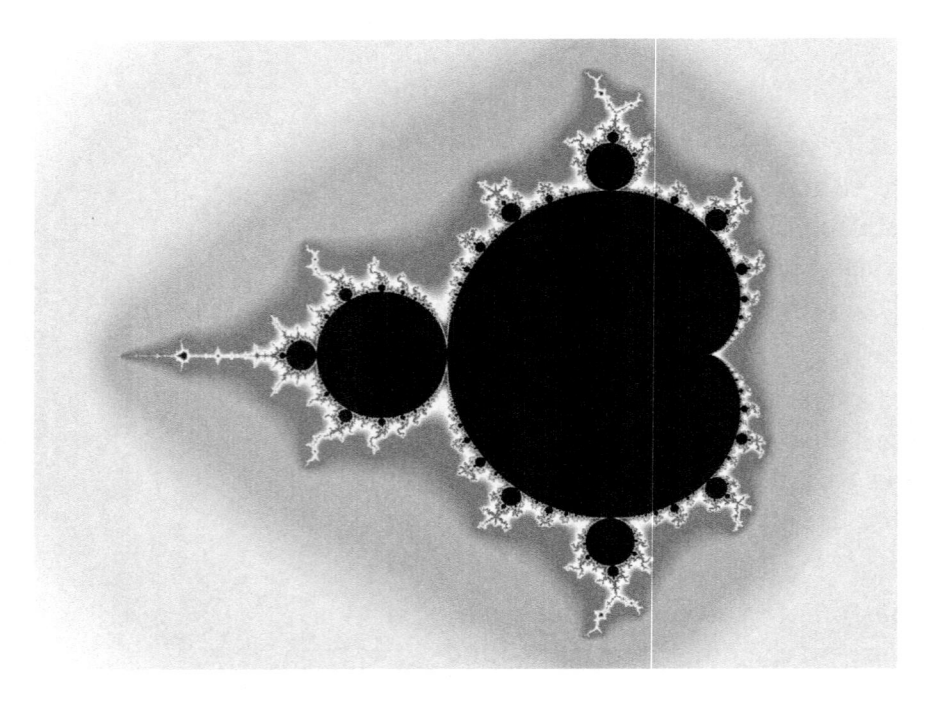

An hour later I had figured it out, and the program was only a few lines long. Bruce and Nancy watched expectantly as I typed RUN and pressed Enter. We waited. Finally a little colored rectangle appeared at the top-left corner of the screen. After another minute, another little colored rectangle.

"This may take a while," I said, emphasizing the obvious. Calculating the Mandelbrot set involved thousands of floating-point operations for each pixel, and the Atari was not a powerful computer.

While we waited for the rendering process, we sat and talked about the future of science fiction. Bruce was certain that cyberpunk would acquire global significance. Movies, comic books, music, even clothing—he predicted that it would become a "fucking juggernaut." Was he sure about that? Yes, Bruce was confident by nature, having grown up in Texas, where I seem to recall that his father ran an oil refinery.

Top: A modern high-res rendering of the Mandelbrot Set.

Bottom: An Atari 800 personal computer.

After an hour or so, four or five lines of little colored rectangles had appeared on the screen. They didn't remotely resemble the pictures in *Scientific American*, but maybe that was because the pixels were rectangular. If I looked at the screen at an oblique angle, to achieve a foreshortening effect, did that help? Well—no, not really.

A new guest arrived: Steve Brown, who edited and published a semi-professional magazine named *Science Fiction Eye* to which Bruce and I had contributed. After he said hello, he looked at the computer screen. "Is that—you know—that thing in *Scientific American*?" he asked. I wondered how he could tell.

Then Rudy Rucker arrived. Rudy was a mathematician, so I was not surprised when he looked at the screen and said, "Are you trying to generate the Mandelbrot Set?"

Then another person arrived. Richard Kadrey, as I recall. Richard had no math background, but he frowned at the video image and said, "Is that the thing from *Scientific American*?"

Much of science fiction had degenerated into simplistic escapism that had nothing to do with science or technology, but cyberpunks subscribed to the nation's premiere science publication, and (even more surprising) they read it.

Here in this little apartment on a back street in a western town, I was among fellow travelers whose optimism regarding technology was undimmed. The only question was whether their writing would find enough readers to catalyze the "fucking juggernaut" that Bruce predicted.

The next day, we all went to the NASFiC convention at a Hyatt in downtown Austin where a panel on cyberpunk fiction consisted of

Three participants from the cyberpunk panel. I managed to dig up some photographs that are approximately contemporaneous. Top left: Greg Bear. Top right: Lewis Shiner. Bottom: Pat Cadigan.

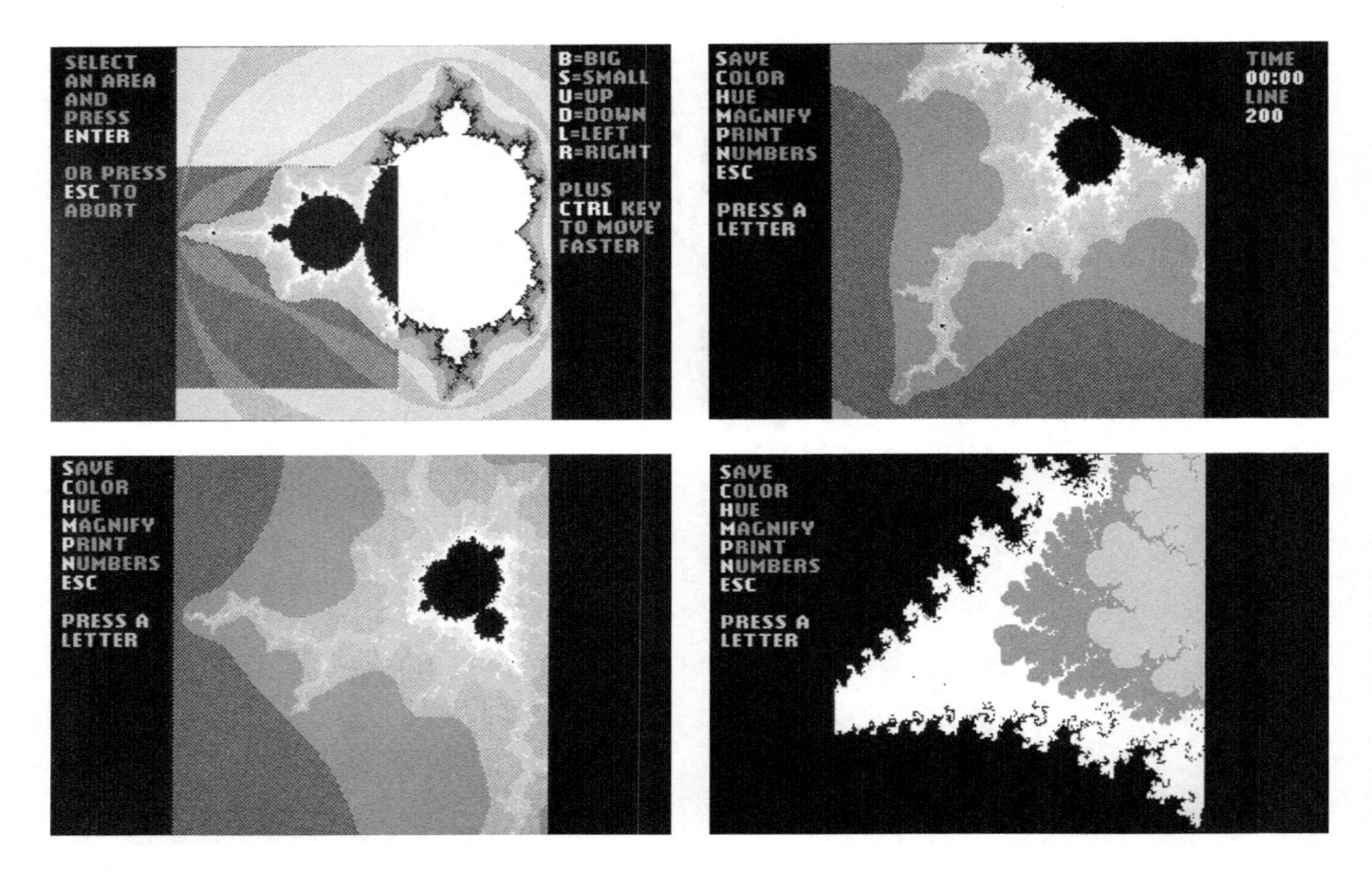

Screen shots of Mandelbrew, my easy-to-use DOS-based software to render the Mandelbrot Set. The image area used a resolution of only 200x200 in the old CGA mode of the IBM PC, but ran in 48K of memory. (Kilobytes, not megabytes.)

At top left, inverse video defines an area for magnification. Subsequent views zoom in. For those of a mathematical inclination, numeric values were available by pressing N for numbers.

Two or three hours were required to render initial views. At higher magnification, double-precision variables kicked in, and I had to leave the computer running overnight. The program will still run on a modern system, rendering the set in about three seconds.

Rudy Rucker, John Shirley, Bruce Sterling, Lew Shiner, Pat Cadigan, and Greg Bear.

This cyberpunk panel later acquired iconic significance in the history of the subgenre, to the extent that it is mentioned in a Wikipedia entry. At the time, though, it looked to me like an Ellen Datlow *Omni* "business dinner," with too many people, some of whom had tenuous excuses for being present. In the end, Sterling, Shiner, and Shirley became so disgusted by the hostility of the panel moderator, they got up and walked out.

I felt that the biggest challenge for the cyberpunks was their lack of an editor who would promote their cause. The New Wave had been nurtured by Michael Moorcock and *New Worlds* magazine, but the only editor explicitly championing cyberpunk fiction was Ellen Datlow at *Omni*.

One time when I asked her to define her editorial policy, Ellen replied: "Near-future stories, urban, depressing—no! *Not* depressing. Did you already write that down?"

Meanwhile, in Australia, William Gibson won his Hugo award. Did this imply that many readers were now eager to embrace the cyberpunk ethos? I didn't think so. Gibson was a singularity.

My Set

After I got back to New York City, I wrote a better-optimized program to generate The Mandelbrot Set. Other people were doing the same thing, but I thought I could make mine easier to use.

I was right—it was easier to use. So what? Well, maybe I could advertise it in the legendary little zine named *Factsheet Five*, and sell it to people in mathematics departments at universities.

I discovered that I could, although in rather small numbers. My software was titled *Mandelbrew* and was distributed on floppy disks. Imagine my surprise when I received a letter from Benoit Mandelbrot, who had invented the algorithm for creating those wonderful, mysterious images. "I never tire of seeing software to generate the set that is named after me," he said. "May I see yours?"

I noticed that he didn't mention the concept of payment. Like so many academics, he seemed to be a freeloader. I couldn't say no, though, so I sent Benoit his freebie.

He never thanked me.

The Big Loft Dream

Now that I had moved a lot of possessions out of my apartment to my office, there was more room in the apartment for Janie, although she still had to commute to her old place in Hoboken every day. She used it as her painting studio, even though she complained that it wasn't large enough.

We still wanted one piece of real estate, instead of three. Ideally it would be a big industrial loft in which we could both live and work, and she could fulfill her ambition to create really big pieces of abstract expressionist art.

She became so fixated on this idea, I avoided questioning it, even though I thought it was hopelessly unrealistic. She imagined that her father would buy a loft for her—somewhere—but he turned out to be like most self-made wealthy people. He wouldn't spend money on anything that didn't seem sensible to him, and he didn't regard Janie's needs as sensible.

Eventually this would make her crazy, but for a while, at least, we put up with an arrangement where each of us commuted to a work place, and we tolerated the inconveniences created by rent-stabilization law, which made rents higher instead of lower.

How to Be Happy

In December, I wrote and illustrated a humorous cat book. I had become fond of Janie's cat, who spent an inordinate amount of time sitting around doing nothing, and I thought he would benefit from a self-improvement guide to actualize his feline potential.

My book was titled *How to Be a Happy Cat*, and was ostensibly written by a cat to motivate other cats. When Caroline came into the city from her rural retreat and visited room 1208, she saw me working patiently and methodically, writing the self-help satire and doing drawings to the limits of my abilities. She looked at me with a skeptical expression, obviously wondering how I could invest so much time with only a nebulous hope of reaping a reward.

The answer, of course, was that my fundamental goal never varied: To avoid fulltime employment. If this book didn't work, I would try something else. If my creative efforts failed too often, I would have to teach more computer classes. This might be depressing, but the alternative would be worse.

If you're a cat... can you afford **not** to read this book?

Is this you? A timid domesticated pet with drooping ears, bent whiskers, and a limp tail?

Dramatic before-and-after pictures show immediate benefits from following the self-improvement plan in "How to Be a Happy Cat"!

Now you can be a **proud feline beast** with bushy fur, stiff whiskers, and human beings completely under your control!

What Kind of Cat Are You?

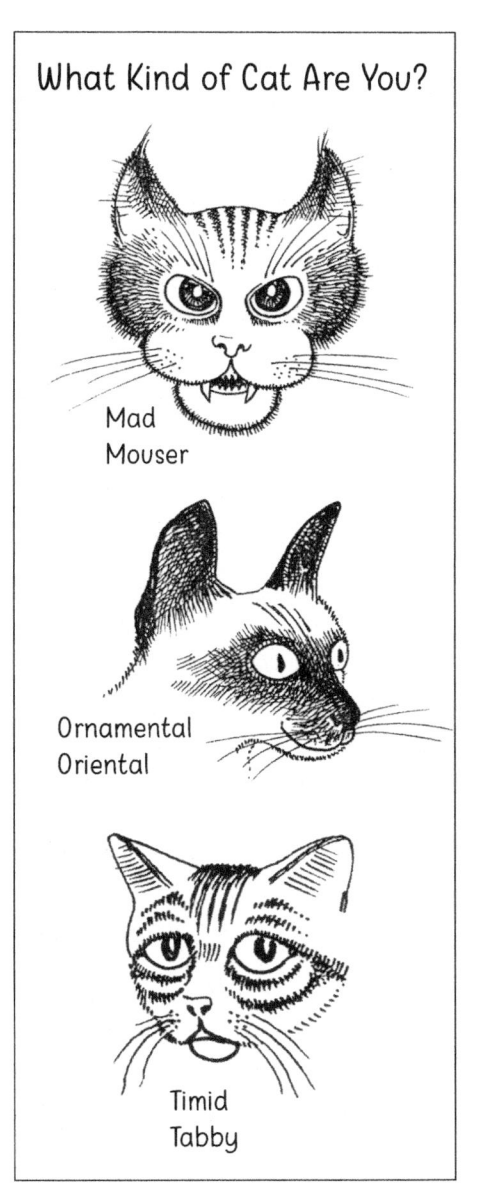

Mad Mouser

Ornamental Oriental

Timid Tabby

A feline fitness program gets off to a promising start!

I've never thought of myself as an artist, but I assumed a publisher could improve my cartoons by getting a "real artist" to redraw them. In 1986, this didn't quite work out as I had expected.

Page 143

1986

A Smelly Piece of Work

One of my students at the Computer Instruction Center worked for Guerlain, the manufacturer of high-end perfumes. When she asked me if I knew anyone who could set up a point-of-sale computer to promote the Guerlain brands in malls across America, I said I could do it for her. After all—how hard could it be?

Soon I was dealing with a British immigrant named Rodney from the sales division at Guerlain. He wanted a computer that would invite women to take a quiz, asking multiple-choice questions such as, "What kind of foods would you serve at an informal party?" The program would then determine the personality of the woman, and would show her a picture of her ideal fragrance: Shalimar, or Habit Rouge, or whatever.

Rodney was an oaf with a leering grin, and he seemed to think that women who bought Guerlain products were idiots. The quiz would ignore all their responses to the questions, until the final question asked what kind of perfume the person liked. Zesty, sophisticated, romantic, or sexy? Those four choices would match four perfumes, and that was it.

I told him we could do better than this. He could build real personality profiles, and could also assemble a database—but he had no interest in any of that. He just wanted a computer that would tell women to buy perfume.

He needed the hardware as well as the software, and since serious laptops didn't exist yet, I recommended a PCjr. It was lightweight and easily transported, and the program that I wrote would be so small and simple, I could put it on a bootable five-and-a-quarter-inch floppy and run it from an autoexec.bat file. I would write it in Microsoft BASIC and build an executable with a bootleg copy of the IBM BASIC Compiler version 1.0 which Hal had kindly shared with me.

My big challenge was to create video images of the perfume bottles. The old BASIC Compiler could only handle two color palettes consisting of three colors each: White, magenta, and cyan, or amber, red, and green. Fortunately the Guerlain perfumes were all amber colored, so one palette would suffice. But screen resolution was only 320x200, and the pixels were rectangular. I didn't own a scanner, so I created my own graph paper with the appropriate aspect ratio, on which I sketched the perfume bottles by referring to pictures provided by Rodney as guidance.

Then I counted pixels and used the DRAW command in BASIC to create the bottle outlines, after which the PAINT command filled them with color. This was all a big hassle. Finally I saved each image by copying video memory to the floppy disk, then retrieved the images by using a BLOAD command to copy them from disk to video memory.

When the job was done, Rodney came to my office on lower Broadway, bringing with him a couple of colleagues and his assistant, a petite, slutty blonde with a sullen pout. She seemed to be in her early twenties, while I guessed that Rodney was about fifty. Judging from the way he stroked and patted her, they had more than a business relationship. When she asked where she should sit, he gave her his leering grin and said, "Why don't you sit on my lap?" She wasn't so sure about that, and compromised by sitting close beside him, resting her hand on his knee. Everyone pretended to ignore this.

When I ran the program, my guests liked the pictures of the perfume bottles, as computer graphics were still an impressive novelty. The only criticism was that Rodney had written so many questions, they would strain the attention span of any woman who took the quiz. Since all the questions except the last one were being ignored anyway, why not get rid of most of them? Rodney wasn't happy about that, because he seemed proud of his creative process.

In the end we reduced the quiz to ten questions, after which I recompiled it and he went away to tour the nation with his computer and his assistant. I guessed that this might be the real goal of his sales campaign: To stay in high-priced hotels and have a lot of sex.

I received $3,000 for this assignment, which was good pay, although it didn't entirely compensate me for dealing with Rodney.

Page 145

Why did Gray Jolliffe draw cats with big noses? We never did find out.

Cats With Big Noses

I made ten copies of a portion and outline of *How to Be a Happy Cat* and delivered them to my agent at Writers House. The cartoons had received good reviews from friends who had seen them; even Tom Disch, who was difficult to amuse, laughed out loud. But, editors didn't want the book.

All right, then: I refurbished the copies, and my agent sent them to another ten publishers. Still no luck.

I was not willing to concede, so I went on a trip to England and visited my friend Christopher Priest. When he went through the pages of my book, he started laughing. He took a sip of tea, then laughed so much, he had to spit it out. "This is embarrassing," he said. That seemed a good sign.

Christopher sent my proposal to five publishers, including Gollancz, who had published *Micro-Mania*. Of the five, Gollancz was the only one that wanted it. They offered 5,000 British pounds—a relatively high advance for them.

When I mentioned my good fortune to my New York literary agent, she said, "Can I have ten percent?" Presumably she felt she should be reimbursed for her time, even though she had failed to sell the book. From her perspective, I had gotten lucky. Why shouldn't she have a share?

Meanwhile, at Gollancz, Malcolm Edwards came up with a cunning scheme. The company had published a very successful book of cartoons by an artist named Gray Joliffe, about a man with a talking penis. (I am not making this up.) Malcolm suggested that Joliffe could redraw my pictures of cats, giving them the same style that had sold his previous book, including a human cat owner whose head looked like a penis. Motivated by simple avarice, I agreed to this. We knew that Joliffe could draw a penis; what none of us bothered to determine was whether he could draw cats.

After the contracts were signed, we found that his cat-drawing capabilities were a bit limited. For some peculiar reason, he gave all of his cats big noses. Also, he didn't seem to think my book was funny. I had to demand that he should illustrate at least some of the jokes, at which point he became churlish about it.

Next came the editing process. A woman named Liz Knights took on the task, and turned out to be a fanatic about excising "superfluous" words. She spent hours going through my text, cutting a word here and a word there. I was flattered by her attention, but she didn't seem to understand the concept of cadence. To clarify, let me take a simple example:

> Why did the chicken cross the road?
> To get to the other side.

Notice the rhythms in these simple sentences. Containing seven iambic feet, they are almost Shakespearian in their perfection, but Liz Knights might have rewritten them like this:

> Why do chickens cross roads?
> To reach the other side.

I think she would have liked this version, because it is two words shorter. The trouble is, the cadences are clumsy, and even when you are reading text silently to yourself, cadences are important in humor. Liz succeeded in flattening my jokes, and some of them didn't even make sense anymore.

Still, the concept of the book remained, which was enough for Gollancz to sell foreign editions. The book appeared in six languages. The holdout was France, but I was told that the French never buy cat books. Why not? Because they're French, I suppose.

The woman at Gollancz who sold foreign rights for me was so good at it, she even sold them to an obscure publisher in the United States, which paid an amazing $10,000. And so here was another object lesson about the vicissitudes of book publishing: After being turned down by a total of twenty-four publishers, and being illustrated by an artist who couldn't draw cats very well, and being edited by a woman who didn't understand humor, my book still somehow sold more copies than most other books that I ever wrote. You can go crazy trying to understand editorial decisions and sales figures in the book business.

Happily, when I showed the American publisher my text before and after it had been edited, he preferred the unedited version. Maybe I should have surrendered half of my advance if he would have used it to hire a different artist. Or maybe people actually like cats with big noses.

The Piers Anthony Universe

My friend John Silbersack became the science-fiction editor of a new imprint named Roc, and called me in some desperation: He needed writers with name recognition, but they were all contractually committed to other publishers. One way around this would be to find literary territory which had been developed by famous names, and commission lesser-known "sharecroppers" to exploit it. For instance, an obscure writer named Gentry Lee had been commissioned to write two novels "in the same universe" that had been established by Arthur C. Clarke's book *Rendezvous with Rama.*

John wondered if I knew a famous writer who would allow me to write a sequel to something he had already written. My first thought was Alfred Bester: I would be excited if he allowed me to write a sequel to *The Stars My Destination*—and indeed, the ending of the original book would permit a sequel. I called Alfie and mustered the courage to suggest this, but he didn't like it at all. In fact I think he was offended by such a gross venture in opportunism.

All right, then, I could think of only one person who (a) might allow me to take such a liberty and (b) had not authorized similar collaborations in the past: Piers Anthony. I had always admired Piers' first novel, *Chthon*, a very grim narrative set inside the lava tubes of a volcanic planet. The protagonist was a convict obsessed with a quasi-human woman who required pain in order to experience pleasure. I felt Piers had never developed this implicitly sadomasochistic relationship to its conclusion.

I wrote to Piers, and received a reply in which he sounded amused by the idea. He was doing well by writing Xanth novels, and had no interest, himself, in going back to *Chthon*. "Go ahead," he wrote. "I have so much money these days, you wouldn't even need to pay me." Very kind of him! Maybe he had a soft spot for me because he had enjoyed *The Patchin Review.*

He only imposed one condition. Unlike most novels of this type, it should be published ethically, in a way that wouldn't deceive the reader. My name would be at the top of the cover in type that was at least as big as Piers' name.

John Silbersack said he could go for this unusual requirement, so I notified Piers' agent, Kirby McCauley. Kirby was shocked by the idea that I wouldn't be paying anything to Piers, perhaps because if Piers didn't receive any money, Kirby wouldn't be able to take ten percent of it. He demanded that I should pay at least $500.

This was annoying, as I had known Kirby since he was an insurance salesman in Minneapolis, and had helped him to start his agency in New York. Since then, he had made many millions by representing Stephen King and other famous names, so I didn't think he needed ten percent of my $500. Quite recently, he had told me he was in the middle of a tax audit with the IRS, but he thought it should be settled easily enough, as the amount in dispute was "only $700,000." Alas, it is in the nature of any literary agent to want a percentage of everything.

Contracts were duly signed, and I was ready to start writing my book when Piers sent me another letter asking if I had read the sequel to *Chthon* that he had already published many years ago, titled *Phthor*.

What? A sequel, which he had written? I knew nothing about it, so Piers sent me a copy. I read it, and was horrified to discover that all the characters died at the end. I wrote to him in some agitation. He had killed off all the characters! Why hadn't he warned me?

His reply was succinct. "You think I remembered?"

I ended up using a typical science-fiction workaround: An alternate universe in which everyone hadn't died. A harder problem was to find a title. After *Chthon* and *Phthor*.... "How about *Shlock*?" a witty friend suggested.

I ended up with *Plasm*. It didn't have an H in it, but it would do.

A harder problem was my old inability to suspend disbelief. I dealt with it by reading a few pages of Piers' work, then writing a few pages of my own, and going back-and-forth like that. I also avoided anything that severely stretched my credulity, such as a giant orange talking telepathic spider.

In retrospect, I think developing the sadomasochistic element of *Chthon* was an interesting idea, but I went too far. I wrote a deranged book which was a bit disturbing, and I wonder why my editor didn't have any problems with it. Maybe he had to fill the slot in the schedule, and he may not have allowed time for a rewrite.

The Year Before Yesterday

Ed Breslin moved to the position of Editor-in-Chief at Franklin Watts, an obscure hardcover publisher for which I had written a crafts book about decorating T-shirts back in the 1970s. Watts was struggling to survive by selling its books to libraries, and I wondered what Ed was doing there.

He asked me to drop in, so I stopped at his office in my typical attire of an old T-shirt and ragged jeans, with hair sticking out in all directions after a windblown bicycle ride through urban traffic.

"I want you to meet the president of the company," Ed said.

Now? Looking like this?

"He won't mind."

Soon I found myself chatting with a friendly man who had learned about some of my dubious achievements from Ed, although my failure to deliver a tetralogy to Warner Communications was not mentioned. "I was thinking Charles could acquire science fiction for us," Ed said. "We can start with just six titles a year. Charles knows all the writers in the field."

Yes, I knew them, but that didn't mean I could persuade any of them to write books for Franklin Watts. Still, my doubts were swept aside, and I found myself in a new position as a consulting editor, receiving a $1,500 fee per book and $1,000 per year expense money.

The royalty advances would have to average $3,500 per title, and I was afraid that this wouldn't make any sense for most writers. In "the old days," a writer would want to have a hardcover edition, because the hardcover would be taken seriously by reviewers, and the reviews would then help to sell paperback rights, bringing in additional money, of which the hardcover publisher would take half. By 1986, this system barely existed anymore: Many paperback publishers were now doing their own hardcover editions.

Still, I could call in some favors. Alfred Bester hadn't allowed me to write a sequel to *The Stars My Destination*, but it was out of print and had never been in hardcover. He liked the idea. Maybe other "classic" novels enjoyed a similar status—but when I investigated, I found that they had all been snapped up by David Hartwell for his series published by Gregg Press.

In desperation, I asked Brian Aldiss if he had any oldies that could be rebuilt and resuscitated. Brian had warm feelings of nostalgia for our mutual bad behavior over the years, and suggested that I might like to do a book version of an old novella that he had written titled "Equator." Well, no, I wouldn't really want to do that, and nor would I like to add another old novella that he suggested, "The Impossible Smile." I swapped letters with him for a while, and finally he said he thought he could stitch the two novellas together with some additional text to make something that would look more like a real book. I wasn't totally enthusiastic about this, but I had to do something, so I agreed.

Now came the problem of a title. Brian was a wonderful friend, but was a pain in the ass as a writer. He insisted on "a Brian Aldiss kind of title," but could not tell me what this might mean, and rejected everything I suggested. In the end we settled for *The Year Before Yesterday*, which was meaningless, and still wasn't really a Brian Aldiss kind of title, but he decided he could put up with it.

Brian's agent duly negotiated an advance of $4,000 instead of the offered $3,500, thus covering her own commission. As for the book itself—it was quite odd, including a character named after one of Brian's own pseudonyms from long ago. Still, everyone was happy that I found a writer whose name was recognizable.

One of my singular achievements while working for Franklin Watts was to persuade the art department to allow this wonderfully retro wraparound cover for Brian Aldiss. I especially like the skirt as suitable attire for a moon walk, and the boots with fins to radiate excess heat.

In my efforts to find more books for Watts, I went back again to Piers Anthony. Vaguely I remembered someone telling me that he had an old novel that he had been unable to sell, despite his new-found fame as a fantasy author. Was it still available?

He said that it was. He had written it in the late 1960s for Essex House, the legendary publisher of gross-out pornographic science fiction, and with his usual talent for being recalcitrant and rebellious, Piers had decided to violate all the usual conventions of porn. For example, instead of having a protagonist with a large penis, his protagonist had a penis that was unusually small—hence the title of the book, *3.97 Erect*.

Essex House had gone out of business before this quixotic weirdness could be published, and the manuscript was so unappetizing, no other publisher had been willing to touch it.

I asked to see it anyway, and when it arrived, I was enchanted by its ingenuity in finding so many ways to disgust the reader. It was too offensive for Franklin Watts, so I wondered—could I find a way to get it into print myself? *Could I, in fact, start a small press?* This thought later became the seed of a venture which would be like so many others in my life: Time-consuming and unprofitable.

After I rounded up my first three novels for Franklin Watts, my efforts became increasingly desperate. Maybe I could lead a bold new initiative to publish Japanese science fiction? I got into a lengthy correspondence with a science-fiction fan in Tokyo who sent me synopses of novels that he would be willing to translate—but they didn't make any sense, and I never figured out if the problem was in the original books or in his descriptions of them.

At some point I wrote a letter to a friend: "Being a hardcover editor is a terrible chore right now; everyone's doing it, and there are no books I can afford except for those which have already been rejected everywhere else. God knows how [editor] Pat LoBrutto manages at Doubleday, paying even less than I do. Well, actually, he manages by publishing people like Kit Reed, who sell to about 700 libraries, and that's it."

Really Franklin Watts was an anachronism left over from the 1960s, and its business model didn't make sense anymore. It was sold to the French company Hachette in 1988. And even Doubleday couldn't survive as an independent imprint: The legendary company which had once seemed synonymous with book publishing was sold to the German company Bertelsmann.

As for my friend Ed Breslin: He moved on to much better things.

A Poster at MIT

Rudy Rucker got me interested in a truly fascinating topic: Cellular automata, also known as "artificial life." Beginning with a random array of pixels on a screen, you could apply a "growth rule" to make them multiply—and they did acquire a lifelike quality, like bacteria, or maybe slime mold.

I liked CAs because they were so easy to program. Throw the pixels on the screen, apply the growth rule, and then apply it again, and again—and wait to see what happened. Often nothing happened, as the cells died, but sometimes amazingly complex nonrepeating patterns would appear, as if by their own volition. It really looked as if the software was defying entropy.

I had a mailing list of mathematicians who had bought my Mandelbrot program, and most of them seemed willing to buy a cellular-automata program, although it had no imaginable applications. I think they just enjoyed playing with it.

Rudy was in contact with Stephen Wolfram, a brilliant mathematician who was organizing the First Conference on Cellular Automata at MIT. He invited Rudy to attend, and Rudy asked me if I'd like to come too, although I didn't understand why.

"I'm a college dropout," I pointed out. "And a self-taught programmer."

"I don't think anyone cares," Rudy said. "When it comes to software, all that matters is whether you can—you know, do it."

Okay, I put together a poster presentation, and Rudy and I went to MIT. He was right: No one cared that I had no qualifications. I did a demo of my program, and it attracted some interest. "User-friendly CAs!" one man with a German accent

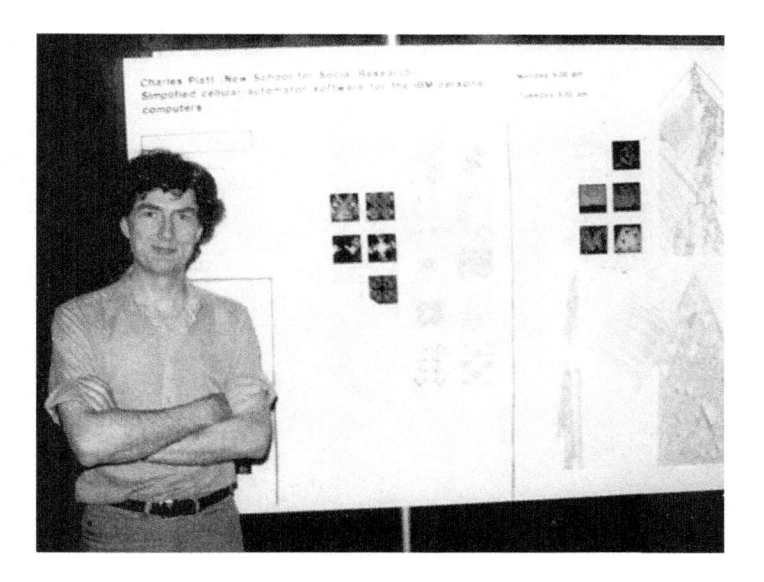

Photographs: Rudy had no poster, so he pointed to mine. Bottom image: Output of a 2D program that I wrote.

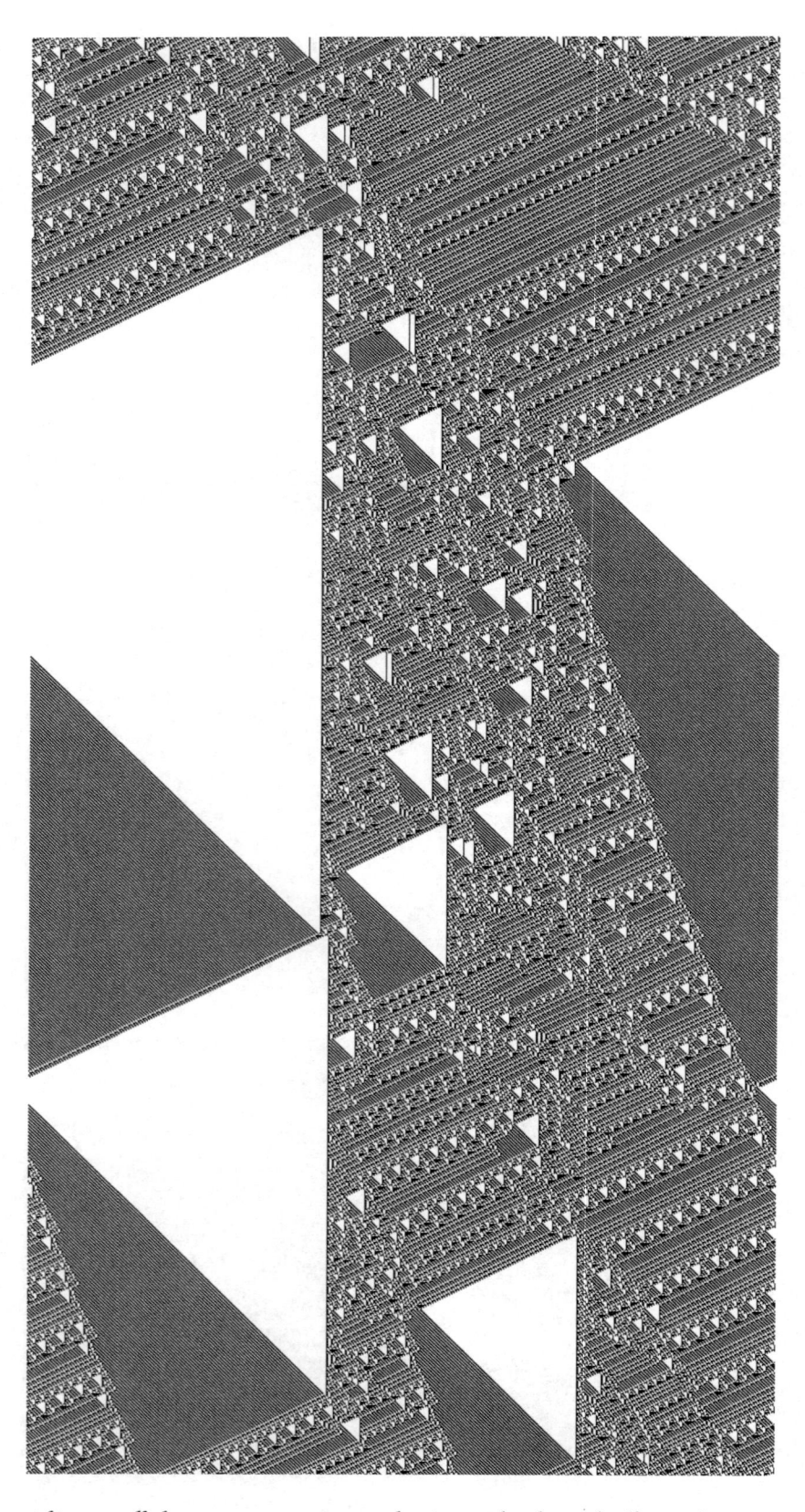

A linear cellular automata program begins with a line of cells, applies a rule to each cell to create a new line of cells below it, and continues this iterative process. In this example there are about 1500 lines of 640 cells per line: Approximately a million cells altogether.

exclaimed. He exchanged a sardonic smile with a colleague. The elitist subtext was obvious: Real academics didn't point and click, they did numeric data entry, no matter how inconvenient it was.

Real academics at the conference didn't want to pay money for software, either. They were like Benoit Mandelbrot. They expected freebies.

The conference was unusual in that no one could explain how CAs evolved from simplicity to complexity. It was just—inexplicable! No one even had a theory for it, and if you're in academia, what are you going to talk about, if you don't have a theory? Still, the mathematicians pretended to come up with theories.

Then it was Rudy's turn, and he didn't play that game. He did what he usually does, and went straight into metaphysics. Maybe, the universe is a giant CA. Maybe God is a programmer. Maybe—

A man in the audience interrupted him. "I don't hear much mathematics in this, Dr. Rucker," he said.

Rudy looked annoyed. "I guess that's just the kind of math I do," he said. Then he sat down.

Suddenly I understood why he had invited me to attend the conference. He'd dealt with academics before, and knew what to expect from them. He had needed some moral support from a fellow science-fiction writer.

The Book Co

Just supposing I started a small press to rescue orphan books such as *3.97 Erect*—how would I go about it? I asked some editors, and someone told me about The F&SF Book Co in Staten Island, run by book lovers who specialized in distributing titles from small presses. I gave them a call and asked them if they would talk to me. Yes, of course! They knew who I was. They had been readers of *The Patchin Review*. I should drop in and say hello.

This was not so easy, as Staten Island was—well, an island. No subway trains served it, so I had to take my bicycle across on the ferry, and then there was a five-mile ride around the edge of the island to the Book Co. Still, once I was there, they were wonderful, welcoming people. They said they would take ten percent of cover price of each book, and would do the warehousing and the shipping. All I had to do was typeset the books, and get them printed, and tell the printer to deliver the copies to the Book Co.

Actually, this was a bit of an oversimplification. I would have to solicit the bookstore orders, which would entail creating sales literature to advertise the books, and then I would have to nag the bookstores on the phone. And I should develop name recognition for my enterprise, which would mean buying ads in *Locus* and *Science Fiction Chronicle*. And—more stuff like that. All right, then: I would hire someone who would help me to deal with the chores. That should work.

I wrote to Piers Anthony to tell him about my investigations and my hope to rescue *3.97 Erect* from obscurity. He stunned me by offering to get me started with a $10,000 loan which I would repay on an indefinite basis, with annual interest at 10%. He was still making money by writing Xanth novels, and liked the idea of bankrupting a small idealistic publishing business. No, wait—wrong word! That should be, "bankrolling."

So, how could I find someone to help me with the work? I could advertise in *The Village Voice* for part-time assistance. But would a Hewlett-Packard LaserJet printer generate text that looked good enough to serve as typesetting in a book? Till I figured that out, I asked Piers to put his offer on hold.

I continued to think about the project, and I came up with a great name for my small press: Black Sheep Books, because every book I published would be the black sheep of the family.

I went downtown to the Municipal Building and checked their

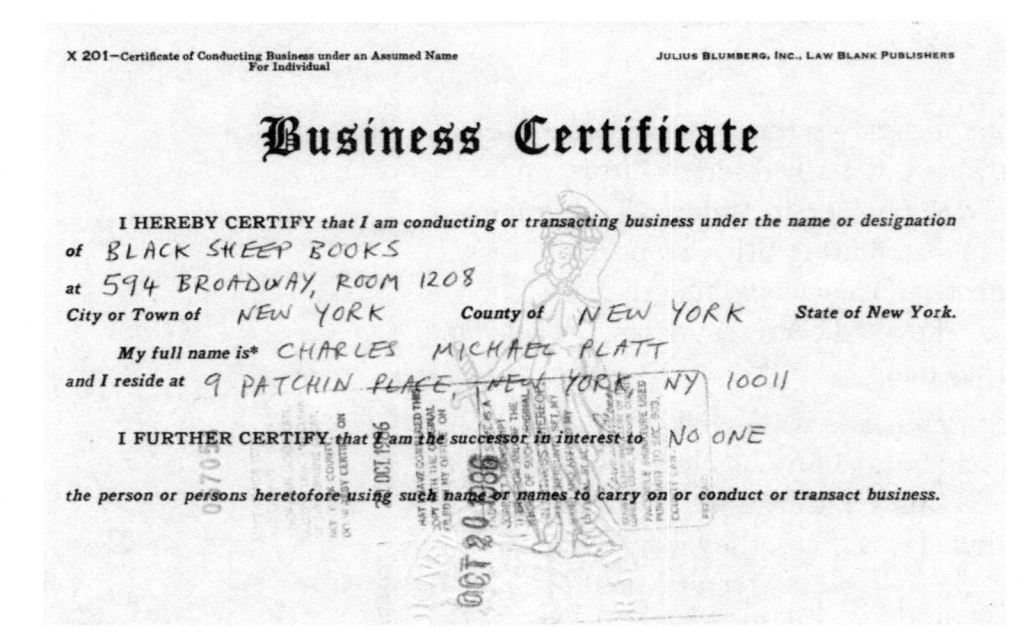

huge leather-bound volumes of business names. Black Sheep Books did not exist, so I registered it, for some trivial sum. And then I went to a bank and opened an account, and went to the post office and opened a PO Box. This, of course, was all the easy stuff.

I contacted Alfie Bester and asked him if I could publish his orphan novel, *Tender Loving Rage*. "Sure," he said. "Do whatever you want with it."

I wondered how many other writers had their own "black sheep books." Probably a lot of them. I conceived a slogan: "Publishing the unpublishable."

Austin Again

I learned that Bruce Sterling's wife Nancy was pregnant, so I decided I should visit them while they were still sane. Soon enough they would be racked with anxiety, besieged with relatives wanting to perform impending-birth rituals, and desperate for money. That would be bad enough, but after the baby was born, an uninterrupted conversation while visiting them would be impossible.

When I hung out in Bruce's living room, I found that his optimism regarding the future of cyberpunk fiction was undimmed, even though every sign suggested that intelligent science fiction of any kind was now doomed unless you were a pre-existing Well-Known Name, as David Hartwell had said. Unfortunately for Bruce, he was not quite a Well-Known Name—at least, not yet.

He did acknowledge that the cyberpunks now had to deal with some backlash from naysayers who rejected techno-optimism and described themselves as "The Humanists."

"Who are they?" I asked.

"Well Kim Stanley Robinson, for a start! Read this!"

Any visit to chez Sterling would entail reading assignments, and resistance was futile. Dutifully I sat down to read Robinson's "Down and Out in the Year 2000" in the April 1986 issue of *Isaac Asimov's Magazine*.

"Actually I quite like it," I said, upon finishing the grim depiction of street blacks hustling spare change from high-tech yuppies of tomorrow. "It has verisimilitude."

"That's not the point!" Sterling seized the magazine and flipped to page 73. "Look at this description of the holo-TV programs that the panhandlers are watching."

"Who the fuck is this?" said Ramon.
Johnnie said, "That be Sam Spade, the greatest computer spy in the world. . . . Watch out now, Sam about to go plug his brains in to try and find out who he is."
"And then he gonna be told of some stolen wetware he got to find."
"I got some wetwear myself, only I call it a shirt."

Kim Stanley Robinson. The humanists were not known for their sense of humor.

There was more, and it was suddenly obvious: The show which the characters were mocking was a parody of William Gibson's novel *Neuromancer*. Robinson's story was a *satirical rebuttal*, using wretched urban poverty to mock the glitz of techno-fetishist power fantasies.

Bruce dumped more issues of *Asimov's* magazine on my knees. "Your problem," he told me, "is that you are *culturally offline*."

"Empty jargon," I muttered.

"It only sounds empty to you because you are so totally out of touch. Or, to rephrase it in a dated idiom that you might be better able to relate to, *unhip*."

"There may be some truth to that," I admitted.

"Your shame is admirable," said Bruce, "and too seldom seen." He put on a tape of Handel played by a Japanese koto orchestra, assuming correctly that I would be unable to cope with anything more modern. "You probably even have a weakness for the Humanist stuff. Deeply meaningful mood pieces evoking insight into the human condition—that's what your 'new wave' was all about back in 1968, wasn't it?"

"Well, somewhat. I didn't really like a lot of it."

I read some more of the magazines that Bruce placed before me, but was interrupted by a sudden call to action. "Hey, we have to make it down to the copy center before 5:30 to Xerox the agitprop."

Bruce was referring to *Cheap Truth*, of course, his broadsheet which promoted the cause of cyberpunk while sneering at most other subcategories. He grabbed a battered file folder stuffed with anonymous diatribes against the status-quo, and slipped into his plastic Korean sandals.

I accompanied him outside into the heat. "I gather David Brin doesn't actually believe there is any such thing as a cyberpunk movement," I remarked as we got into Bruce's rust-riddled Volkswagen and he nursed it along Main Street, seeking a parking meter with free time left on it.

"There's a trenchant quote from John Shirley about that." He parked his car and plucked from his folder a transcript of the 1986 Science Fiction Research Association's conference panel on cyberpunk literature. He quoted Shirley: "You don't want to believe there is a movement, because it frightens you, because you think you're not competent to handle the new idiom of it."

"It seems to me," I said, "that if John Shirley thinks he's competent to handle a new idiom, I might be able to deal with it."

Bruce grimly shook his head. "Not until you get *culturally online*."

In the air-conditioned comfort of the copy center, he commandeered a self-service Xerox machine and commenced working it with obsessive intensity. Then we drove back to the apartment. "Come on," said Bruce, "we have important work to do."

"I'm not entirely convinced about its importance."

He shook his head dismissively. "Cyberpunk is the first new movement in science fiction in twenty years. Its best-known member has won every major award. It is the only literature with an informed, online world view. And you question its importance? When you finish folding the broadsheets, we have a couple hundred stamps to stick. And when you finish reading those *Asimov*'s magazines, there's three years' worth of *Omni*."

After I visited Bruce, just one more issue of *Cheap Truth* appeared. I was unsurprised; becoming a parent does tend to discourage dalliances that don't make money.

As for cyberpunk fiction—it did enter public consciousness, but never quite became the juggernaut that Bruce had imagined.

Big Paintings

During a break between classes at the Computer Instruction Center, I went into the men's room, glanced at my reflection in the mirror, and discovered that half of my hair had turned white.

That was impossible. It had to be a trick of the light. Hair couldn't just turn white within a matter of days, could it?

The South Bronx in 1980. Still looked much the same in 1986.

Actually, it could, under appropriate conditions. Nightmarish stress would do the trick.

The cause of my stress was my significant other. I was finally beginning to realize that beneath her shy, gentle exterior, Janie was angry with the world and most people in it, including her landlord (*the rapacious monster who wanted to turn her apartment building into condos!*) and her fellow tenants (*the philistines who complained about the smell of her oil paint!*) and her father (*the tightwad who wouldn't give her the money she wanted!*).

Now my name had been added to the list, because of my unsympathetic attitude toward her requirements for painting space.

Her desire for a Very Big Loft where she could create Very Big Paintings had escalated to become a raving obsession. If she could not paint Very Big Paintings, her life would be meaningless, she would subside into a bottomless pit of depression, and the deprivation would be so intolerable, she might as well give up and die. Why was this so hard for me to understand?

I did understand, but there were practical issues. After her father had refused to bankroll a Very Big Loft in Manhattan, Janie was fixated now on a cheaper location. The South Bronx was probably the only place where she could get what she wanted.

It was not conveniently located, but that wasn't my primary concern. Many buildings in the South Bronx had been arsonized, the nearest subway station would be ten blocks away, and if you valued your physical safety, you'd be advised not to walk home after sunset. Streets were full of garbage, roaming gangs settled disputes with lethal weapons, and if you called 9-1-1, the police might decide that they were too busy to pick up the phone.

To Janie, these were minor inconveniences. She was an artist! Creativity was her life blood!

I started to live in fear of her diatribes, which reminded me too much of my childhood, during which I used to hide from my mercurial mother. I also started to worry about Janie's bouts of depression, and persuaded her to ask her therapist for antidepressants. Reluctantly, she agreed, and to my amazement, the medication actually worked. She felt more cheerful, and became a bit more mellow.

Unfortunately, she said that being mellow interfered with her art, so she went off the meds—at which point the raving obsession resumed. I now felt that our relationship was doomed, because as much as I cared for Janie, I was not willing to exile myself in an urban wasteland populated by gangs and drug addicts who torched tenements for the pleasure of watching them burn.

I offered a suggestion. Maybe she could consider doing smaller paintings?

Smaller paintings! Only a totally self-centered dickhead could say something so insufferably insensitive. What was *wrong* with me?

Our arguments made me feel as if my stomach was digesting itself. And now my hair was turning white.

In desperation, I went with her to visit her therapist—but joint therapy sessions turned out to be a bad idea, because the therapist took my side. He told Janie she was being unreasonable, and this of course triggered more anger. "I AM NOT BEING UNREASONABLE!" she screamed at him.

I thought back to the days when I had been getting to know her, and had asked how her ex-boyfriends would describe her. Moody—difficult—unable to compromise—can be a real bitch—yes, here it all was. I had asked a clever question, but I had not been clever enough to believe the answer.

On the fourth or fifth visit to her therapist, I said I was giving up. I went back to my apartment, alone. Intestinal spasms rippled through me, and I sat on the toilet for a while. Then I lay in bed for an hour or so, wondering if I was ever going to have a successful relationship with anyone. Waves of self-pity and self-loathing overwhelmed me. I was a loser! I was hopeless!

Suddenly it occurred to me that Friday was the deadline for placing personal ads in *The Village Voice*. I struggled out of bed, grabbed the text of an old ad that had done well for me in the past, and rode my bicycle to the offices of the *Voice*.

Time passed.

A couple of years later, I called Janie out of curiosity, to find out what had happened to her. She said she had a new boyfriend, and they were happy together—

"Where are you living?" I asked.

"Oh, still in my old apartment."

"But—it's not big enough."

There was an embarrassed pause. "I'm doing smaller paintings."

Again and again, this has happened to me. A woman makes an absolutely non-negotiable demand, which I am unable to satisfy. Our relationship breaks up, and then—she gets involved with some other man, and relinquishes her demand as if it never existed.

Why does this happen? I have no idea.

No Dogs Allowed

How to Be a Happy Cat was published in UK, and I went there to promote it, although it wasn't really the kind of book that anyone could promote very easily.

While I was there, I gave Malcolm Edwards my proposal for a follow-up humor book about dogs.

"I had been expecting something like this," he said. He promised to discuss it in the next editorial meeting.

What Malcolm had not been expecting was that my book would denounce all dogs weighing more than 20 lbs as sociopathic vermin that should be euthanized and eaten for the greater benefit of humanity. I saw no other way to approach this important topic, although I did try to make it entertaining.

"Our editorial meeting was divided," Malcolm reported later. "The people who were negative about your proposal were the ones who owned dogs, while the people who were positive about it didn't own dogs."

"But the dog-lovers prevailed, didn't they?" I said.

"Well, yes, they did."

No surprise, there. That was exactly what I expected from authoritarians who enjoyed mindless canine obedience. They could not tolerate dissent.

Cats and PEN

The PEN American Center hosted an annual party for writers whose works had been published during the previous year. I read the instructions carefully, and there were no rules regarding the type of book that was eligible, so I submitted a copy of *How to Be a Happy Cat*.

At the party, my work attracted some attention. The effete literati frowned at it in the manner of museum curators examining a primitive artifact, or microbiologists trying to evaluate a new kind of pathogen. "What is it about?" was the most common question.

"It's a self-improvement guide for cats, written by a cat," I explained.

I had wanted to meet women at PEN, but found they were all too dour and embittered by their poor sales figures.

Bugfuck!

In November, I heard that Harlan Ellison was being sued by someone for defamation. Then I learned that the suit would be heard in Manhattan, and I couldn't stay away.

Seven years previously, in an interview for *The Comics Journal*, Ellison had described a writer named Michael Fleisher as "crazy." Unfortunately for Ellison, Fleisher had a thing about being called crazy, and complained that he was so "devastated and appalled" by the remarks, he wanted $2 million in damages.

I went downtown to the Southern District Federal Court building, found the court room, and seated myself in one of four plywood pews reserved for (nonexistent) visitors. Fleisher's attorney had just started making his opening statement, in which he told the jury of five women and four men that Ellison was a controversial person who had gone a little too far when he described Fleisher as "crazy"; "certifiable"; "twisted"; "derange-o"; "a lunatic"; and "bugfuck."

What was this word, "bugfuck"? So far as anyone could tell, Ellison had invented it. In which case, what did it mean? Maybe it was similar to "crazy," but Ellison and his attorneys wouldn't get trapped into defining it. As the trial dragged on during ensuing days, discussions persisted about the exact meaning of "bugfuck" as if the attorneys couldn't resist being allowed to say "fuck" in front of a judge as often as possible.

Ellison's attorney argued that it didn't matter, because Fleisher had described himself as "a lunatic" in an interview that he gave some other magazine. Nor could Fleisher claim that being called "crazy" would damage his literary reputation, because everyone in the comics field knew that his work was deranged. In one of his comic-book stories, "The Night of the Chicken," a farmer picked up a prostitute in a bar, got her to dress up in a chicken costume, hacked her to pieces with an axe, then fed her to his chickens.

So Ellison had described himself as crazy; and Fleisher had described himself as crazy; but the trouble started when Ellison said that Fleisher was crazy.

In case the jury might think that there wasn't much to choose between these silly people, Ellison's attorney reminded the jury of the vital importance of writers who take a radical stance. The work of Thoreau had been a powerful influence on Gandhi, who liberated a whole continent from colonial oppression. Gandhi then inspired Martin Luther King, whose marches through the South ushered in liberation for American blacks. And Harlan Ellison had participated in those historic marches. (Had he? I wasn't so sure about that, but disproving it would be difficult.) Ellison, like Thoreau, was a brilliant writer, and he had won every imaginable award for excellence. He was outspoken sometimes—even using hard-hitting language like "bugfuck"—but that's how great radicals are! He certainly shouldn't be confused with a mere comic-book writer.

Michael Fleisher: "Don't call me bugfuck!"

Fleisher's attorney didn't buy this. He got Ellison on the witness stand, and forced him to admit that—unlike Thoreau—he had written his own comics scripts. The attorney pulled out a stack of lurid magazines whose paper had turned yellow during the years it had taken for the legal machinery to bring this case to trial. Wasn't it true that Ellison once planned to do a comics adaptation of a story he co-wrote titled "Would You Do It for a Penny?"

Imagine the confusion in the mind of a juror at this point. There you are, a retired subway token-booth clerk, or a sanitation worker. The term "writer" makes you think of poets, perhaps, or bestselling novelists, but the plaintiff, here, writes comic books describing motorcycle gangs, zombies, and psychopaths carving up scream-

Above: The U.S. edition.

Opposite page, top: The Japanese edition, published in 1994.

Opposite page, bottom: The German edition, published in 2020, with a cover by Michael Marrak. Just goes to show, if you live long enough, you may get a cover that you really like. Note especially the details: The laurel leaves on T. Rex (indicating his status as an emperor), and the Mickey Mouse ears on the motorcycle rider. And, I love the giant ants fitted with death rays!

Page 164

ing women with axes and power saws. He's the one sitting meekly at the table nearest the judge—a shy, stooping, self-effacing man with glasses and thick bushy hair, like the protagonist in the movie *Eraserhead*. Meanwhile the defendant, Ellison, is wearing a dark blue blazer with gold buttons, like an elderly diplomat, with his gray hair immaculately coiffed, and he has an air of grim detachment. He even helped to liberate the American Negro, for heaven's sake! But now Fleisher's attorney is showing him back issues of a comic titled *Creepy*, and he's saying, "Is this your story, here? Did you write this?" And Ellison has to admit—well, um, yes, actually, he did.

The implication was clear: Ellison didn't exist on some loft literary plane. He knew all about the comics field, and therefore he must have known that Fleisher wasn't really crazy, but he said it anyway, with reckless disregard for the truth.

Okay, then, what about the harm? Was there any harm? Fleisher needed to show professional damage, and—there wasn't any. When Ellison's attorneys held up a poster showing the income that Fleisher had declared on tax returns, the line went steadily upward from about $27,000 in 1979 to $50,000 in 1983. Being called "bugfuck" wasn't necessarily a bad thing, for the writer of "The Night of the Chicken."

Despite its ludicrous aspects, the trial dragged on for four weeks. It was like watching bad streaming video, with no fast-forward, but I became addicted to the quibbles between lawyers, scurrilous attacks on the integrity of witnesses, half-truths delivered under oath, and a final summation by the judge that took most of one morning and referred repeatedly to "Harvey" Ellison.

Finally, the jury deliberated for less than ninety minutes before acquitting Ellison and *The Comics Journal* on all counts. When I spoke to a juror afterward, she said that the key factor causing them to reach their decision had been lack of professional harm.

Fleisher refused to say how much the case had cost him, but I suspected that a large part was covered on a contingency basis.

After my four-week stint as an observer, I felt happy that I hadn't sued Ellison for hitting me. Fighting a law suit takes a huge amount of time and energy, even if you win. Tormenting him in print had been much less time consuming, and had been enjoyable in many respects.

Metafiction

I called my long-suffering editor-friend John Douglas and told him I had an idea for a novel that he would be unable to resist. I had compiled a list of every key concept ever used in science fiction, and I had devised a plot that would include all of them. Seriously! It could be done! Space travel (of course), telepathy, robots, immortality drugs, time travel, barbarians from the Earth's core, intelligent dinosaurs, Martians, and even intelligent talking dogs. They would all be there, and therefore my subtitle would be, "The only science-fiction novel you ever need to read."

John listened to my pitch, pondered for a moment, and said that other writers whom he published might not appreciate Charles Platt implying that no one needed to read their work.

All right, forget the subtitle. What about the idea? John seemed tempted. "Let's see your list," he said.

For the next half-hour, we went through it. John thought that some of my choices were too obscure to be worthwhile, and he suggested a couple that I had missed, but in the end, probably against his better judgment, he decided to acquire this piece of foolishness. He offered an advance of $5,000, which did not remotely cover the time that I would spend writing the novel, but I couldn't resist the challenge.

The result was published under the title *Free Zone* and is my favorite of all my books. Alas, it was misunderstood as mocking science fiction, when really it was my homage to science fiction. I explored the humorous aspects of the concepts, but that didn't mean I was mocking them.

The book was unsuccessful in the United States, but I remain proud that no other writer ever attempted to do what I did. Maybe there are good reasons why they didn't do it, but still *Free Zone* remains a singular achievement.

1987

From Playmate to PostScript

MacPlaymate was an outrageously offensive, utterly inexcusable interactive game conceived for the Macintosh. It depicted a sultry character named Maxie who invited the user to take off her clothes by clicking on them. Once she was naked, she lay on her back and the user could apply dildoes such as the "Mighty Mo Throbber," "Deep Plunger," or "Anal Explorer" from a toolbox on the screen. This would cause Maxie to kick her legs and moan until she reached a climax.

Such gross objectification of women was tolerated (barely) in 1987, because enlightened companies such as Google did not yet exist, and no one was ready to shame rogue males into submission.

An artist named Mike Saenz developed the visuals for MacPlaymate, while a programmer named Bill Bates helped with the animations. They took their wares to the annual MacWorld conference, and were so successful, they received a purported $60,000 in three days by selling it for $50 per copy. The highlight of the event (Bill told me later) was when a man in the throng became so desperate, he threw his Amex Platinum card over the heads of people in front of him, into Bill's eager hands.

The windfall from MacPlaymate would now underwrite Bill's more serious ambition: To revolutionize the printing industry. He developed probably the world's first desktop publishing program, named JustText, which seemed as radical in 1987 as word processing had seemed ten years earlier.

Bill lived in an apartment on Sixth Avenue between 10th Street and 11th Street, a three-minute walk from my home on Patchin Place. I met him by chance through Tom Disch, who was briefly connected with software publishing when his text-adventure game *Amnesia* was published by Electronic Arts.

Bill seemed to be around forty (like me), amiable, habitually smiling, slightly overweight, looking more like a businessman than a computer nerd. He was the sole author of JustText, just as Fred Beyer had been the sole author of WP6502, and he was buoyantly optimistic, as Fred had been. When he learned that I was a writer who was thinking of starting his own small press, Bill saw me as an obvious customer for desktop publishing. When I mentioned that I had graduated, barely, from the London College of Printing, he realized that I could help to beta-test his software.

How strange, the way that history repeats.

When I visited Bill to learn more from him, he explained why a Macintosh computer connected with a LaserWriter was conceptually revolutionary. It all came down to a language named PostScript, and once I understood it, I realized that it was the most exciting thing to happen to typesetting since Gutenberg.

To justify this claim, I have to back up a bit.

The first two screens of MacPlaymate. Subsequent views cannot be reproduced in a family publication.

Those Damned Dots

Back in 1981, when the IBM PC was introduced, video displays of text were horrible. Each letter consisted of glowing dots on a cathode-ray tube, and because each dot required storage in computer memory, engineers tried to use as few dots as possible.

You might wonder if RAM was really so expensive that no one could afford a nicer looking alphabet by allocating a few more dots. Well, in those days, RAM for the IBM-PC retailed for about $5,000 per megabyte. As I write these words, forty years later, RAM costs less than 1 cent per megabyte, and from this you can conclude that memory in the original IBM PC used to cost 500,000 times as much

Upper alphabet: This was standard on the original IBM PC fitted with a graphics adapter.

Lower alphabet: If you paid extra, you could get the monochrome adapter card which generated this alphabet. I spent years writing books in this horrible font, but it was better than the alternative.

as it does now. This is one reason why each character on a screen used to be formed in a grid of just 8x8 dots (or 9x14 if you used the special IBM monochrome adapter card—which also allowed the display of underlining, a radical concept at the time).

As for printed output, some progress occurred when dot-matrix printers started using more wires to create more, smaller dots. Then proportional letter spacing became available, and then Hewlett-Packard introduced its first LaserJet printer, in 1984, offering fonts named Times Roman and Helvetica—which sounded exciting, but there was no copyright on a font name, so the guys at HP saved on licensing fees by designing their own versions, hoping that no one would notice the difference.

Actually anyone with any aesthetic sensibility whatsoever could see a big difference, but this was not the only drawback. You couldn't change the point size of a font, so you had to buy multiple versions in fixed sizes such as 10pt, 12pt, and 18pt, which were sold on cartridges, which were expensive.

It was a tangled nightmare of ugliness, inconvenience, and expense until mathematicians John Warnock and Charles Geschke created the PostScript language, which used formulae instead of bitmaps to describe the subtle curves of each font. Now the letters were elegant and scalable, because if you wanted the point size to be, say, 1% bigger, you just changed the values in the formula by 1%—or, rather, you told PostScript to do it for you. In addition, PostScript could describe almost any other printed object on a page.

Warnock and Geschke founded a company named Adobe Systems to sell their concept, and because Warnock was a part-time painter and his wife was a formally trained graphic designer, they really did have some aesthetic sensibilities. They licensed real fonts from type foundries, and I think it's safe to say that without Warnock and Adobe, computer graphics would not have evolved in a civilized way.

To print a PostScript document, you needed a device which contained a PostScript interpreter. Apple obliged by introducing the LaserWriter, which created output almost indistinguishable from real typesetting, unless you looked closely.

For professional purposes, a printing company could use an imagesetter able to create output at 2,400 dots per inch. The same PostScript formulae could drive any PostScript printer, and the output would improve in quality up to the limits of the device. The language was *device-independent*, which was a brilliant concept.

Warnock had a vision that every computer and every printing device in the world would eventually use PostScript, so that all documents would be compatible with all devices, and everything would look beautiful. Later, Adobe's Portable Document Format partially achieved this dream. It is the foundation for every PDF file that exists.

Only one snag remained: Previewing a PostScript document on a screen. The Macintosh generated its display using an earlier, simpler, and more primitive drawing language called QuickDraw. Translating PostScript into QuickDraw was so difficult, Bill Bates decided to skip it when he wrote JustText. You couldn't see your formatted output on the screen, and you had to proof it on a LaserWriter. Still, this would be okay for formatting the pages of books, and Bill sold his software on that basis.

What he didn't realize was that a company named Aldus had already hired a team of programmers to overcome the QuickDraw conversion problem, and within a year or so they would achieve the holy grail of screen preview with a program called PageMaker. It was limited by the tiny screen on the Mac, and it crashed a lot. Still, it would satisfy most users, and at that point, JustText would become obsolete.

When I met Bill, this hadn't happened yet. His software was still state-of-the-art, and I realized that I could finally accept Piers Anthony's kind offer to bankroll Black Sheep Books. His $10,000 would be just enough to buy a Macintosh, a hard drive, and a LaserWriter.

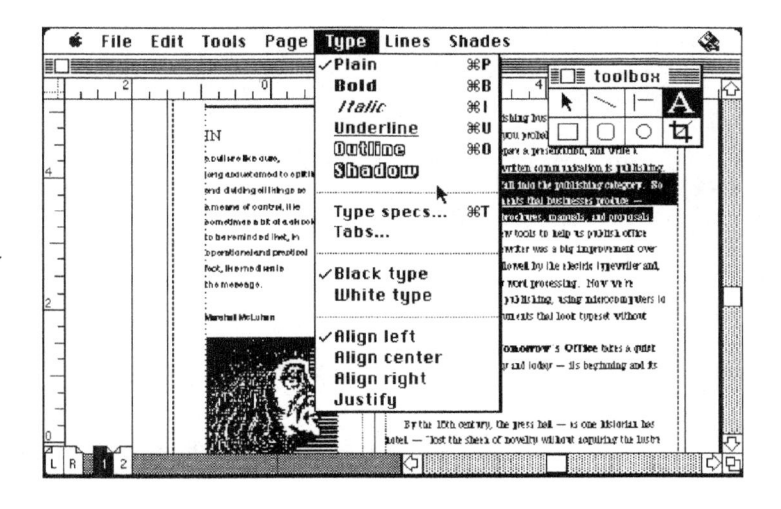

Top: The very first Apple Laserwriter was a beast. I never did figure out what was inside it, making it so heavy.

Bottom: A screen shot of Page-Maker 1.0. Yes, that was the entire screen of the original Macintosh. There was barely enough room for the menus.

A Friend From Osaka

In March, at the inevitable Lunacon, I met a Japanese science-fiction fan named Hiroshi, who introduced me to a friend of his named Fumiko. They had known each other in Japan before she relocated in the United States.

Fumiko roused my curiosity. "There's something about you," I said, "that doesn't seem quite like most Japanese women."

"Oh, because I am sitting like this," she said. She was reclining in a chair with the relaxed body language of an American woman. "I can do this if you prefer." She sat up quickly with a straight back, clasped her hands between her knees, and inclined her head modestly while she gave me a coquettish smile.

Was this intoxicating, or *what?*

I was disappointed when she told me she lived near Boston. I was more disappointed when she said she was married. Worse still, her husband raced motorcycles and had a large gun collection. Oh, well, so much for that! She had to go back to Boston, so I offered to drive her to La Guardia Airport in my Camaro, and Hiroshi said he would come along for the ride.

I had never driven to La Guardia before, and got lost. This was quite embarrassing, and when we finally arrived at the airport, the last flight had left—which was even more embarrassing.

Hiroshi and Fumiko conferred briefly in Japanese. "She doesn't have enough money to stay at the convention hotel," Hiroshi told me. "But I suggested she can stay at your apartment."

Oh. But if her husband was expecting her—

"He is away, traveling right now," said Hiroshi.

I observed a strict rule, never to trespass into a marriage, and this would be especially important if the husband owned numerous firearms. Still, the situation could be dealt with in an ethical and appropriate manner. "I only have a small apartment," I said. "But I can sleep on the couch. Fumiko can have the bed."

Some more Japanese talk ensued, taking much longer this time. The outcome was surprisingly brief: "Thank you very much," Fumiko told me.

First I had to take Hiroshi back to the hotel, because he was staying there. As I got out of the car to say goodbye to him, he leaned closer and dropped his voice to a conspiratorial level. "I told her, many women would be excited by the privilege to stay in Charles Platt's apartment."

What? Before I could question him, he grinned, waved goodbye, and disappeared into the hotel lobby.

Fumiko was now behaving in a new style, which was neither demure Japanese girl nor uninhibited American woman. She was like a formal business person, which I guessed was her way of indicating that I should not expect anything of an intimate nature. That was okay, as I didn't.

A while later I installed her in my loft bed and said goodnight. She gave me an odd look, which I didn't know how to interpret, but I was tired of trying to divine the mysteries of Japanese people. I went to sleep on the couch in the living room.

The next morning, Fumiko had a suggestion. Her husband was still traveling, and she was in no hurry to go back to Boston. Maybe I could show her around New York City?

Oh, all right. Why not?

It happened to be a beautiful sunny day, offering a hint of springtime. We rode the Staten Island Ferry, we went to the top of the World Trade Center, and did some more touristy things. She was vivacious and funny, and great company. We ended up back at my apartment to eat lunch, and then, finally, she was ready for the airport. Suddenly she leaned close. "Goodbye, Charles," she said.

Her face was only inches away, and I realized something that should have been obvious: The business mode had been a facade. Now I witnessed a new transformation, from formal to insatiable. I had never felt so incompetent at judging a person's intentions, not that she seemed to care.

The last flight to Boston wasn't until much later, so she stuck around for a while longer. She explained that she was estranged from her husband, she was planning to leave him, and would do so as soon as she found a new job. She was a financial analyst and wanted to move to Manhattan, where she was applying to work at a

Japanese company.

This all sounded quite dangerous, and I noticed an intent look in her eyes that had not been there before.

I drove her to the airport, and she went back to Boston—but called me a few days later. Her current employers were sending her to a Florida conference, at the end which she would have the weekend free in Orlando. How about if we went to Disney World?

This sounded even more dangerous, but I decided to give up trying to fight the inevitability of her intentions. I met her at Disney World, and we enjoyed ourselves, and then she went back to Boston while I returned to Patchin Place.

In the middle of the night, I got out of bed to go to the bathroom and saw the light flashing on my answering machine. Evidently I had slept through the phone ringing, so I played back the message—and heard Fumiko telling me that she had crashed her car. She had some minor injuries, and her husband was traveling again. She was very reluctant to ask such a big favor, but—would I drive up there to help her?

I was still a bit concerned about the husband, but she told me not to worry; he was competing in a motorcycle race somewhere. "He is never here when I need him," she said.

I went to join her for a few days, and discovered still more layers of her personality. She loved to drive recklessly, which was how she had crashed the Porsche that her husband had bought for her. She asked to try my Camaro, and soon we were cruising the freeways around Boston at 110. She expressed some grudging appreciation for my car, but said she would prefer a new Porsche, which her husband would probably buy for her with the insurance money from the old one.

A couple of weeks later, she got the job in Manhattan that she had wanted, and now came the inevitable request: Could she share my place with me while she was finding an apartment of her own? I agreed, but by this time yet another transition had occurred. She was now *genuinely* businesslike. Almost every waking minute was spent studying for her job, and I saw the Japanese work ethic kick in. It allowed room for no other use of time.

After a couple of weeks, she found an apartment, moved into it, and that was the end of my affair with Fumiko. As for the husband, I don't know what happened to him. We never met.

She had been so much fun, I didn't mind. Also, it was a valuable learning experience. When a somewhat repressed British male comes up against a smart, ambitious, and multifaceted Japanese female from a culture in which women have played a complicated, ambiguous role for centuries, he doesn't stand much of a chance.

"You are part of a fine British tradition," Bruce Sterling remarked, when I told him my story. "Just like John Lennon and Yoko Ono."

I wrote a story for *Penthouse Forum* based on Fumiko, titled "A Friend from Osaka." Unfortunately the magazine had just hired a new female fiction editor who disliked my portrayal of a Japanese woman who was sexually precocious but had a hardcore work ethic.

"This is a racist stereotype," she complained.

"It's an accurate description of a real person," I said.

Didn't matter. The magazine was happy to have explicit porn—indeed, they required it—but stereotyping was offensive, and the editor knew it when she saw it.

The first edition, which eventually appeared from Tafford Publishing.

Pornucopia

I received my $10,000 from Piers, spent it on a Macintosh system, and was ready to start production of his novel *3.97 Erect*—but first, I couldn't resist a new temptation. I wanted to write programs in PostScript.

Could Bill Bates recommend some books on the subject? Oh, he could do better than that. He could loan me a couple, free.

The first dose is always free.

PostScript turned out to be a wonderful, beautiful language—definitely the most elegantly designed programming language I ever encountered. I loved it. Soon I was writing programs that generated fascinating curves, effects, and graphic objects on my LaserWriter.

I justified my indulgence by telling myself that if I learned PostScript, I could write my own desktop publishing program, which would be easier to use than JustText. After that, I could start typesetting books.

What I failed to consider was that Bill had taken about a year to learn PostScript and write JustText, and he was a more experienced programmer than I was. After a month or so, I had to acknowledge the magnitude of my self-assigned task, and saw that it would exceed my available time. My obligation to publish *3.97 Erect* had to be honored.

All right, then—but I didn't like the title. Would Piers consider a substitution?

For the next three weeks, I suggested titles and he rejected them. I used free association, I looked up synonyms, I asked friends—nothing worked. Finally, the word "Pornucopia" popped into my head, and Piers agreed to it, as he had always liked puns. That was a relief.

I put an ad in *The Village Voice* for a typist, and found a brave woman who was willing to copy-type the disgusting and offensive novel that Piers had written. She spent four days inputting it to the Macintosh. I also advertised for someone to do cover art, and found a woman who delivered a passable drawing of the succubus who was a character in the book.

I generated the pages of Pornucopia at 150% size, so that the 300 dots per inch of the Laserwriter would become a higher-quality 450 dots per inch when they were reduced to fit book pages. That way, I wouldn't need to pay for output on an imagesetter. Now I had to get back to the matter of distribution.

I revisited the F&SF Book Co in Staten Island to establish the formal details of my relationship with them. At this point I couldn't avoid some details that I had brushed aside previously, and I had to think seriously about the issue of money.

The people at the Book Co walked me through every detail. I took copious notes, and then went home to do my own math, which of course was what I should have done originally. And—this was very disillusioning. I had not fully understood how awful the business model for a small press could be. It was really, truly awful.

In fact, there was only one way to make it pay, or at least break even. I would not be able to hire anyone to help me.

This was not good, because it would be like acquiring a full-time job, and avoiding a full-time job was still my top priority. So, I had to wonder, was Black Sheep Books entirely—practical?

I still loved the idea of it, but the reality was a bit different from what I had imagined. It would make me depressed and frustrated, and I wouldn't be any good at it.

I still hadn't finished writing my novel *Plasm* for Roc Books, so I decided not to think about *Pornucopia* for a while. This was difficult, because *Plasm* was set in a universe developed by Piers Anthony, so I did tend to think about my commitment to him—but I tried not to.

After I did finish writing *Plasm*, the problem of Black Sheep Books was still waiting for me. In desperation, I had an idea: Maybe I could subcontract it.

I placed a classified ad in *Locus* stating that I had acquired rights to a couple of orphaned books by notable writers, if anyone else wanted to pick them up, and to my surprise a man named Phil Gurlik contacted me. He already had a small press named Tafford Publishing, and he didn't seem to mind the drudgery and lack of profit associated with running it. He was willing to adopt my orphans, and even had some creative ideas for marketing them.

Great! There was only one remaining issue: I still owed Piers $10,000.

I called him to tell him the good news and the bad news. The good news was that *Pornucopia* had been typeset, and I had acquired cover art, and Phil Gurlik would publish it. The bad news was that I had spent the $10,000 on expensive computer equipment, and I might need a while to pay off the loan.

Piers is notorious for being confrontational with publishers, but where I am concerned, he has always been remarkably tolerant. He agreed to a repayment plan, and we remained on good terms.

The Tafford edition of *Pornucopia* was eventually published, after Phil Gurlik came up with the idea of shrink-wrapping it to prevent young Xanth readers from being traumatized if they (or their parents—even worse) encountered it while browsing in bookstores.

The book now has collectible status, a copy of the first edition being worth about $100, if it is in good condition.

Phil also published Alfred Bester's *Tender Loving Rage*, although sadly not until after Alfie had died.

I'm proud that I rescued a couple of novels from obscurity, but I'm a bit embarrassed that Black Sheep Books is probably the only small press that never actually published anything. I still have the business certificate, though.

Maybe—one day—

Soma

Plasm was now in the production process at Roc Books, so I took the obvious next step and suggested a sequel to my sequel to Piers Anthony's sequel. Titled *Soma*, it would be even more deranged than *Plasm*, because I had been seeing the popularity of militaristic science fiction, and I felt a need to correct its evasions.

I didn't buy into the mythology of principled military professionals honoring an ethical code while blowing things up. Surely, the purpose of warfare was to kill enemies efficiently and ruthlessly, without any principles at all. This being so, how could future technology facilitate it?

It seemed to me, there must be a sexual component in blood lust, which would explain the well-documented tendency of male troops to rape women while killing men. Testosterone was implicated, and the effectiveness of blood-hungry warriors would be optimized if all their sexual energy was channeled into violence, with no other outlets permitted. Could that be arranged?

I called my friend Michael Blumlein, a wonderful writer of disturbing stories, who also happened to be an MD. I asked him if there was a way to sever a nerve bundle from the penis, so that all sensations would be deadened. If this procedure was inflicted, a man could still get aroused from other stimuli, yet could never reach a climax, and would become insane with frustration. Maybe he would be homicidally insane, which would be ideal for my purposes.

Michael didn't know the answer to my question, but he had a morbid imagination and loved medical curiosities, so he took an afternoon to research the answer in a medical library. He came back with his conclusion: Yes, it would be possible, and in fact would be relatively easy.

Thus I described my fighting force of men who went into a kill-crazed frenzy as a result of being deprived of their ability to reach a sexual climax. I also figured out ways to damage them emotionally so that they could feel no vestige of compassion while torturing and killing any living things that they encountered.

Basically I was saying to readers of militaristic fiction: You want combat in space? Here's how to do the job properly. What do you think?

Really, it's never a good idea for a writer to be hostile toward his readers. On some level I did recognize that, but still, I thought it would be interesting.

His Kohlerness

I received a notice that my taxes would be audited, and when I went to the IRS offices in midtown, I found myself sitting opposite a beefy guy named Kohler who had a carnivorous grin.

"I earned less than $20,000 last year," I said. "Why am I being audited?"

His grin widened. "Mr. Platt, it's just like winning the lottery."

Of course, one person's laughter is often derived from another person's pain, but Kohler elevated this principle to levels that I had never imagined.

To be fair, some aspects of my tax return were unconventional. For example, I had depreciated my bicycle. This was not a trivial matter, as the bicycle had been hand-built and cost $1,000—but I used it partially for business when I delivered manuscripts to publishers or met editors for lunch, so why shouldn't I depreciate some of its value?

Kohler had no time for such specious nonsense. He dismissed my bicycle expense with a casual stroke of his pen. He had loftier goals for his jihad: He wanted to disallow *everything*.

During the next two months, he devoted countless hours to my case. He even paid a personal visit to the Computer Instruction Center, because he suspected that I had an office there, in which case he could disallow my home-office deduction. I didn't have an office there, but then—he disallowed my home-office deduction anyway.

He was so relentless and extreme, I started wondering about ulterior motives. During the past two years I had published some mockery of L. Ron Hubbard in my little zine. This had been a source of annoyance for Fred Harris, who promoted Hubbard's work and had hoped that I would help the great man to win a Hugo Award. I knew that Scientologists had tried to infiltrate the IRS, partly in an effort to protect the Church's nonprofit status, but also to attack perceived enemies. My auditor looked and behaved the way that I imagined a Scientologist would look. He was on a mission. He had that carnivorous gleam in his eye.

It was a desperate situation, so I came up with a desperate solution. I called Mr. Kohler and told him I was moving to California.

"But the audit is almost complete!" he complained. "When are you leaving?"

"Tomorrow," I said.

"Are you serious? How long are you going for?

"Indefinitely."

I don't think anyone had faced him with this problem before. "Can you come to my office today?" he asked.

"No. Here's my forwarding address."

Six months later, an IRS office in Los Angeles sent a letter to me at the address that I had provided. I called them and told them I was moving back to New York City.

After another six months, I received a call from a new auditor at the IRS office in New York. This man was a typical bureaucrat, no more, no less. He did not have a carnivorous gleam, and in fact he seemed baffled that I had been audited in the first place. He reinstated most of my expenses (except for the bicycle) and concluded that I owed the IRS about $200.

I could live with that. "But what happened to Mr. Kohler?" I asked.

"Oh, his Kohlerness?" He rhymed it with "holiness."

I was astonished that one auditor would mock another when talking to a taxpayer. "Yes, him," I said.

"He's been promoted. He's investigating organized crime."

Loose Cannon

"This time you have really gone too far!" The voice on the phone was strident and commanding, with a Texan accent. It was Bruce Sterling's voice.

I was standing in my bathtub, where I had been lathering my hair under the shower. Because of my pathological need to answer any ringing phone—always—I had installed a phone in the bathroom. Two phones, in fact, so that if a second call came in while I was on Line One, it would ring through to Line Two. This was a feature which the phone company described as "hunting," and it appealed to my thrifty British nature, as it was fractionally cheaper than paying for Call Waiting on a single line.

I shut off the water, but my hair was still full of shampoo. "Is this Bruce?" I asked.

"You are a loose cannon!" he yelled. "You don't seem to understand! This is the worst thing you've ever done!"

"Calm down," I said, because I didn't know what else to say. The sequence of events that had led to this unfortunate phone call was now pretty obvious.

In *Cheap Truth*, Bruce had published polemical book reviews by a critic who used the pseudonymous byline "Sue Denim." (Sue Denim . . . pseudonym . . . a play on words.) Although *Cheap Truth* was now defunct, "Sue Denim" had continued writing reviews for Steve Brown's magazine, *Science Fiction Eye*. All of the reviews were nasty to the point of maliciousness, and people in the science-fiction field were wondering who was doing it.

Confidentially, Bruce's wife Nancy had tipped me off. Sue Denim was Lew Shiner, a friend of Bruce who regarded himself as a cyberpunk author. At science-fiction events he would socialize on a cheerful, friendly basis with the people he skewered in his pseudonymous reviews, and they didn't know he was being nasty about them behind their backs. I disapproved of this, because personally I wrote nasty reviews under my real name.

I wondered how to use the privileged information about Lew in an entertaining way, bearing in mind that Nancy had sworn me to secrecy. Then inspiration struck. I could write my own reviews, in my own little zine, under the name Sue Denim. The fun part would be to use the Sue Denim byline for scurrilous attacks on cyberpunk fiction, so that Sue Denim would appear to have turned against her fellow travelers in *Science Fiction Eye*, and Shiner wouldn't be able to set the record straight, because to do so, he would have to reveal that he had been Sue Denim all along.

I went ahead with my prank, and waited for the fallout.

The fallout was now turning out to be a bit more toxic than I had expected. "A writer's name is his most fundamental asset!" Bruce yelled at me. "You are debasing a writer's currency! This is totally unacceptable!"

"But Sue Denim isn't Lew Shiner's name," I objected. "In fact, he didn't want anyone to know that he was using it."

"That's not the point!" And so it went on, while I stood waiting to continue my shower.

I so much enjoyed Bruce Sterling calling me a loose cannon, I made a pun out of it when I eventually published a book of my lit-crit writings. The cover depicts my wish-fulfilment dream of an old-school rocket ship bombing the iconography of fantasy literature back into the stone age.

> **Obituary:**
> **The Man who Nobody Knew**
>
> Many readers will be saddened to hear of the death of James Colvin, the science fiction writer who contributed actively to New Worlds while it was under the editorship of John Carnell, and who went on to write progressive fiction and regular book reviews, after Michael Moorcock took over as editor in April 1964.
>
> Two of Colvin's best stories were *The Mountain* (NW 147) and *The Pleasure Garden of Felipe Sagittarius* (NW 154). His novel, *The Wrecks of Time,* was serialised in NW 156 to 158, and a collection of his short stories, *The Deep Fix*, was published by Compact Books.
>
> Colvin was born in 1941 in Surrey, came to London and lived on his own in a Kensington bed-sitter. He avoided personal encounters, and was seldom seen by his colleagues.
>
> Tragically, a heavy filing cabinet full of manuscripts fell over, crushing his chest, early in November 1969. After two weeks in hospital he died from pneumonia and other complications associated with a punctured lung.
>
> As one of the few people who knew Colvin personally, I feel the science fiction field has lost a talent which never quite came to fruition. To the end, Colvin was a man who nobody really knew.
>
> —William Barclay.
>
> *Colvin at a science fiction convention: one of the few pictures ever taken of this little-known writer*

My obituary for Moorcock's pseudonym James Colvin was written under the name William Barclay, which itself was another pseudonym used by Moorcock, just to complicate the prank. The photo was of Pete Taylor, a friend of Mike's who had a suitably anonymous face and was not widely known in science fiction.

"Well, I'm sorry it upset you," I said.

"If I find out that you wrote it, our friendship is over!"

That seemed a bit harsh, as the whole thing was just a prank which didn't affect Bruce personally at all. My best bet would be to wait and hope that he would calm down.

At this point my second phone rang. "Sorry," I said, "I should answer that." Still with soap in my hair, I hung up the first phone and picked up the second.

"Charles?" asked a male voice that I didn't recognize. Whoever it was, he didn't sound friendly.

"This is Charles, yes."

"This is Lew Shiner."

Well—who else would it be?

"Hello Lew," I said. "How are things?"

"You're an asshole." And he hung up on me.

Bruce eventually did calm down, but Shiner never did. He stopped writing reviews—and later stopped writing science fiction, so ultimately it didn't really matter that I hijacked his pseudonym.

Really pseudonyms open up all kinds of amusing opportunities for pranks, which I consider justified, as a fake name is really a prank in itself. Back in my days working on *New Worlds* in the UK, I ran an obituary for a writer named James Colvin, which was a pseudonym used by Michael Moorcock. I just—killed him off! My obit stated that Colvin had died after being crushed by a file cabinet full of unpublished manuscripts. Mike seemed a bit annoyed about this, although he still maintained a couple of other pseudonyms, so it didn't impair his writing options significantly. At least, that was how I saw it.

Brighton Redux

I stumbled off the plane at Gatwick Airport after three hours of sleep, and took the train to Brighton for the 1987 World Convention. Soon I was checking into a hotel where the only missing element was John Cleese playing Basil Fawlty. Then I went out in search of breakfast, and wandered along a nearby quaint little back street, experiencing traumatic spasms of intestinal aversion from smelly little caffs offering fried eggs and greasy chips for 95 pence. I passed the window of a local laundromat, glanced in—and saw Charles N. Brown, the editor of *Locus*, who normally lived in California. He was holding a plastic basket full of wet socks.

Every human brain has its limit, beyond which it yields to disorientation and stress. This was mine.

I went back to my room and napped for a while to regain my equanimity, then walked through the Metropole Hotel and noticed that British science-fiction fans looked distinctly unhealthy compared with their US counterparts. They seemed to subsist entirely on cigarettes, warm beer, and greasy animal residues. They were much slimmer, though, and when I inquired why, I was told, with some disdain, it was because British people can't afford to eat as much as Americans.

This world convention became notorious for its unwise decision to allow some sponsorship by Bridge Publications, which published the work of L. Ron Hubbard. Hubbard's work was a bit—unsubtle, really—and he was primarily known as the founder of Scientology. World science-fiction conventions had always been free from commercial exploitation, and Algis Budrys made a sensitive situation worse by preceding the Hugo Awards ceremony with a special announcement. In his capacity as the promoter of Hubbard's "Writers of the Future" enterprise, which trained young people to write science fiction, Budrys announced a forthcoming series of workshops in Britain which would "fully validate the legacy of L. Ron Hubbard" using "methods developed by Writers of the Future."

Supposedly his intention was to impress the audience with the

Top: Brian Aldiss, making a speech of some kind.

Bottom: Algis Budrys, from a Writers of the Future publication.

benevolence of Ron, so that if Ron turned out to have won the Hugo for Best Novel, people would be less likely to rise up in wrath. In fact the novel came in sixth place, below No Award, which placed fifth. Still, many attendees felt that Hubbard's name had tainted the Hugo Awards.

After the ceremony, an inebriated David Langford (the much-loved atomic scientist and tireless publisher of the newsletter *Ansible*) got into a little dispute with Fred Harris, the PR man for Hubbard. Dave had just won a Hugo, and he felt that it was tainted by indirect Scientology sponsorship. And so, 1) He bickered with Harris. 2) With ironic intent, kissed him on the cheek. 3) Harris poured his beer over Dave's head. 4) Dave threw his glass at Harris, and missed. 5) The glass smashed against the wall.

This was a rare episode of *principled* bad behavior at a science-fiction convention.

Brian Aldiss also was gifted with a Hugo Award. He didn't seem to care about the Scientology association, but had his own concerns. Upon receiving the trophy in front of the throng, he remarked: "It's been a long time since you gave me one of these, you bastards."

I have no photographs of the croquet game at the Aldiss mansion, unfortunately, but some kind of gathering also occurred at the home of John and Judith Clute. Top: A bad photograph out on the roof of John, Bill Gibson, Judith, and me. Below: Judith and John.

On the Wednesday following the convention, a few residual attendees made their way to an all-day party at the country mansion where Brian lived with his wife Margaret. I demanded to play croquet in the drizzle, Brian tolerantly disinterred cobwebbed equipment from the tool shed, and we set it up in a disused tennis court.

Unsurprisingly, in a game as viciously competitive as this, the editors triumphed over the writers, with David Hartwell winning the first game and Susan Allison the second. In croquet, as in life.

Black Art

My novel *Plasm* was published, and it had one of those covers that make you stare at it in confusion, muttering, "How did this happen?"

I had not imagined that anything could be worse than the green which had dominated *The Whole-Truth Home Computer Handbook*, but now the art department at Roc had come up with a dominant color that was worse than green. It was black.

I now felt convinced that yet another book was doomed. Still, I completed and delivered *Soma*, the sequel. I thought I had done a good job, but maybe it would be doomed, too.

To reiterate: Most books are doomed.

Ackermania

They called it "The Auction of the Century," and advertised it in *Omni* and *The New York Times*. Actually, it was the garage sale of the century, and the garage belonged to Forrest Ackerman.

Ackerman was a collector who never knew when to stop. He spent decades accumulating books, magazines, comic books, movie posters, stills, costumes, Buck Rogers zap-guns, latex monster-masks, severed heads, bleeding eyeballs, decaying chunks of artificial flesh . . . 300,000 items altogether, filling his eighteen-room home and, yes, overflowing into his three-car garage.

In December, in New York City, a firm of auctioneers was selling off some of the garage-surplus material, plus a few other items of science-fictional interest. The result: a four-day feeding frenzy for collectors, climaxing with the sale of the original screenplay of *The Wizard of Oz* for $36,000.

I first met Forry Ackerman (or "4E," as he called himself) in 1969,

Top: Ackerman gets friendly with the Bride of Frankenstein.

Bottom: A special issue of the wonderful magazine that he created was published in 2016 to mark the centennial of his birth. (He died in 2008.)

A print of Frazetta's famous painting (of which the original did not sell, at the auction) and a photograph of the artist.

when I visited Los Angeles and shyly asked to see his legendary "Ackermansion." He had no idea who I was, but welcomed me genially and provided a detailed tour of the house. He explained how he had invented the term "sci-fi" ("It suddenly came to me: hi-fi, sci-fi!") and invited me out for a meal at a local self-service cafeteria, which he drove to in his powder-blue Cadillac. (I remember he especially enjoyed demonstrating its solenoid-operated door locks.)

The quantity of his collection was impressive; he even had comic books stashed inside his icebox. But the quality of it was, well, a bit sleazy. Somewhere among all the books he probably owned first editions by H. G. Wells, but he seemed far more interested in 1930s exploitation movies. Ghoulish items pleased him most of all: He revelled in them like a mutant kid with a pile of poisoned Halloween candy.

The New York auction was scheduled to take place in December at The Puck Building, mainly known for chic parties attracting fashion models and TV celebrities. It seemed an unlikely place to sell comic books and movie memorabilia, so I went to check it out.

The first two days were previews: anyone could walk in and inspect the merchandise. One large space was filled with old movie posters—a garish montage of mad scientists, fire-breathing lizards, ominous silver machines emitting death rays, heroes killing giant ants with swords, big-breasted women drowning in pits of slime—to put it bluntly, here, in one room, were all the stupid ideas that ever gave science fiction a bad name. The monstrous faces leered down like freaks in a carnival midway, while collectors evaluated them like fastidious museum curators, checking for creases, tears, yellowing paper, and other imperfections.

Adjacent to the posters I found items that the catalogue listed as "artifacts." Here was the head of Mr. Sta-Puft, the marshmallow monster in *Ghostbusters*, enshrined in a glass display case. Close by, I found two decaying "Spock Ears," once worn by Leonard Nimoy,

Page 184

now sealed in a sandwich bag. In another glass case was a miniature mechanical hand from *King Kong;* all of its fur had long since fallen off, leaving nothing but some tarnished aluminum rods.

These "artifacts" looked to me like relics culled by some maniac bag lady who had spent a lifetime raiding dumpsters outside movie lots. They took the whole concept of collectibility beyond all normal bounds. To the outsider, they literally looked like trash.

But this auction wasn't for outsiders (or *mundanes*, as Ackerman called them). This was for a subculture of movie freaks and magazine buffs suffering from what I can only describe as "Ackermania": The obsessional desire to collect anything involving monstrosity, mutilation, and the macabre.

I found Forrest Ackerman sitting at one side of the display space, behind a table whose wood-grain Formica was chipped at the edges and spotted with bits of old masking tape. He wore two red "I Love Sci-Fi" buttons pinned to the lapels of his plain brown suit, and beamed genially at everyone who wandered by. Although over seventy, he had the rounded cheeks and pink, unlined skin of a man in his middle fifties. He posed for flash photographs with unpretentious pleasure, as if his celebrity status was still a novelty to him.

I asked him why he had decided to have the auction.

"Well, now that I'm seventy-one, I'm really not making any money. When the auctioneers came to me, I decided to empty out my three garages of duplicate material. I mean, if I have six autographed photographs of Karloff, I should be able to live with five. So, the thousand items that you see here are just the tip of the iceberg."

I walked into the next room, where I found a gallery of original artwork by Frank Frazetta, Boris Vallejo, Carl Lundgren, Tim Hildebrandt, and others. These paintings did not belong to Ackerman; most had been commissioned originally as book covers, and had been added to the auction by the artists. And here, standing in front of "The Barbarian"—the famous painting that once graced the cover of *Conan the Adventurer* and inspired a thousand imitations—was Frank Frazetta himself.

He turned out to be an earthy, matter-of-fact, plain-spoken man. I could have mistaken him for an electrician or a plumber. At the same time, he had no false modesty about his work: "This one painting," he told me, "has revolutionized the industry. It made the Robert E. Howard estate millions. See, when I'm at my best, I produce masterpieces. But of course, no one hits a home run every time. Sometimes, when I'm tired or I'm just not working right, I produce stuff that's junk."

After two days of previews, the auction took place in an adjacent ballroom where the decor was Renovated Industrial Chic: refinished hardwood floors, cast-iron pillars painted white, with spotlights angled at the white vaulted ceiling. An audience of around three hundred sat on white plastic folding chairs, clutching copies of the $18 silver-covered catalogue and free copies of *Omni* magazine. Sandwiches were available from a table in one corner, to sustain us through ten hours of bidding that lay ahead.

I found a seat beside a young man who was studying his catalogue with singleminded intensity. He had already made his first purchase: two curved objects that looked like dark-brown fortune cookies. I asked him what they were.

"Abraham Lincoln's chin, and the pouch from under one of his eyes. They were in an episode of *Star Trek*. Here, you can touch them. Go ahead!"

I picked them up. They felt squishy, like Dr. Scholl foot pads.

"I got a real good price on them," he told me. "Forty-five bucks."

Other "artifacts" were soon selling for much more. King Kong's hairless hand went for $1,400. Mr. Sta-Puft fetched $375. Spock's ears, in their sandwich bag, drew $425.

Original cover art from magazines of the 1930s was popular, selling for $1,000 to $2,000, and most of the originals by Boris Vallejo made $2,000 to $5,000. The real excitement, however, centered around Frazetta's "Barbarian" painting.

"We will accept opening bids of $100,000 for this work," the auctioneer announced. She was greeted with stunned silence; and then, people started laughing.

Well, would anyone offer $50,000 for "The Barbarian"? Or how about $25,000? Finally, someone raised his hand. From there, offers climbed gradually to $42,500, where they stopped. "Don't get excited," she told the winning bidder. "We haven't sold it to you yet."

Frank Frazetta had gone back home to East Stroudsberg, but was listening in on the auction by telephone. He promptly rejected $42,500. The audience booed. What they didn't realize was that, according to one of the auction staff who spoke to me off the record, Frazetta's confidential reserve price on "The Barbarian" had been two million dollars.

I went home and wrote about the auction for *The Magazine of Fantasy and Science Fiction*. I seem to recall that I was paid about $65.

1988

The Guide

No one ever seemed to understand the title of my little zine *REM*, so I changed it to *Science Fiction Guide*. One of the tenants at 594 Broadway happened to be a cartoonist, so I asked him if he could draw a picture for the cover. I wanted a girl scout, because in England they are known as girl *guides*, and I liked the idea of a totally obscure pun that hardly anyone would understand.

"What do you want her doing?" my friend asked.

"I don't know. Something related to science fiction."

"How about if she does the Vulcan salute?"

"The what?"

"From Star Trek."

I decided not to mention my loathing for Star Trek. "Great!" I said. And that was how I acquired the cover art for, I think, $10.

Science Fiction Guide continued for many more issues than *The Patchin Review*, because it had fewer pages, which entailed much less work for me. Somehow, though, it attracted much less attention, and sold only about 150 copies instead of the 950 that *The Patchin Review* managed to sell of every issue. I have never figured out exactly what there is about a publication that creates a magnetism which readers find difficult to resist, but the *Guide* didn't have it. Maybe I should have revived a gossip column.

A Destructive Scan

The 1988 Nebula Awards were held in March in Los Angeles, where I found myself talking to Vernor Vinge, a wonderful writer and brilliant man who was also one of the most gentle and generous people I ever met. I told him I was planning to write a serious novel exploring the prospect of uploading human intelligence into hardware. The "Max Headroom" TV series had popularized that idea in a silly

SCIENCE FICTION
GUIDE
rowth rule: 5DA2D248
NUMBER 14
JULY 1989
$1.50

SCIENCE FICTION
GUIDE
$1.50
Number 13
February 1989

Special
HUMOR
issue
June 1988
$1.50
SCIENCE FICTION
GUIDE

SCIENCE FICTION
GUIDE
NUMBER 11
MARCH 1988
$1.50

way, but I wanted to make it serious and plausible.

Vernor, of course, had already considered this topic in detail. He was, after all, a mathematician and a computer scientist, in addition to being a serious science-fiction writer. "It would probably be a destructive scan," he remarked.

I hadn't considered this, but of course, he was right: The brain would have to be peeled or sliced to reveal its structure. So, being uploaded into hardware would be a one-way trip, and there wouldn't be any second chances.

"One thing you may also consider," he added, in his low-key style, as if he thought I probably wouldn't be interested, but he would mention it anyway. "You could have an accelerated clock speed."

He was writing my book for me. And of course he was right again: There was no reason why a computer simulation in silicon had to run at the same speed as a biological brain. It would be unconstrained by the limits of biochemical nerve impulses, and could be dozens or hundreds of times faster.

"Do you mind if I use these ideas?" I asked him.

"I'm not going to write about this," he said. "So go ahead."

A man I recognized as Stanley Schmidt had been standing nearby. He was the editor of *Analog* magazine. "You should read *Mind Children* by Hans Moravec," he told me. "It's directly applicable to your idea."

Later, I did read *Mind Children*, which was an amazing book.

So here it was again: The generosity of science-fiction people. I felt sure than Stanley Schmidt didn't share my tastes in science fiction, and probably regarded me as an annoying troublemaker in the field, yet he was happy to suggest ways to improve my book. And, his advice was valuable.

The suggestions from him and Vernor later grew into my novel, *The Silicon Man*, for which I had one goal: I wanted to write at least one book in my life which would receive good reviews. Eventually it did fulfill this goal, but of course there was a snag: it not sell many copies.

Above: Vernor Vinge

Opposite page: A selection of "Girl Guide" covers. I tried to include cellular automata on each one.

Jerry and the Tape Player

The 1988 Nebula event featured some especially memorable bad behavior, as if to make up for the 1987 Nebulas where nothing much happened. In a pseudo-baroque "banqueting hall" (the nearest Hollywood ever gets to historic architecture) some mellow socializing was in progress when a writer named Arthur Byron Cover switched on a tape player. Norman Spinrad, who organized the event, had commissioned Arthur to provide some background music, and here he was, doing his duty.

"Turn that thing off!" The voice was loud and military in tone. It was Jerry Pournelle's voice.

Arthur had the pacific demeanor of an ex-hippie. Long-haired and unassuming, he was known to avoid confrontations—but something about Jerry Pournelle triggered him. Maybe, distantly, he heard echoes of flower children chanting "Off the pigs! Don't trust anyone over thirty!" For whatever reason, his posture straightened, he made eye contact, and he placed himself between Jerry and the tape player. "No, Pournelle!" he shouted. "This is not your party."

Jerry seized one of the steel-framed, stackable chairs scattered around the room. He raised it menacingly. ("I was only aiming for the tape machine," he later claimed.) Within moments, a bevy of women converged upon him, clutching his arms and twittering in dismay. Norman Spinrad inserted himself and somehow got poked in the stomach with a chair leg. "Ow!" he exclaimed. He sat down, looking surprised.

Grudgingly, Jerry allowed himself to be restrained. He returned to his seat, and the party resumed—but the music was still playing. It was at a very low level, and truly was background music, but something about it maddened him. Once again he charged forward, this time brandishing a Swiss Army pen knife. He seized a wire and made as if to cut it.

Arthur grabbed the other end of the wire and dragged it free from Jerry's grasp. "No, Pournelle!" he shouted again, like a trainer confronted with an especially disobedient dog. "No, no, no!"

There was a scuffle. Jerry pushed Arthur. Arthur pushed back. Somewhere in the melee, Jerry sustained a bruise in the back of his head.

The next evening I ran into him on the way to the awards ceremony. He was formally attired in a tuxedo. "Here," he said. "See what they did to me. Feel the lump."

I hesitated, feeling disconcerted by the intimacy of his invitation. Still, I touched the crown of his head.

"Not there." He grabbed my wrist and guided my fingers to a point about four inches above the back of his starched white collar. "There!"

"You're right," I said. "There's a lump."

"Yes," he said. "And you know, they still haven't given me back my pen knife."

I miss Jerry, as I miss many of the participants in those science-fiction events, where a lot of people dressed up formally as if they were going to a presentation of Oscar awards, but their behavior might be a bit . . . unpredictable.

The dissonance was always a delight.

The Horror

The 1988 Nebulas had additional significance for me, in that I met someone who would be important in my life. Her name was Clarissa, and she was a school teacher who also wrote horror fiction.

I had never understood the appeal of horror, because its implicit world view is opposite to that of science fiction. Typically a horror story entails something paranormal or irrational which kills people who are powerless to prevent it. Thus, horror is fundamentally a literature of fear, and shows no interest in human transcendence and empowerment that may be achieved through technology.

In science fiction, typically people overcome a threat. Anything that seems supernatural or irrational is explained, usually via the scientific method, and there is a bias toward optimism and the eradication of fear.

Still, Clarissa was smart and interesting, and was a California blonde around my own age. She said she was married, but she gave me her phone number because she would like to have someone to talk to about writing. Okay, I could understand that. I said I would give her a call when I got back to New York.

A couple of days later, I managed to find a story of hers in a collection. It described a girl ritually killing her father, then having sex with his corpse, and then mutilating it.

I told myself not to take it too seriously.

The apartment on Beverly Glen Boulevard was located immediately above the garages.

Disembodied Audio

I telephoned Clarissa on a Sunday afternoon, just out of curiosity, and we ended up talking for an hour.

Talking on the phone became a regular weekly event for us. The hour became two hours each time, and the frequency doubled to twice a week. It was a fascinating way to get to know someone, without any visual cues. She said that she felt lonely and alienated from her environment, and she wanted to write more stories.

Two months later, during a week of vacation from her teaching job, she jumped on a plane and came to New York. At that point, the relationship was no longer purely verbal, and she started talking about getting a divorce.

Normality Issues

In September I found myself relocating just west of Century City, in the greater Los Angeles Area. Clarissa had a two-bedroom apartment on Beverly Glen Boulevard, where she was now living alone. I joined her there to start a new life in an environment which in many ways was benign yet turned out to be so alien for me, moving into it was more confusing than when I had relocated in the United States from England in 1970.

On the plus side, I now had a girlfriend who was nonpromiscuous, didn't do drugs, was willing to engage in conversation, and was not an artist who was angry with the world. This was encouraging.

However, instead of my spacious office on lower Broadway, I now worked in a tiny room that had no furniture. I sat on a cushion on the floor and used a laptop resting on my knees, but told myself that it didn't bother me, because I have always enjoyed the feeling of impermanence and adventure associated with camping out.

Southern California was like a permanent vacation from the harsh, gray urban environment of Manhattan. I had brought my lightweight touring bicycle with me, and when I studied a map I found that I was within an easy five-mile riding radius of the ocean on one side and West Hollywood on the other. In the mornings, before the day became too warm, I went riding through suburban neighborhoods, enjoying the modest architecture of little 1930s-vintage houses amid the copious exotic vegetation. A lot of this scenery found its way into *The Silicon Man*, which I started to write in the afternoons before Clarissa came home from her teaching job. She then became a perceptive and supportive critic of the chapters that I showed her.

A typical back-street house in the Studio City area.

Really, it was idyllic—except when I had to deal with the peculiar human need which may be described as "fitting in."

While I was growing up in England, I used to stay home and read about mathematics, or draw comic books, or build electronics devices, because if tried to fraternize with normal children, they laughed at me and beat me up. This was how I learned the sad truth: I didn't fit in.

As an adult, I only had to look at magazines on sale in a supermarket to see how different I was from normal people. The magazines featured team sports, food, and clothes, which I found incomprehensible and boring. Fortunately nonconformists in the science-fiction community provided a refuge from all that, and computer nerds were even more reassuringly dysfunctional. But now I found myself in a suburban zone where normality was unavoidable.

Worse still, it was in the greater Los Angeles area, where people were style-conscious. Back in the 1970s, as a guest at Harlan Ellison's house, I had noticed that Los Angelenos all had sun tans. Tans were important, hair was important, fingernails were properly trimmed, clothes were important, shoes were important, a wristwatch was important, and the car that you drove was extremely important. No one was trying to dress like a movie star, yet the presence of Hollywood seemed distantly tangible, polarizing everyone in the direction of Looking Good.

Now I found myself embedded in this nightmare. Clarissa's friends were very pleasant toward me, but they shared that comfortably normal Los Angeles look, and I wondered what to do. Even if I bought new clothes to acquire protective coloration, I didn't think it would fool anyone. In the past, whenever I had tried to look normal, it hadn't worked. And even if it worked this time, then what? I would have to follow through and *talk* normally, which would be an even greater challenge.

In England, I had acquired local linguistic habits such as false understatement, self-deprecating humor, irony, and sarcasm. Then I moved to New York and fell in with writers and editors who often expressed themselves similarly—and even the ones who didn't were not surprised by it. They had watched Monty Python on PBS. They understood that if an English person said "Very nice!" he might mean just the opposite, or if he said "I was a bit worried" he could be referring to a state of mortal panic.

When I listened to Clarissa's friends, they spoke literally, and they took me literally, so I had to suppress my normal style of speaking and express myself literally, too. This was tiring—and then there was the problem of conversational topics.

The men didn't talk much about sports when women were present, but the other two big topics were inescapable. Clothes and food could sustain literally hours of conversation, and where clothes were concerned, shopping was a large part of the dialogue.

Gradually I realized that most people, of both genders, could actually enjoy shopping, and they still enjoyed it *even if they didn't buy anything*. The process itself was engrossing, and after they shopped, they talked about it. They described where they went, what they discovered, how high the prices were, how diverse the inventories were in different stores—I timed one conversation about clothing, and it went on for almost two hours.

My confusion became more intense when I realized that after a conversation, most people didn't remember what was said. The process of talking was a recreation in itself, creating a sympathetic resonance which made people happy—except for me, of course. I felt my life ticking away, until my restlessness became intolerable, and I couldn't sit there any longer. Sometimes I excused myself, saying that I needed some fresh air, and I went out for a walk. When I returned, the same conversation was still going on. At least, it sounded the same to me.

As for food—everyone enjoyed comparing notes on where to find the best sushi, or enchiladas, or exotic ice cream, or peculiar imported beer, or gourmet jelly beans with organic flavoring. I had never known that such foods existed, and I didn't need to know, because I had almost no interest in food.

Desserts were the worst food topic, because the conversation became as predictable as an approaching locomotive. In any restaurant, I could foresee the inevitable moment when a waiter would show dessert menus or bring a dessert cart. Everyone would inspect the options avidly, and then the anguished expostulations would begin. That chocolate cake looked *so good,* but look at the number of calories! Could they be justified, just this once? Maybe if the person suffering this torment spent an extra half-hour on the exercise machine, as penance?

I felt bad that people were torturing themselves like this, but still I felt like screaming at them: "You go through this exact same monologue every time. Every single time! Just buy it or don't buy it, and if you do buy it, stuff it down, and let's get out of here!"

I speculated that if I learned more about the people themselves, that would alleviate my boredom, because people's skills or life experiences are always interesting. One of Clarissa's friends was a nurse, so I asked her about her work—and saw her go through a strange series of responses. First she was surprised, then disconcerted, then nervous, and finally seemed reluctant to talk at all. Later I was informed that I had made her very uncomfortable. Why was I digging for information? Did I have some ulterior motive? And, there was a subtext: Why couldn't I just relax and enjoy the mood, and take it easy? Well, I couldn't. Because, I didn't. Conversations without content put me in a *very bad mood.*

I wondered if I could find some writers in the Los Angeles area with whom I could enjoy "shop talk." I had a few tenuous contacts—but when I visited them, they were guarded and diplomatic, unlike my outspoken friends in New York. Succeeding as a writer in Southern California was a very serious and competitive matter; the chance of success in movies or TV was small, but the rewards could be huge, and people were circumspect about interacting with a possible competitor, especially as they didn't know me very well.

In New York, the situation was opposite. Instead of producers picking and choosing among thousands of desperate writers doing elevator pitches, you had editors struggling to find enough publishable books to fill their lists. Really, if you were reasonably competent as a writer in the 1980s, your chance of an editor buying your book could be relatively good. On the other hand, you could feel pretty sure it wouldn't make much money, and therefore, the stakes were low, and no one had to protect their turf. You might hear something like, "Did you know Hartwell is moving to Tor? He's going to be looking for hardcovers. Maybe you could write something for him." I never heard that kind of tip about finding writing work on the West Coast.

The final impediment to a social life in Los Angeles was topography. The dispersion of human beings meant that you couldn't just drop in on someone. A car journey would be involved, and in any case, people liked some advance warning. They wouldn't want their homes to be a mess when visitors arrived.

In New York, my apartment had always been a mess, and I didn't care. Tom Disch used to ring my door bell when he went food shopping on Sixth Avenue, and I enjoyed him dropping in unexpectedly. When writers from out of town came to New York to meet editors, they would often visit me, and Ed Bryant usually stayed for two or three days. When I went out somewhere, if I had a little spare time, I might call someone from a pay phone: "Hey, I'm in your neighborhood, what are you doing? Shall I drop in?" Or I would stop at the computer store, to say hello to the people there. I think they regarded me as being like a character from a sitcom. I was their Kramer.

I had never thought of myself as an especially social person, but when I added it up, I realized that I had known at least fifty people in New York City. In Southern California I knew about four, and they were scattered over that huge area.

Perhaps if the internet had existed, I might have found new friends, but it didn't, and I had no context in which to meet people. What was I going to do, start chatting about the weather with a stranger at the local mall? I did find a couple affinity groups, such as a bunch of libertarians who met and talked about politics in Long Beach, but I had to drive for two hours through rush-hour traffic to get to one of their meetings, and when I did finally get there, they were—well, as dull as political people usually are.

I tried to make the best of the situation, even renewing acquaintance with people whom I didn't really get along with very well, such as a writer whom I will refer to here as John Smith. He was style-conscious and seemed to take everything very seriously, but he was friendly—quite hospitable—when I visited him at his house.

Two days later, an editor friend happened to call me from New York. She was wondering if I was okay. What was I doing with myself, on the West Coast?

"Well, I spent an afternoon with John Smith," I said.

There was a silence. "My God," she said, "you must be desperate."

I felt stunned. I couldn't imagine anyone in Los Angeles speaking with such ruthless, in-your-face candor. And that was exactly the problem. I missed that candor, and I had to monitor myself so that I didn't slip up and blurt out something like that. It was a major challenge, trying to fit in.

Poverty

I was starting to worry about money. I figured I might finish my novel in about four to six months, at which point I would submit it to a publishing house—but even if they bought it, how much would that bring in? Maybe $10,000, if I was lucky.

I wasn't teaching classes anymore, so I lacked that income to fall back on. I had imagined that some source of income might materialize in Los Angeles, but without a network of friends, I wasn't sure how to find it. Almost all the opportunities I ever found in New York had come through knowing people. I had never answered a job ad in my life. I didn't have a resume. I didn't even know how to write a resume. I had never been in a serious job interview, ever. At the age of 43, without any history of full-time employment, and lacking any qualification other than a totally useless Higher Diploma in Printing Management, I might be unemployable.

Waking from a Quake

I woke in the night from a dream in which someone had been screaming at me. And—someone was screaming at me. Clarissa was standing in the doorway of the bedroom, yelling "Wake up, wake up!"

Feeling bleary and confused, I asked her what was going on.

"Earthquake!" She stared at me as if I were an idiot.

But there was no earthquake. Nothing was shaking.

"You slept through it," she said, returning to the bed.

I was skeptical about this—but then I heard the distant sound of multiple car alarms, which had been triggered by the tremors. I really had slept through it, while Clarissa, as a seasoned resident of Southern California, had leaped out of bed to seek the relative safety of a door frame.

What a disappointment. I had always wanted to experience an earthquake.

Scalpel Terror

I made an appointment for a vasectomy, as I was certain that I wouldn't want to procreate again during the rest of my life. The idea of someone sticking a scalpel into my scrotum was difficult to deal with, but I told myself it was a routine procedure which no rational person would find disturbing.

As my appointment date came closer, I started to worry. Now that I had slept through an earthquake, I realized that they did actually happen in Los Angeles from time to time, and were unpredictable.

I couldn't help wondering—what if there was an earthquake at the specific moment the surgeon was making an incision? Obviously the odds were against such a coincidence, but—it could happen! The razor-sharp blade would be just touching my scrotum when the room would start shaking, and—oops!

In the end, on the day of the appointment, I canceled. I decided that it just wasn't worth the risk.

Later that day, my father telephoned from England. I had told him that I was planning to have the vasectomy, so he was calling to see if I was okay. "I'm glad to hear you speaking in your normal tone of voice," he said.

Very droll! He was sympathetic when I told him I'd backed out of the plan. He was even more terrified of medicine than I was.

The Head Freezers

My friend Gregory Benford told me that he had visited Alcor Foundation, a small nonprofit organization which performed the procedure of human cryopreservation, commonly known as cryonics. The idea was simple enough: If the brain could be preserved with minimal injury as quickly as possible after death, the person might be revived by future technology.

Key word: *might*.

This sounded far-fetched even by the standards of science fiction, yet Greg was a physicist as well as a science-fiction writer, and he told me that he was impressed by the Alcor facility. "They may be on to something," he said.

In that case, I wanted to see it. I figured I could get a more forthcoming response from Alcor if I presented myself as a journalist, so I asked Ed Ferman at *Fantasy and Science Fiction* if he would publish something on the subject, and when he said he would, I called Alcor and told them I was ready to write a magazine feature. (Eventually my contact with Alcor would turn into an obsession consuming years of my life, but that didn't begin until the 1990s.)

Alcor was located in Riverside, out at the eastern edge of the Los Angeles sprawl, far beyond my range on a bicycle. I rented a car, found my way through the web of highways to the Riverside Freeway, took the appropriate exit into an industrial park—and got lost.

I saw a couple of construction workers digging a hole in the sidewalk, so I stopped to ask directions. They were beefy guys wearing hard hats with American flags painted on the side. "Do you know where I can find Alcor Foundation?" I asked.

"Alcoa?" one of them said. "The aluminum company?"

"No, no," said his partner. "He means that place where they cut that woman's head off."

"Oh, yeah," said the first guy. "Well, you make a right up there by the Taco Bell—" He knew about Alcor because he'd seen them on the local TV news.

I found their facility on a cul-de-sac. I think it was next to a plumbing supply company, in an anonymous concrete building with a parking area just big enough for six cars. Their front door was locked and the windows were mirror-coated, presenting an enigmatic and uninviting facade. I pressed a bell-push and waited.

Eventually the door was opened by a thin person who had a friendly face. He had a normal short haircut, he wore a normal shirt

This wasn't the specific back issue that I picked up during my visit, but most of them in the late 1980s and early 1990s shared this kind of cover image, like war-zone photographs of improvised emergency medicine.

and pants—but somehow I felt as if he was acting a part that didn't come naturally to him.

I told him I had an appointment to see Mike Darwin, the president of the organization. "I'm sorry, Mike Darwin is not here right now," he said.

"Well, can I wait?"

He thought it over for a while. "I suppose so."

He allowed me into a waiting area about eight feet square, with two brown velvet-covered armchairs and a big splash of silk flowers in a vase on a table. The thin man stood nervously, hovering over me while I sat on one of the chairs. After a few minutes he muttered something and slipped out of the waiting area, and I heard the door lock itself behind him.

On the table were some back issues of *Cryonics* magazine, Alcor's monthly in-house publication. The cover of the first one showed a grainy monochrome photograph of a procedure involving a body that was probably not alive. This looked interesting, so I opened the magazine at random—and found myself reading about the separated human head that the construction worker in the street had referred to. It had belonged to a woman named Dora Kent.

Decapitation was a routine procedure at Alcor, because you should be able to grow a new body when you were revived in the future, and preserving only your head would save money on storage costs. In Dora's case, for reasons which were unclear, the routine procedure had run into some legal complications.

This was interestingly weird, so I started reading more attentively. Gradually I managed to put together the details.

Dora was the elderly mother of an Alcor director named Saul Kent. She had been near death when Alcor moved her into their facility, where they figured they could achieve optimal preservation. If she died on-site, immediate intervention was available.

Death duly occurred, after which they removed her head and perfused it with cryoprotectants. So far, so good, but because she had died without a physician present, she was now a coroner's case.

The Alcor people surrendered the body, hoping that this would be sufficient, but the coroner went public with a statement saying that he had to autopsy her brain to rule out foul play. This of course would mean unfreezing it.

In response, the Alcorians said, "Oh, no, sorry, we don't allow that."

The coroner then did what one might have expected him to do: He obtained a search warrant. Soon men with guns were raiding the Alcor facility (in which I was now sitting), shouting "Give us the head of Dora Kent!"

In response, the Alcor people said, "Actually Dora's head isn't here. Someone took it away in a dewar. Too bad about that."

A dewar was a stainless-steel insulated vessel which could be filled with liquid nitrogen, and the coroner was surprised and disconcerted to learn that a head-sized dewar would fit conveniently in a minivan.

Some of the cryonoids were hauled off to jail, and the coroner started talking about charging them with homicide, although they were released after a few hours. The coroner's office then arranged for another raid on Alcor in which computers, laboratory equipment, and a lot more items were seized and removed.

At this point I imagined that the people of Alcor were no different from any wacko cult that crossed a line by defying authorities, and they would be punished. This turned out not to be the case, however: When I opened the most recent copy of *Cryonics* magazine, I learned that the Dora Kent case had been settled in favor of Alcor, as a sympathetic judge granted an injunction to prevent autopsy of the brain.

Eventually the confiscated items were returned, and the coroner never did get possession of Dora's head. In fact, its location remained a subject of speculation. Maybe it was at her son Saul's house, or in someone's basement, or in a mini-storage facility somewhere—who could tell?

This was a wonderful story, but it got better. The coroner lost his bid for re-election, because he had mishandled other cases. The Alcor employees who had been detained were granted financial compensation. In due course, the legality of cryonics was affirmed in the State of California, and the cryonoids went back to business

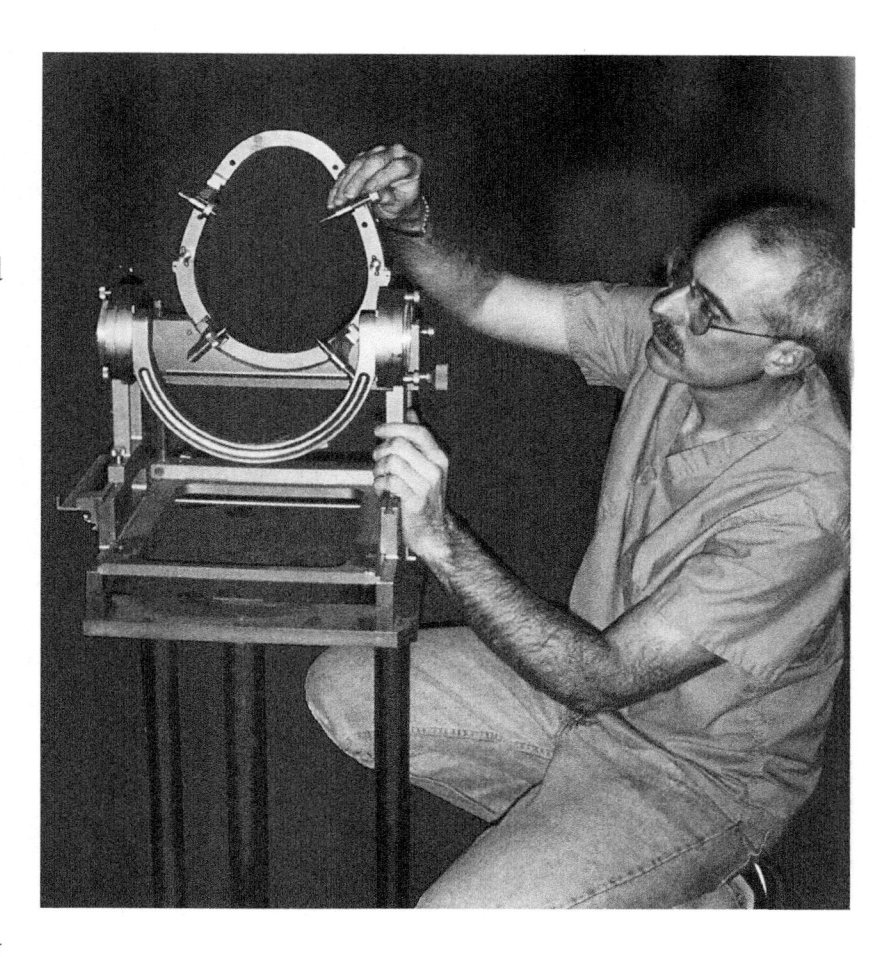

Mike Darwin posing with a device for clamping a human head. He had a passion for obscure medical equipment that was likely to freak people out.

Page 201

as usual, pumping freshly-dead people full of exotic chemicals, removing heads where their clients expressed a preference for this option, and dunking them in liquid nitrogen. Alcor had paid a lot in legal fees, but in every other respect had emerged stronger from the confrontation.

Perhaps most people would have had a laugh-or-barf reaction to the stuff about decapitation and autopsies, but I loved it. If the people at Alcor were able to do such crazy shit and get away with it, I wanted to join the party, especially as I had always felt angry about mortality. So far as I was concerned, even a futile gesture of rebellion would be better than no rebellion at all.

At this point, Mike Darwin turned up. He was tall and angular, with a melancholy, brooding look. He apologized for being late, but he didn't really seem apologetic. He acted as if there were a thousand other things he'd rather do than talk to a journalist, but here I was, so he showed me every inch of the facility, from the operating room to the very large dewars in which people who had chosen whole-body preservation were stored.

I saw that Alcor was a low-budget operation with improvised fixtures and furniture that looked as if it had been picked up in yard sales, yet at the same time the place was crammed with bona-fide medical equipment which appeared to be highly functional. Everything was clean, properly labeled, and neatly stored, and all the equipment and devices had a properly thought-out purpose which Darwin articulated with an impressive air of authority.

When I asked him how much a cryopreservation would cost, he explained that it could be covered by taking out a life-insurance policy naming Alcor as beneficiary. For someone my age, the premium would be around $500 per year.

What a deal! "I might be interested in signing up," I said.

He gave me a skeptical look and said nothing.

"Seriously," I said.

"All right," he said, still looking skeptical. "If you give us your address, we'll send you the documents, and our signup administrator, Arthur McCombs, will get in touch."

Later I discovered that of the hundreds of journalists who visited Alcor over the years, I was the only one who ever showed any personal interest. Yet again I was reminded of my status as an irredeemably idiosyncratic person, far from the center of any bell curve—even in cryonics.

Fateful Fantasy

At the annual World Fantasy Convention in the UK, a British writer named David Garnett told me over a pint of warm British beer that he was making 10,000 pounds by writing a novel in a new fantasy series, and he suggested that I could do it too.

"I don't think that's a good idea, David," I said. "I've published essays denouncing fantasy novels as a kind of literary cancer."

"You could use a pseudonym," he suggested.

I was rewinding my memory tape. "Wait a minute, did you just say *ten thousand pounds?*" That was more than $20,000 in those days, or around $50,000 in 2021 dollars, for maybe a month's work. Of course, I had never written fantasy, but—how hard could it be?

David explained to me that Warhammer was a role-playing game like Dungeons and Dragons, and the manufacturers now wanted to diversify into books that shared the "Warhammer universe."

"These people aren't like book publishers," he said. "They've got real money, and they don't understand the pittance we normally work for. You already write columns in *Interzone* for David Pringle. Well, he's the editor that Warhammer have hired."

Pringle? He was a hardcore J. G. Ballard fan. Now he was commissioning books about men with swords hacking up goblins and trolls?

Indeed, it was so, and when I caught up with him at the convention, he showed no shame. He was determined, he said, to publish *high-quality* books about men with swords hacking up goblins and trolls. And so, I succumbed. Like several other writers, I hid my shame behind a pseudonym and said, "Yes, yes, please send me the necessary source materials so I can produce for you the exciting Warhammer adventure that deep down inside, I've always known I wanted to write!"

The magnitude of this appalling error would become painfully apparent soon enough.

A couple of Warhammer figures, or action characters, or whatever they are called. Apparently people move them around a game board while players throw dice. Eventually Warhammer became valued at a billion dollars. Billion with a B. There is even a Warhammer version of Monopoly.

Page 203

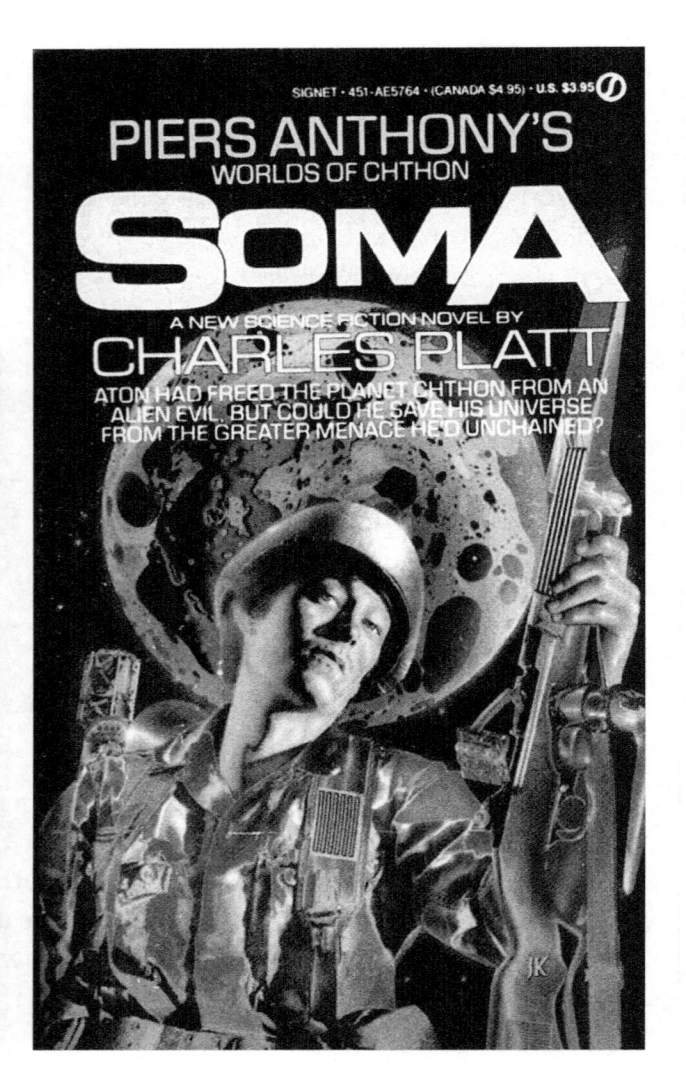

The British edition, left, embraced the deranged spirit of the book and took it beyond anything I expected, while the American edition, right, looked as if the warrior was proposing some perverse sexual encounter.

On the British cover, I feel sure that the poorly painted rock at bottom-right was added to conceal the woman's severed neck.

A Man With a Gun

I never liked to admit defeat, so I doubled down on my decision to live in Southern California. I went back to New York to retrieve more of my possessions.

While I was in the city, I met old friends including my indefatigable editor, John Silbersack. After the disappointing sales of my novel *Plasm*, he vowed to do better with the sequel, *Soma*, and used the most powerful sales tool at his disposal: A cover depicting a man holding a very large gun.

Personally I would have preferred a totally nutso cover such as the one that my British publisher had commissioned for this book, showing a ritual scene of decapitation reminiscent of the fate experienced by Dora Kent, although administered with less finesse. The British artist had accurately captured the deranged mentality of warriors in a state of raving sexual frustration, and it looked to me as if he had even shown the bleeding neck-stump of the decapitated victim before someone insisted that the stump should be concealed with a hastily painted rock.

But, this wasn't John's idea of a selling cover. He wanted a man with a gun, because it was *the one thing that always worked*—except that when my book was eventually published, it didn't work.

John was baffled, but the problem seemed obvious to me. The man with the gun in the painting that was acquired for the book had a sleazy, sardonic leer, as if he wanted to fondle the reader's genitals. What John should have done was commission a cover showing a macho guy who looked as if he wanted to kill the reader.

John disagreed. "What I should have done," he said, "was put Piers' name at the top of the book in large type, and your name at the bottom in very small type, and we should have set it in the Xanth universe instead of the Chthon universe."

He was right, of course. If you're going to sell out, it should be a wholehearted sellout with no self-serving nonsense about doing it "ethically." The root of our problem was that Piers really was an ethical person, and we made the mistake of respecting that.

Death Questions

When I got back to California, Alcor's membership documents had arrived. I read them with mounting discomfort, because they forced me to confront my own death in a way that I had not anticipated. They included questions such as—if I died in a way that caused brain damage, did I still want Alcor to preserve me? How much of my brain should be viable, to make it worth preserving? What if I was lying around at room temperature for a couple of days before anyone found me, and I started to decompose? Should they preserve whatever was left?

I had always felt that I was realistic about mortality, but now I realized that I had been just as evasive about death as everyone else. The documents intimidated me. I kept them, but I didn't sign them.

1989

Rage Against the Beasts

Via air mail from the UK, I received a stack of books a foot thick crammed with more than a million words of pedantic detail pertaining to the Warhammer fantasy realm. These books would be my guide to hundreds of different creatures, each with its own unique powers. The books also listed towns, weapons, costumes, magic spells, rituals, and gods.

Warhammer seemed to be the life's work of obsessive-compulsive anal-retentive maniacs. Was I really supposed to remember all of this?

Still, I reminded myself: *10,000 British pounds*. I had to give it a try. I started to conceive a plot under the title, "Rage Against the Beasts." That sounded good, didn't it?

As plowed through the books, I discovered that they were not only verbose, but disorganized and inconsistent. Some "facts" contradicted other "facts," and additional "facts" weren't mentioned at all. David Pringle, for instance, happened to mention that the Warhammer world was two or three times as big as Earth, even though I didn't find this detail in any of the books. (Two times as big, or three? I never did discover which was correct.) It also had two moons.

Worse still, the books were very derivative, and I wondered why Warhammer hadn't been sued. Did Michael Moorcock know that the games in Games Workshop involved battles with "chaos lords"? Was Terry Pratchett aware than in the Games Workshop world, there were "colors of magic"? Was the Tolkien estate aware that Games Workshop described endearing little guys who bore an uncanny resemblance to hobbits?

Submerging myself in a fantasy scenario was humiliating for me, but embracing a set of second-hand concepts derived from other writers was even more humiliating. Well, I wasn't willing to give up, so I finished a detailed outline of my proposed novel and sent it in.

The Green Monster

While riding my bicycle through the back streets of Studio City, I noticed a 1972 Cadillac Coupe de Ville parked at the curb with a FOR SALE sign in the window. "Best offer over $900," the sign said.

The Cadillac was a beast. A monster. It was classic early-1970s, complete with vinyl roof. The paint and the roof were swamp green, and I eyed the car with admiration, remembering those halcyon days when General Motors built dreamboats with unlimited quantities of steel and chrome. I thought I heard the car calling to me. "Hey, let's go cruising!" it said.

How could I say no?

When I found the seller, he told me that it had belonged to his girlfriend's father, who had died of a heart attack after maintaining the car religiously for seventeen years. It had all kinds of extras that were state-of-the-art at the time of its manufacture: Signal-seeking FM radio, central door locking, power windows, fully automatic climate control. The only thing I didn't like was the green leather of the seats, but what other color could they be?

I offered $850, which was accepted, and the deal was done.

Clarissa wasn't entirely happy when I brought the behemoth back to our apartment building. After she got into the car, she had difficulty getting out of it, because the doors were so huge and heavy. If the Cadillac was parked on a slope, she might not be able to escape from it at all.

The big issue was where I was going to park it. I had assumed I could keep it outside the building, but she asked me not to do that. She felt—well—a car like that—of that vintage—and, you know, swamp green—it would be a bit embarrassing.

Here it was again: The Los Angeles concern about appearances, which always blindsided me. I thought the car was a wonderful joke,

Me and my Cadillac, in a parking lot on the roof top of the local mall.

but for Los Angelenos, cars were as serious as desserts, and there was no room for humor. Somewhere at the top of the "desirable car" list would be a Bentley or a Rolls Royce; further down would be a Porsche; below that a BMW or a Mercedes; and right at the bottom of acceptable marques might be a Toyota Camry, if it was reasonably new and the paint hadn't faded. A 1972 Cadillac was off the list completely. Owning it would be like having a skin tumor.

In the end I agreed to park the car on a back street, outside someone else's house. For their sake, I hoped that no one might think they owned it.

Drachenfels

My Warhammer outline came back to me with a lot of notes. The fanatics at Games Workshop told me that trolls would be too stupid to lay siege to a town in the manner I had described. Beastmen and mutants were indigenous to many areas of the Warhammer world, not just the Chaos Wastes. The soul of a mere Chaos Champion would serve no purpose bound into a sword; it would have to be of a Daemon Prince. And on and on, in relentless detail.

This was all very depressing and annoying. Maybe I should just forget the whole thing—but I had invested so much time already, I didn't want it to be fruitless. Economists think of this as "the sunk cost fallacy," which tempts people to devote additional time to a futile endeavor. Playing more hands of blackjack in an effort to win back your losses is a classic sunk-cost fallacy.

I resigned myself to making the revisions, and rewrote my outline. A couple of weeks later, it was duly accepted, so I got down to the serious business of writing the book. It took four weeks, working every day, ten or twelve hours a day. I researched the names of parts of sailing ships. I made sure my goblins were the right color. I gave my Daemon Prince the correct deformities. I got into the spirit of the thing when my Bad Guy plunged his sword into an orc's ear. I really *tried*.

When I had almost completed my task, an unexpected package arrived from England. It contained a book titled *Drachenfels*, the first Warhammer novel, by Jack Yeovil. In case anyone wondered who Jack really was, the creators of Warhammer cheerfully revealed (in their magazine *White Dwarf*) that he was the well-known British writer Kim Newman. Evidently the Warhammerians couldn't imagine that Newman might be embarrassed by his association with them. If he wanted to use a pseudonym, I guess they assumed he was just being a bit shy.

The cover of *Drachenfels* looked like an under-exposed photograph of a block of granite, printed in magenta and black and overprinted with the "Warhammer" logo in such a way as to make it unreadable. And when I turned to the back cover, I found the following:

"In a castle as grey and jagged as the mountains around it.... Detlef Sierek, the greatest playwright and impresario in the Warhammer world, is to recreate on stage the death of Drachenfels."

The greatest—*playwright?*

I checked inside. Sure enough, it was a book about the staging of a play. There was some court intrigue, a lot of elegant little quips and Victorian mannerisms—it was like an Olde English drawing-room comedy.

I felt stunned. Were David Pringle's literary ethics so powerfully entrenched, he commissioned a novel in which there weren't any swordsmen, goblins, or trolls *at all?*

I went back to my Warhammer rule books. They contained stirring scene-setting passages such as:

> Many sink into an abyss of despair, mindlessly running and gibbering with the warped and unnameable beasts of the Chaos Pack. Their fate is a minor mercy, for with mindlessness comes oblivion. Some arise as dreaded and terrible Chaos Lords, the leaders of the Chaos Beastmen that slaughter and rampage across the Wastes and beyond.

That was the stuff I understood, squarely targeted at repressed fourteen-year-olds with power fantasies. I understood their primitive yearnings; I'd been like that myself. They were my people!

But now, with my book almost finished, here was this droll, mannered little farce by Kim Newman about a bunch of noblemen staging a play. And it was the *first in the series*, setting the tone for all that would follow.

I finished my manuscript and turned it in. Then I went back to writing *The Silicon Man*.

The front cover of the first Warhammer novel. Reproduction in monochrome is difficult, as the cover was entirely printed in black and magenta. The word "Warhammer" is almost invisible at the top of the cover, printed in black. It was embossed, so readers who were blind might have been able to detect it.

Page 209

Back to the City

In June my feelings of alienation in Los Angeles became too much to bear, so I returned to New York City for a month. I had been happy living with Clarissa, but I never did figure out how to develop social relationships with her friends, and my 1972 Cadillac was like an advertisement confirming that I was an aberrant life form.

Clarissa promised to join me in New York in July, during the weeks of vacation that she enjoyed as a teacher. After that, I didn't know what was going to happen.

I had sublet my apartment at Patchin Place, but the one-year sublease was up, and I repossessed the apartment. Even the screaming brats in the school yard outside my window now seemed like a welcoming chorus. I had also sublet my office, and repossessed that, which induced intense feelings of gratitude. My record albums were still there, and so was my desktop computer, and other bits of technology that made life worthwhile.

I walked to the local health-food store and bought my favorite packaged sandwich made by an obscure collective calling itself Sister Shorter. I always loved the caption on their label: "Contains no harmful spices." Sister Shorter understood that all spices are potentially hazardous to the taste receptors of a civilized person, and therefore should be omitted. Yes!

I called friends and caught up on publishing gossip: Who had paid a huge amount of money for an embarrassingly bad book by a famous name, who had discovered a wonderful new author whose sales figures turned out to be a disaster, what was the latest absurd excuse from a well-known procrastinator regarding nondelivery of a manuscript, and stuff like that. Quips were traded. Sarcasm and irony were employed, and I realized how much I had missed these conversational habits. And, no one talked about clothes or food.

The next day I went to the New School Computer Center, which was lining up instructors for its summer classes. I was not enthused by the idea of teaching Adobe Illustrator all over again, but I needed some money, and I still had my set of course notes which would make the class run itself, almost. Would the school take me back? They were annoyed that I had absconded to California, but I had always taken a lot of trouble to maintain a friendly relationship with the woman who did the scheduling, and my student evaluations had always been good—so I was forgiven.

I was home again.

On My Own

Clarissa visited me in New York City, but couldn't relocate there permanently, as she needed her teaching job. I was no longer willing to live in Los Angeles, as all my strategies had failed.

I felt guilty, as usual, about my inability to make people happy. Any normal person should surely be able to adjust himself to a new environment—but, I wasn't normal. At the end of July, in a state of great sadness, feeling angry with myself for being so easily defeated, I went back with Clarissa to her apartment, to pack most of my possessions into boxes which I shipped to New York via UPS. Then I loaded everything else into the Cadillac, which I would drive from coast to coast.

With Philip Jose Farmer in Peoria, Illinois.

Clarissa said she wanted to accompany me on the cross-country trip, even though there was an air of finality about everything. So, we started driving.

The huge trunk of the car was completely crammed with stuff, including an air conditioner and my bicycle. Inside the car, on the back seat, I had my computer, printer, two video monitors, and a VCR, plus Clarissa's very large suitcase and some other oddments.

We averaged 12 miles to the gallon, and the price of unleaded 92-octane fuel varied from $1.10 to $1.40 per gallon. Total fuel cost: About $300, considerably cheaper than air tickets for two, quite apart from the expense if I had shipped all the large items.

Our journey took us through Illinois, where we stopped in Peoria to see Philip Jose Farmer and his wife Bette. I had kept in touch with Phil over the years, by phone and the postal service. He seemed fond of me, as if I were a wayward son, and I loved him for his kind, philosophical disposition—and his strangeness.

He had been truly radical in his early days. His stories about people having sex with alien creatures had astonished and delighted me when I read them as a fourteen-year-old. Yet here he was in a totally conventional house, in the American heartland, with his lovely conventional wife, who tolerated his peculiarities by ignoring them.

If he could seem contented in a normal environment, why couldn't I? I wondered how he dealt with conversations about clothes and food. Probably he just sat there in his own little world, thinking about more weird adventure stories that he wanted to write. He was a very patient man. I was not.

After I reached New York with Clarissa, we unloaded the Cadillac and I parked it on a back street. That night someone broke open the trunk and stole the spare wheel, which seemed like an omen. I advertised the Cadillac in *The Village Voice* and sold it for, I think, $500.

Clarissa stayed until she had to return to California to resume teaching, and after that, I was on my own.

The Fantasy Novels

Back in December, 1981, Harlan Ellison had given an interview to *Twilight Zone* magazine in which he waxed lyrical about his relationship with his publisher, Houghton-Mifflin. "I was paid $154,000 for [a novel titled] *Shrikes* just on the basis of telling the plot to the editor." he claimed. "My novels *Blood's a Rover*, *Nights in the Gardens of Trepidation*, and *The Prince of Sleep* will all be out in the near future."

Actually, he hadn't written any of these books.

In September, 1989 the world science fiction convention was in Boston, which happened to be the home of Houghton-Mifflin. So it was that at one of the parties, I ran into a woman employed as one of the Houghton-Mifflin editors. I don't have a verbatim transcript of our chat, but I kept notes, and it went something like this:

"Let's see," I said, as if searching my memory. "Your company publishes Harlan Ellison."

"I'm his editor."

"Really! Didn't your company offer a lot of money for a book called—what was it—*Shrikes*?"

Her expression became stony. "It will not be published."

"Oh! Sorry to hear that." I wondered how much he had actually received of the alleged $154,000, and how he would be paying it back, but it would be rude to ask. "What about those other books by Ellison—what were they called? *Blood's a Rover*, *Nights in the Gardens of Trepidation*, and *The Prince of Sleep*."

"They will not be published. So you know him?"

"A bit." I didn't mention that he had been so enraged by my mockery, he had assaulted me physically a few years ago. "Now, tell me," I went on, "what about *The Last Dangerous Visions?*"

"We have a new deadline for delivery of the manuscripts."

"Why, that's good news! You know, I have a story in that collection. I sold it to him quite a long time ago. In fact, come to think of it, just over twenty years ago. How time flies! I've been waiting."

She didn't seem surprised. "I can assure you," she said, "the collection will be published."

"Really? There have been several missed deadlines—"

"This is now our sixth deadline for him at Houghton-Mifflin." Finally, she gave up her pretense of professional detachment. Like every editor I had ever met who had dealt with Ellison, she was weary and annoyed. "You have to understand," she said, "I inherited *The Last Dangerous Visions* when the previous editor retired."

I couldn't help laughing.

"I do see the humor in it," she said. "But really—we are going to issue it. In four volumes."

I asked if they would be a subscription deal, as in a book club, where people would continue to receive volumes until they remembered to cancel.

"No, no. They will be published all at once." She sighed. "What I don't understand is why you contributors don't all get together and assemble the books yourselves."

I was astonished. It was Ellison's job to assemble the books, not ours. He would be keeping half of the royalties, while the (approximately) 100 contributors would share the remainder between them. So, on average, he would be paid 100 times as much of each of us. Why should we do the work for him? All he had to do was write the introductions, and if he just wrote two a day, he could finish the whole thing in less than a couple of months.

I decided not to make that little speech. I wished the editor luck in her mission, although I felt confident that she would fail, just as her retired predecessor had failed.

And of course, in the end, she did fail.

At the time of my conversation with her, Houghton-Mifflin had published two short-story collections by Ellison. After that, the company published only one more collection, because he never delivered the promised novels, or anything else.

Documents

I received a call from Arthur McCombs, at Alcor Foundation. "I was wondering," he said, "if there's any problem with you signing the membership documents that we sent. It's been almost a year."

I had brought the documents back with me to New York City, and they were sitting in a pile of all kinds of unfinished business, on my desk. "I have them right here," I said.

"So, are you intending to sign up? Can I help you in any way?"

Could he help me? That was a very interesting question. "I honestly don't know," I said.

"Do you need advice regarding insurance arrangements?"

"No, I took care of that." I happened to know someone who sold life insurance, and he had drawn up a policy naming Alcor as beneficiary. I had signed it and paid the premium, because I really did intend to make arrangements with Alcor, as soon as I figured out a way to cope mentally with their documents. "The insurance is in place," I said.

There was a silence. "You made the insurance arrangements, but you haven't completed our documents?" Arthur sounded as if he had never heard of such a thing, and probably he hadn't. So, I was wacky even by the standards of head-freezers. "You do realize," Arthur went on, "even if we receive the insurance money after you die, we can't freeze you till you sign the documents."

"I suppose so," I said.

"So—why—"

I felt like screaming, "I haven't signed the documents because I don't want to think about dying!"

But that didn't make sense, because Alcor membership actually offered a small but nonzero chance to evade the finality of dying. "All right, I'll do it," I said.

"When?" said Arthur.

"I'll get them notarized tomorrow." And I did.

A week later, a little package arrived containing a stainless-steel med-alert bracelet for me to wear, engraved with Alcor's emergency 800 number and instructions for intervention if I was found in cardiac arrest. While I had been living in Los Angeles, I had looked at the fancy watches and other jewelry worn by normal people, and wondered if I needed to wear something like that to fit in. Now I had my own piece of jewelry, but it just confirmed that I was incapable of fitting in.

I wondered how much of a weirdo I really was, statistically speaking. Well, there were two cryonics organizations, and when I added up their memberships, fewer than 1,000 people in the world had made arrangements to be cryopreserved. Therefore, I was one weirdo in six million.

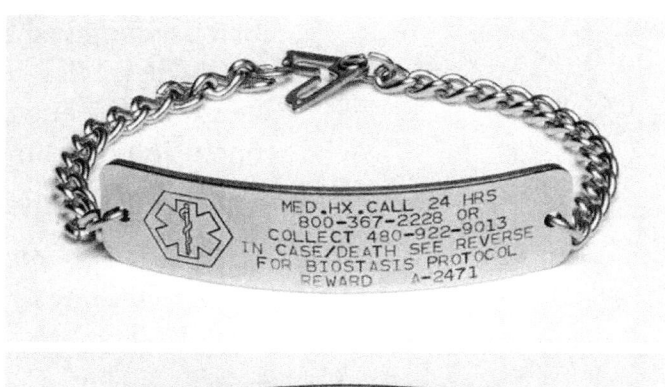

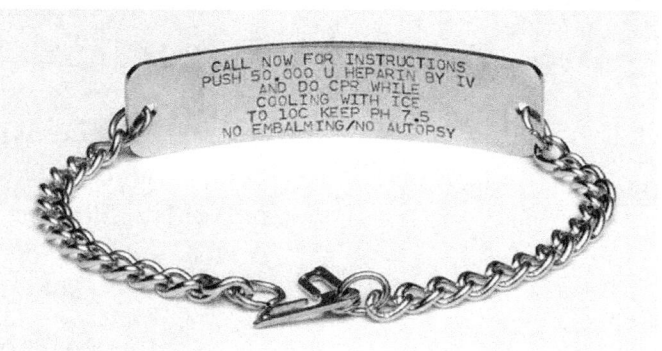

I had assumed that science-fiction writers would be interested in joining Alcor, and indeed, Gregory Benford had done so, but he seemed to be the only one. Robert A. Heinlein wrote *The Door into Summer*, a novel featuring the concept of cryonics, but when Alcor offered him a free membership, he declined. Frederik Pohl wrote *The Age of the Pussyfoot*, about a man who wakes up after 500 years in cryostasis, but when Alcor offered him a free membership, he declined. When Arthur C. Clarke was asked to make a statement to assist Alcor in its legal battle with the Riverside coroner, he obliged, and wrote: "Although no one can quantify the probability of cryonics working, I estimate it is at least 90%—and certainly nobody can say it is zero." Ninety percent! But Clarke never made arrangements for his own cryopreservation. Evidently one of the most prescient futurists in the world wasn't that interested in seeing the future.

A stainless-steel medalert bracelet of the type that Alcor Foundation distributed to its members. (This particular bracelet is not the one that was issued to me.)

I was in the habit of eating lunch every couple of weeks with writer Barry Malzberg. He understood the concept of cryonics, but had never explored the details, so the next time I saw him, I gave him a quick summary.

"Alcor is like a company selling tickets to Mars," he said thoughtfully, "except that they don't have a rocket." He thought some more. "They don't even have the money to build a rocket." Another pause. "They don't know how to build it." His voice was rising in pitch. "There aren't even any plans for a rocket! This is outrageous!"

"It's better than being cremated or buried," I said.

Barry disagreed. He thought it was fraudulent.

Many years later, some time around 2010, I had an opportunity to make an hour-long presentation about cryonics to Jeff Bezos at a Silicon Valley event. He was a brilliant, wonderful man, and he obviously enjoyed himself asking all the same questions that I had asked when I first visited Alcor, except he went through them twice as fast. By the end of the hour, I could see he had reached the same conclusion that I had reached: It might actually work.

"So are you interested?" I asked.

"You mean—me personally?" He looked shocked. "Oh, no!" And he hurried away to a presentation on some other topic.

Street Life

As fall turned to winter, my euphoria at being back in New York City began to fade. I was alone, and lonely, in one of the richest but also one of the most stupidly mismanaged cities in the world. I now had to deal with obnoxious behavior which New Yorkers seemed to feel was an inevitable feature of their environment.

When I was knocked off my bicycle by a cop throwing open the street-side door of his parked car, I remarked to him, as I picked myself up off the street, that a New York City law prohibited people from exiting on the street side of a vehicle

He eyed me without interest. "Do you know what this is?" he said, pointing to his car.

"That would be a police car."

"Right." He turned his back and walked away.

I had pulled a tendon under my knee, so I couldn't ride my bicycle for a couple of months. Now I had a problem, because the other options were unappealing. Subway service was unreliable, and on a crowded train, odious people breathed on me, making me wonder about drug-resistant tubercle bacilli. Taxicabs were driven by crazed immigrants who were clueless about geographic fundamentals. Buses stopped every two blocks, causing them to advance slower than walking pace in midtown. So, I might as well walk, but if I did so, I would have to deal with street people. Initial feelings of concern and sympathy tended to be eroded fairly quickly by their aggressive attitude. A typical dialogue would unfold like this:

Street person (with a facial expression indicating severe pain and deprivation): "Spare change?"

Me: "No, sorry."

Street person (with sarcasm): "God bless you."

Me: "Hey, don't talk to me about God!"

Street person: "Fuck you, asshole!"

But, my friends were still here, and the West Village was a congenial environment, because it was convenient, and nobody was normal. Gay male couples could hug each other on the sidewalk. Drag queens could wander in to The Jefferson Market to buy groceries. I could dress in old clothes and plastic sandals, looking like a bum. No one cared, and their indifference was a pleasure. I could be a misfit, and it didn't matter at all.

Talking Dogs

In October, I attended the annual writers-editors party hosted by Science Fiction Writers of America. A stranger saw my name tag and exclaimed, "You're Charles Platt!"

"I might be," I said cautiously. "Or I might have just stolen the tag. Who are you?"

He identified himself as James Morrow, a name that I had seen on a book cover, although I didn't think I had read the book. That made me feel more secure, because if I hadn't read it, I would not have written a negative review of it, and James would not be angry with me.

"I have been dealing with an advertising agency," James said, unaware of my thoughts. "You might be interested to know that they have made one of your books compulsory reading for their employees."

One of my books? "Which one?" I asked.

"I can't remember the title," he said. "But it's the one which contains the talking dogs."

That was funny. "You may find this hard to believe," I told him, "But actually I have two books in print right now which contain talking dogs."

Indeed, I had written a nonfiction book about future technology, in which I speculated on far-fetched concepts such as enabling dogs to talk by modifying the larynx. But I had also written my humorous novel *Free Zone*, in which one of the characters was a talking dog.

The nonfiction book was probably the one that the ad agency had been interested in. But, you never know.

Everyday life on the streets of New York. Los Angeles had not been like this. At least, not back then.

Left to right: Robert Heinlein, James Beard, and St. Thomas Aquinas. Christina Whited was on good terms with all three.

Channeling Bob, Jim, and Tom

One evening, as I left my office at 594 Broadway, I found myself sharing the elevator with Christina Whited, the tenant who channeled spirits of the dead. She had just received some publicity in *New York* magazine, because she claimed to be channeling the spirit of James Beard, the legendary chef, who had been giving her some exciting new recipes. When James Beard's literary agent was asked to comment, he said that if Christina felt tempted to put James's new recipes in a book, he would be expecting his usual ten percent.

Christina was a slim blonde woman who dressed fashionably, although I got the sense that she might be having trouble paying her office rent each month. An idea occurred to me: Could she channel the ghost of Robert A. Heinlein?

"Get me Robert's birth date," she said, "and I'll see if I can find him."

I liked the way she was automatically on first-name terms. I wondered if she called James Beard "James." Also, the magazine feature had quoted her as saying that she often talked to St. Thomas Aquinas, in which case I wondered if she addressed him as "Tom."

Still, I was not wanting to make fun of Christina. I had a serious motive. I had been annoyed that Heinlein's wife, Virginia, prevented me from interviewing him for my *Dream Makers* books. He was now dead, but she was still alive, so I wondered if I could bypass her with a direct line of communication into the spirit realm. Of course, I didn't really believe that Christina could do this, but on the other hand, I didn't disbelieve it. Everything in my perception of the world is believable until disproven. Christina charged $75 per hour for her services, and I decided that I was willing to pay it if there was even a fractional chance of getting through to "Robert."

I obtained his birth date and passed it to her, and the next time I saw her, she said that he had a "do not disturb" status for a while, because he hadn't been dead for very long and needed to finish processing the accumulated memories from his life. However, if I could put together a list of questions, she would probably be able to do a seance in a month or so.

Well, all right! I was especially interested in knowing how Heinlein felt about Charles Manson claiming to have built his cult using the novel *Stranger in a Strange Land* as a do-it-yourself manual. I felt sure that other people would have their own questions, too, so I sent out a few letters inviting suggestions.

Among the replies was a short letter from Forrest Ackerman, which he wanted me to read to Heinlein via Christina. "You left life without clearing the slate with me," Ackerman wrote, "without reconciling our differences, without extending apologies for the affair of the kidnapped Hugo, the Mexican magazine suspicion, and your Denvention speech imbroglios numbers one and two."

I didn't know anything about any of this, but maybe Christina could come up with some answers.

Eventually, she told me that Robert was up and running, and she agreed to do the session, although she was moving out of her office because of financial difficulties, so we would have to get together at my apartment. She turned up on time, well-dressed and vivacious as always, and sat at a table where I had set up a tape recorder. I sat opposite her while a third chair remained empty, although she assured me that Robert was now sitting in it. "He was waiting for me outside the building when I arrived," she said.

At no time during the next hour did she go into the mystic fol-

Page 219

de-rol traditionally associated with psychics, and she spoke in her normal voice. She seemed to have no doubt whatsoever that Heinlein was there, and felt no need to dramatize it.

Unfortunately, her sincerity was her undoing. If she had been a fake, she would have done some homework—but she was so confident of her powers, she hadn't bothered. Consequently her responses showed total ignorance of the man whose spirit was supposedly talking to her. When I asked her what "the affair of the kidnapped Hugo" might mean, she said, "I think he's telling me it may refer to a rare edition of a Victor Hugo book."

So, nothing to do with a Hugo Award? So much for my $75! Maybe her James Beard recipes would be a bit more authentic, but I had my doubts.

Too Juvenile

I finally finished writing *The Silicon Man* and submitted it to Betsy Mitchell, who was editing for Bantam Spectra Special Editions, probably the most prestigious imprint for a "serious" paperback-original science-fiction novel.

Meanwhile, I was still waiting for a response regarding my Warhammer book. My editor was taking longer to read it than I had taken to write it, so I asked my British literary agent, the indefatigable Christopher Priest, to give him a nudge. The word came back quite quickly:

"He doesn't much like your book and he doesn't know what to do about it."

So it was that after writing thirty-five books during a period of twenty years, and selling all of them, my comeuppance had finally come up. And the opus that turned out to be my nemesis was, of all things, a Warhammer novel.

When pressed for an explanation, David Pringle said it was "too juvenile." But—but—surely, it was supposed to be juvenile! The entire Warhammer universe was juvenile. Trolls, wizards, fearless warriors—how could it not be juvenile?

Christopher was in no mood to put up with their rejection. He took a hard line. They had approved my outline of the novel, and I had followed it precisely, so I should get paid.

Within a couple of weeks, he seemed to change his mind. I never learned the details, but I suspect the response from Warhammer was something along the lines, "Pay you? Ha ha ha. Sue us."

This was the down side of dealing with a company that had a lot of money. They could pay writers a lot, but they could choose to pay nothing at all, with the confidence that their lawyers on retainer would protect them from upstarts such as myself.

Maybe that was why no one had ever tried to sue them for plagiarism.

In the end I received 1,000 of the 10,000 pounds that had motivated me through so many dark, desperate hours studying maps, monsters, and other half-baked bullshit. Of course, it was rough justice: Lured by a lump of easy money, I attempted to betray my most strongly held, widely self-publicized principles regarding fantasy literature—and failed!

1990

Undersold

Betsy Mitchell accepted *The Silicon Man* for publication under the Spectra Special Editions imprint. That was the good news. After decades of equivocation, I had finally written an ambitious novel and sold it right away. I had great respect for Lou Aronica, the publisher, and felt that it was the right home for my book. They could publish it within a year—but they were only willing to pay $6,500.

I thought about this. "How would you feel," I asked Betsy, "if you let the manuscript sit on your desk for a couple of weeks?"

"If you want to shop it around, that's fine by me," she said. Which was very nice of her, as she certainly didn't have to.

I created another copy and delivered it to Susan Allison at Ace Books. She read it quickly, and was willing to buy it. "I can pay you an extra $500," she said, "and I think I'll be able to publish it better than Bantam. But I have a lot of inventory. I won't be able to publish it for two years."

Two years! I wasn't willing to wait that long, so I went back to Bantam and accepted their offer.

In retrospect, I probably under-sold my own book. Probably I should have tried it on some general-fiction lists initially, at hardcover houses. But offering the book to other publishers would have consumed even more time, and as I approached the age of 45, I didn't feel that I had time to spare.

Documenting Weight Watchers

I received a call from my old computer mentor, Hal Pollenz. Weight Watchers International was planning to open retail stores, and somehow they had found Hal. He would be setting up an ambitious system to handle checkout and inventory, transmitting daily reports via modem to company headquarters—a visionary concept in

1990. He would be assisted by four programmers at Weight Watchers headquarters in Kansas City, and wondered if I had time to join them there. "I need you to write the documentation," he said.

Well, that was nice of him. I wasn't planning to teach at The New School during the summer, so I accepted his offer.

Hal told me he would be in touch again when the schedule was definite. I thanked him, never imagining the consequences.

Killer Keyboards

On my forty-fifth birthday, I adopted a philosophical attitude. The Warhammer book had been a fiasco, but that was all over, and best forgotten. Payment for *The Silicon Man* had been disappointing, but, it was going to be published. My life could have been a lot worse.

Within a few weeks it *was* a lot worse, as my brain and body suddenly experienced failure modes that I had never known before.

The issues began when I received phone calls from a female friend who described odd tingling pains in her wrists. I was fond of her and felt an obligation to listen, but as she went into relentless, excruciating detail, I found myself feeling wanting to hang up the phone. I have always felt that if I listen to people telling me about health conditions, I am more likely to acquire those conditions myself—which sounds like a foolish superstition, except that I don't perceive a strict separation between mind and body. At least, not between my mind and my body.

My friend was suffering repetitive strain injury, commonly known by its acronym, RSI. This was a hot news story in 1990, because a lot of journalists were happy to promote the concept that RSI was caused by that dangerous "new" device, the computer keyboard. Typewriters had been around for more than a century, and computers for more than a decade, so why should RSI suddenly become a consequence of people typing on keyboards? It didn't make sense, but a good scare story never needs to make sense.

Within a few days, I started to experience pain in my wrists. I ignored it, because I refused to believe it. I continued my usual regimen of typing 5,000 words per day, more or less, which turned out to be a very bad decision. Within ten days, merely applying light pressure to the keyboard with one finger created pain around the tendons under my wrist. I still didn't believe that this could be happening, because I didn't see how or why it could be happening, yet now I had to accept that it was happening.

I went to my regular MD, who explained that muscles in the forearm pull tendons that pass through the carpal sheath inside the wrist on their way to the fingers. My tendons were hurting because they were inflamed, although he couldn't understand why. I had been typing on a computer for ten years, and using a typewriter for twenty years before that, with never a trace of RSI.

"I think you're doing this to yourself somehow," my MD concluded.

All right, then, I went to see a psychiatrist. She didn't buy the self-destructive theory, because in her experience, people with psychosomatic symptoms tend to disassociate from the affected part of the body, and they become fatalistic about their condition. I wasn't fatalistic; I was in a state of panic.

How could I earn a living, if I couldn't use a keyboard? How could I get around town, if my wrists hurt when I gripped the handlebars of my bicycle? I even had trouble on a bus or the subway, because my wrists hurt if I tried to steady myself. I couldn't open a bottle of orange juice, brush my teeth, or wipe my ass without hurting my wrists.

I went to see a physical therapist in Brooklyn who normally dealt with sports injuries but was starting to see patients with RSI. The condition was so fashionably new, no one was sure how to treat it, but that didn't stop self-described specialists from making recommendations. Finding "the right keyboard" was important, although no one could agree exactly what that meant. Sitting with a straight back, resting your wrists on a rolled-up towel, pausing every ten minutes—such suggestions were made with an air of authority.

Personally, I needed an explanation: I wanted to know how and why it had happened to me, because this would be a necessary precursor to finding an appropriate treatment and then preventing it from ever happening again.

My PT didn't see it that way. He wasn't very interested in how and why. Etiology wasn't his thing. He just told me to sit with a straight back, rest my wrists on a rolled-up towel, pause every ten minutes, do some exercises, use wrist splints, and my wrists would get better.

They didn't get better.

I tried typing with my knuckles, but even that caused some discomfort. I tried handwriting—holding a pen in my fist, so that my fingers would not stress the tendons—but it was horribly slow, and after I paid someone to type it for me, I wanted to make edits, and

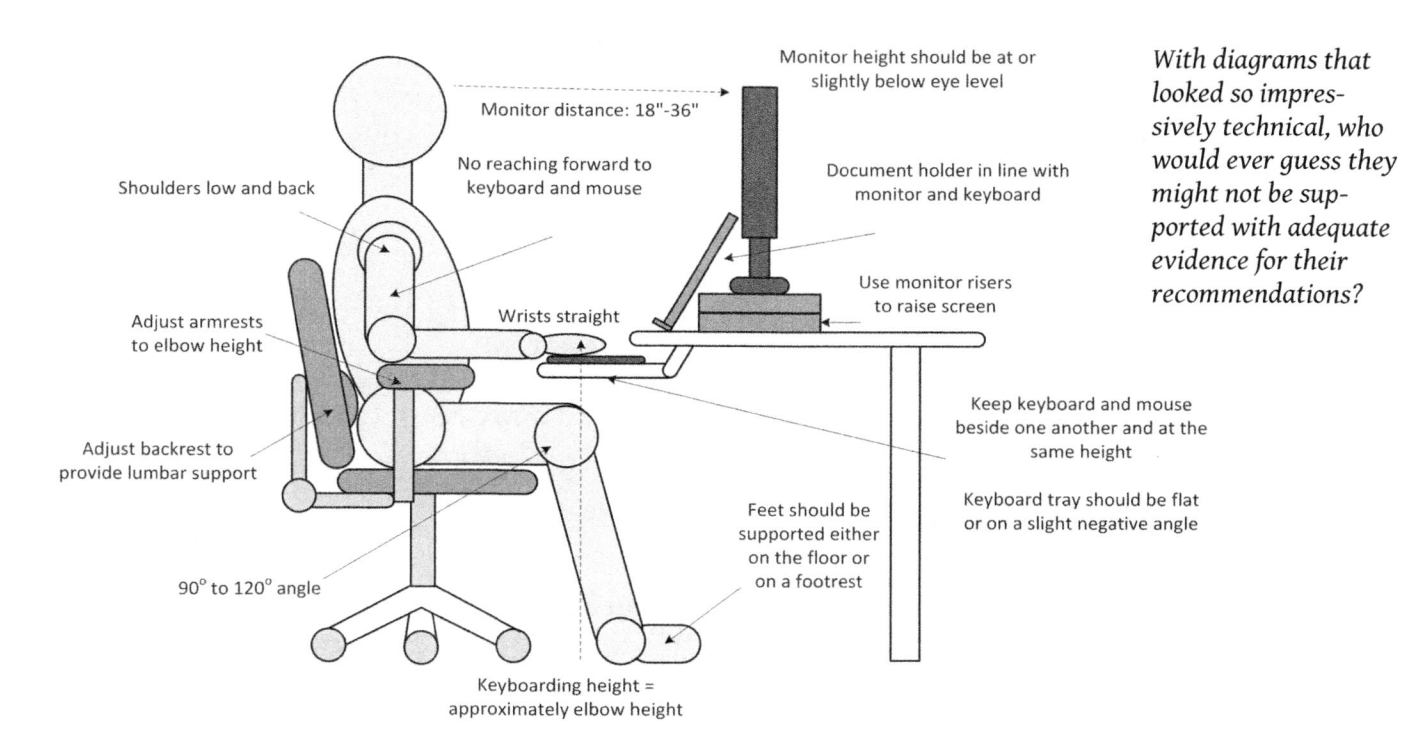

Diagram of ergonomic workstation setup with labels:
- Shoulders low and back
- Monitor distance: 18"-36"
- No reaching forward to keyboard and mouse
- Monitor height should be at or slightly below eye level
- Document holder in line with monitor and keyboard
- Adjust armrests to elbow height
- Wrists straight
- Use monitor risers to raise screen
- Adjust backrest to provide lumbar support
- Keep keyboard and mouse beside one another and at the same height
- Keyboard tray should be flat or on a slight negative angle
- 90° to 120° angle
- Feet should be supported either on the floor or on a footrest
- Keyboarding height = approximately elbow height

With diagrams that looked so impressively technical, who would ever guess they might not be supported with adequate evidence for their recommendations?

couldn't. I tried voice recognition software, but it was in its infancy in 1990, and was hopelessly inaccurate.

For several days I lay around in a state of despair. My whole life had been based around expressing myself in text. I felt like an athlete who could no longer walk. Finally I came up with an idea: If I couldn't do any work, maybe I could find a new girlfriend.

Helpful Advice

I remembered a woman named Sharon who had been involved with my friend Richard (the one who went to St. Vincent's emergency room after consuming a bit too much of Sally's crystal meth). She was unusually smart, was a playwright and TV writer, and had a lovely smile. Richard had broken up with her a couple of years ago, and I wondered where she was.

I knew where she worked, and by using some trickery, I managed to get her contact information. A couple of days later we were talking on the phone, and after we swapped news about our lives, I asked her if she would like to get together. She was a little surprised, but cautiously receptive.

Within days, we were experiencing a powerful chemistry. My wrists were still unusable, and I would experience moments of sudden anger and despair about being unable to do the simplest things, but Sharon had a very rational, reassuring attitude. Her father was a surgeon, and she grew up with the assumption that any medical condition will probably get better, one way or another. She told me I should just take it easy while we enjoyed each other's company.

Eventually I met her father. He was a Korean immigrant with a very down-to-earth attitude. "So your wrists hurt when you use them," he said.

"Yes, they do," I said.

"So—" He paused. "Don't use them!" He barked with laughter and walked out to the kitchen to make himself a cup of tea.

This advice actually turned out to be the best I received, although it wasn't very welcome at the time.

Nightmare in Missouri

The Weight Watchers project that Hal had mentioned took a bit longer to get rolling than he had expected, but he called to tell me that the team would be convening two weeks hence. Hotels had been booked, and we were good to go.

That was nice, except that I still couldn't use a keyboard. I had postponed telling Hal, because I clung to the hope that my wrists would—somehow—get better. They weren't getting better, so I had to confess to him now about my miserable condition.

"Talk to Neil," he said.

Neil was the project manager. I think he was ex-Marine; he sounded that way when he came on the line. I have always tried to avoid characters like Neil, because they didn't have a very tolerant attitude toward undisciplined nonconformists such as myself.

"Can you dictate text to a typist?" Neil asked.

"I—suppose so," I said. "But I'm sure you don't want the expense—"

"We'll hire a typist." And that was that.

Or was it? Somehow—without knowing why—I felt a strange premonition of disaster. I had never tried dictating text to a typist. It ought to be okay, but, would it? The idea made me anxious, and then I started to wonder if my anxiety would itself be a problem, preventing me from functioning as a productive team member in a group which Neil would be supervising in the manner of a drill sergeant.

All I really wanted was to stay in New York with my new girlfriend, but here was another issue: She had pre-existing plans of her own to go on vacation for ten days in Spain. This also made me anxious, although I didn't know why. Maybe I felt dependent because my bad wrists seemed to be such a liability. Throughout my whole life, being self-sufficient had been essential to me. Being unable to use my hands properly was a nightmarish experience.

I flew out to Kansas City one day before Sharon left on her trip. I stayed overnight in the allocated hotel room, and turned up the next morning at a suite of offices where I would be working with Hal, Neil, four programmers, a manager named Diane from Weight Watchers, and a woman who was going to be my typist.

Neil was a beefy guy with short hair, pretty much the way I had imagined him. "How are you doing?" he asked giving me a penetrating look.

"Fine!" I said, trying to sound like a gung-ho new recruit. In reality I felt like the soldier suffering shell-shock in the movie "Patton," just before blood-and-guts George slaps his face and tells him to shape up.

The programmers were a miscellaneous crowd. One was a young, hardcore Mac enthusiast whom the others regarded with condescending smiles, although he turned out to be the best of the bunch. One was an expert in point-of-sale equipment, and he demonstrated how a computer could use an RS232 connection to open the drawer of a cash register. This was a novelty to the rest of us. We were impressed.

I felt embarrassed by my need for a typist, but when I started to dictate the documentation, the process was much easier than I had expected. In fact, it was no trouble at all. Well, that was a big relief, except that somehow I was still feeling anxious, which didn't make sense, because I didn't know what I was anxious about.

I had never experienced an anxiety attack before. It was a nonspecific feeling of overwhelming dread—the kind of feeling you might experience if, perhaps, you were the only English-speaking person on a ship without lifeboats that had started to sink during a typhoon in the middle of the Pacific Ocean. That kind of feeling.

At the end of my first afternoon, Diane reviewed everything that I had written and handed it back without comment. My coworkers were astonished; they told me that she was never normally satisfied with a first draft of anything. I now had a special exalted status, in their eyes. Wonderful! But it didn't allay my anxiety.

In the evening, in my hotel room, I spoke to Sharon on the phone shortly before she was heading out to the airport. "Can you, er, call me when you get to Spain?" I asked, with a tightness in my voice.

"I can do that." She sounded cheerful and warm. Normally I would have been happy in the knowledge that I would see her again soon enough, and in the meantime would be earning a bunch of money. But my state of mind was far from being normal.

I slept very badly, waking every hour and checking the time. When she did call, as she had promised, I was relieved, yet afterward the anxiety returned. It had acquired a presence like a dark, amorphous thing that wanted to devour me from the inside.

The anxiety seemed powerful enough to make me start screaming for help, although that would be futile, as I sensed that there was nothing anyone could do to help. "Can you—call me tonight, somehow?" I asked, feeling embarrassed to be making such a request.

Sharon said she wasn't sure about using Spanish phones, but she would do her best, using some kind of telephone credit card.

My second day at the office was not easy. I had trouble concentrating, but struggled through it somehow and hurried back to the hotel. Then I sat by the phone—

She called, for which I was grateful, but at this point my sense of identity was disintegrating, and I felt that if I stayed in Kansas City, I really would start screaming. "I may have to go back to New York," I told Sharon. "Can you call me there tomorrow?"

She was surprised, but agreed. So, I threw clothes into my suitcase, hurried out of the hotel, and by midnight I was on an airplane.

When I arrived in my apartment in the middle of the night, the familiarity was a relief. I actually managed to sleep for a while, and when Sharon called—wondering what was happening—I almost felt relaxed. This didn't last long: Within ten minutes after the call, my internal monster was eating me again, as fiercely as before.

I had to speak to the people in Kansas City to explain my absence, and I didn't feel that I could tell them the truth, because I was ashamed. It sounded so self-indulgent and crazy. In desperation, I made up a story: I told them my girlfriend had suffered a car accident in Spain, and I had to go there to take care of her.

"Talk to Neil," Hal said.

Neil was the last person I wanted to talk to, and of course he was in his usual assertive mode. "Let me call the hospital there," he said.

I tried to think of a way to stop him. "The language problem—"

"I speak Spanish," he said.

Well, of course he would, wouldn't he? I was cornered, but I knew if I tried to return to Kansas City, I would self-destruct. "I just have to go!" I said.

I don't remember very much about the ensuing days. I don't know how I filled the time. Sharon called every day, and when she did, I tried to sound normal. I talked to some of my friends—but how could I tell them I was almost incoherent with anxiety, when I still didn't know why?

I became so exhausted from being unable to sleep, I didn't know what I was doing. I stepped off the curb on West 10th Street and was almost run over by a car. In desperation, I went to St. Vincent's Hospital and told them I was afraid of getting hurt. Could they admit me to their psychiatric wing, so that I would be safe?

They suspected me of having suicidal impulses, but I emphasized that this was not the case. Eventually they believed me—and lost interest. A doctor gave me a prescription for Ativan and sent me away.

The Ativan turned out to be my salvation. Beautiful, wonderful benzodiazepine! I could almost think normally with 2mg of Ativan twice a day. I couldn't do much work, but at least the anxiety was assuaged, partially at least.

Finally Sharon returned to New York. Our affair resumed, and my anxiety abated—but it still returned unpredictably. Now that the monster had enjoyed the freedom to run around inside my head and cause mayhem, it seemed reluctant to go back into the hole where it had lurked for most of my life. I was happy when I was with Sharon, but somehow I had lost my lifelong ability to feel confident when I was alone.

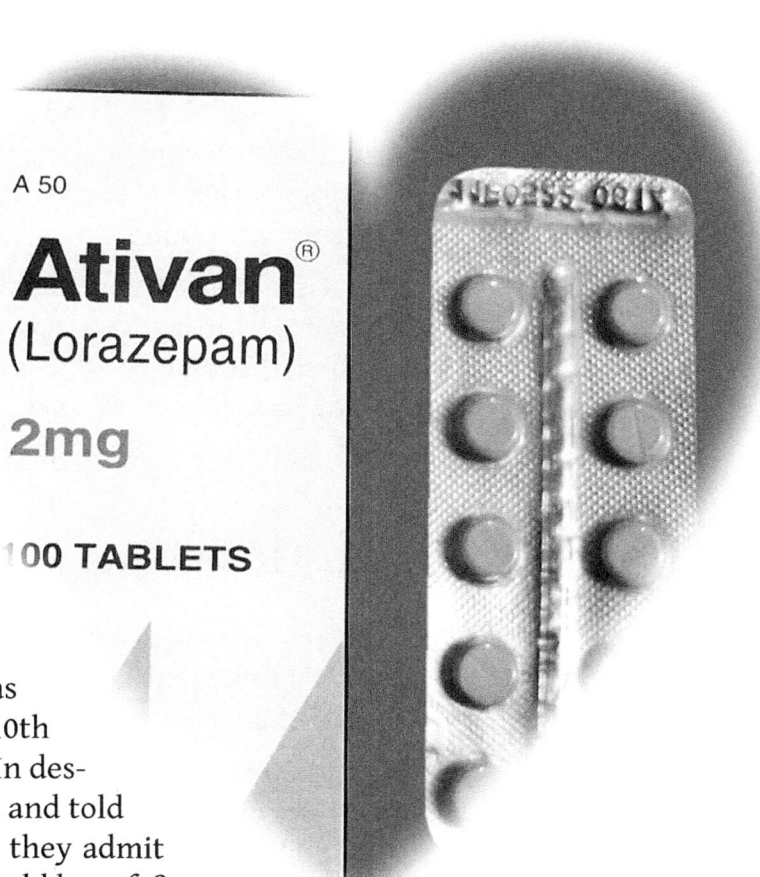

I saw a therapist who had treated patients suffering post-traumatic stress disorder, and she argued that I was recapitulating my experiences as a very young child when my mother suffered migraines and would disappear into her bedroom for days at a time. At a certain age, the infant has not yet developed a separate sense of identity. He experiences the world *through* his mother at that age, so when she disappears he feels that he ceases to exist.

This was a very good description of the way I felt when my sense of identity seemed to be disintegrating. Unfortunately, knowing why something is happening doesn't necessarily mean you can stop it from happening.

This problem continued, intermittently, for another two years. Eventually it sabotaged my relationship—but when the relationship ended, the anxiety attacks ended, for reasons that remain unknown. They have never returned, and I don't know why.

I still keep a bottle of Ativan around, just in case.

No Theorizing

As for my wrist problems, they diminished over a period of months when I forced myself to do almost nothing using my hands. Sharon's father had been right about that.

My physical therapist now regarded himself as an expert on RSI, and since I had recovered my ability to use a keyboard, I asked if he would like to collaborate on a book. He liked that idea, so we entered into a formal agreement.

Now came the tricky part. As a doctor, he took a dominant role, telling patients what to do—but I had transitioned from being a patient to being a journalist, and my job now was to get him to provide information, which I would want to check for factual accuracy.

Imagine my surprise when he couldn't answer my questions properly, especially the "how and why" issue. I had assumed that the phenomenon would have been properly studied by this time, with people using keyboards under various properly controlled conditions. But, so far as I could tell, such studies had never been attempted. All the treatment recommendations were still based on suppositions and anecdotal case histories.

I felt that in my case, the power of suggestion had to be relevant, as the pains had begun immediately after my friend described hers. In my physical therapist's mechanistic view of the world, this idea was a non-starter. Tendons became inflamed because someone did something to stress them, and if a friend had described her condition, that was totally irrelevant.

But was it? Anxiety could cause muscle spasms, and if the muscles in the wrists constricted the carpal sheath while the tendons continued sliding inside the sheath, surely this could create friction, which could cause inflammation. Swelling would occur, and then there would be more friction, creating a vicious circle.

My PT collaborator became annoyed. He wasn't interested in my bullshit theories. But then he undermined his own mechanistic model when he said he had been approached by *Newsday*, a newspaper that had offices in New York City and Long Island. The workstations in the two offices were identical. Everything was identical, yet in News Room 1, numerous people had developed repetitive strain injury, while in News Room 2 there were no cases at all.

Here was a real-life experiment under controlled conditions, and it confirmed my suspicions. Maybe one nervous person in News Room 1 had learned about repetitive strain injury from a friend, or by seeing a report. She became anxious and developed the condition. Her coworkers saw it, and they became anxious, too. The condition then spread like a contagion.

At this point my physical therapist lost patience with me. RSI was caused by bad keyboards and sitting positions, and could be alleviated by better keyboards and sitting positions. End of story!

I resolved to write a portion of the book describing RSI, and leave the "why" questions till later. I passed the portion and outline to my literary agent—and the next day, when he had read my graphic description of wrist pains, he reported that he started to develop wrist pains, too. "I feel as if your book has trained my wrists to feel this way," he said.

How much more evidence did I need? And now I had a new concern: If RSI really could be induced by muscle spasms caused by anxiety, my book could communicate it. I had hoped to write something that would help people, not make them sick, so I told my physical therapist that I was opting out, and our collaboration was over.

Later I talked to Stanley Hoppenfeld, an orthopedic surgeon who had authored seven highly regarded text books on musculoskeletal disorders. He was a world expert in the field, yet he couldn't come up with a theory explaining how small, low-impact movements created tendonitis. From his point of view, it didn't matter: He didn't deal with theories. He wasn't any more interested in etiology than my PT had been. As a surgeon, he knew that opening the carpal sheath to reduce pressure on the tendons would usually alleviate RSI. End of story.

Maybe my theories really were bullshit. All I know is, if someone starts to describe wrist pains to you in graphic detail, you may consider changing the subject.

Top: The original Bantam paperback. Bottom: The hardcover that I produced for myself.

Farewell to Science Fiction

Gollancz issued a contract for British rights to *The Silicon Man*, and I received an initial payment. Malcolm Edwards seemed to like the book—but two months later, he confounded my expectations by deciding not to publish it. Sales figures of other "midlist" titles had been so disappointing, he believed he would lose less money if he allowed me to keep my initial advance while he abandoned the project.

He sent me a letter in which he explained this. At the end, he wrote, "I have not enjoyed writing this letter."

Well! I had not enjoyed *reading* this letter.

When the book eventually appeared in the United States, it received a lovely review from Gerald Jonas in *The New York Times*, suggesting that it was one of the three best science-fiction books of the year. But by then, the review was of little use. Bantam Spectra hadn't printed enough copies, so it was out of print within four weeks.

I suggested to my editor that she might like to print some more, but she didn't want to do that. Other books were already in the pipeline, seeking their own shelf space in bookstores. In any case, my book was of that vanishing species, an individual, standalone novel. It wasn't part of a series, and I wouldn't be writing more "in the same universe."

I was annoyed with Bantam for allowing it to go out of print, so I asked them to surrender the hardcover rights for free, so that I could print my own edition. Perhaps because they felt some embarrassment over what had happened, they kindly agreed, and I paid $50 to reuse the very nice cover art that they had commissioned.

I did the typesetting and the cover design for the novel myself. Phil Gurlik put his Tafford Publishing imprint on the hardcover, but I never dared to ask him how many copies he sold.

In years that followed, Wired Books brought out an edition, and then Stairway Press, and currently another American edition is forthcoming. My book was nominated for a Campbell Award, and (I seem to remember) a Libertarian Futurist Award, although it didn't win either of them. A Japanese edition seemed to sell relatively well, but there was never a British edition.

Now let's look at the numbers. I received $6,500 from Bantam for their magically disappearing edition, and around $2,500 for the Japanese edition, and (I think) 500 pounds sterling for the nonappearing Gollancz edition. Obviously, I could not support myself by writing books of this type.

Recently I re-read *The Silicon Man*, and it was more ambitious than I remembered. The characters were drawn from real people, the scenery was vivid, and three of the key figures in the story were women, with complex motivations—quite unusual in science fiction at that time. The ideas were solid, the development was uncompromising, and the action consistently went beyond what a reader might expect. The book became a bit slow in the middle, but overall it seemed to do the things that a reasonably intelligent science-fiction novel should do.

Also, it was predictive. Two decades after it was published, I visited the basement laboratory in San Francisco of my friend Todd Huffman, who was leading research into digitizing the structure of a mouse brain by slicing it with a diamond microtome. Todd's company, 3Scan, was not trying to replicate brain function, but in the long term, that would be the implication of his work. Looking at his lab equipment was a very strange experience. "I predicted this," I thought to myself.

But so what? Malcolm Edwards seemed to feel that the midlist was never coming back, and I suspected that he was right. David Hartwell concluded that serious science fiction written by people who were not well known was almost impossible to sell, and I thought he was right, too.

I once asked Greg Bear about the fate of his novel *Blood Music*, which I greatly admired. In fact, it had been a significant influence on me while I was writing *The Silicon Man*. When I asked how Greg dealt with the disappointment when *Blood Music* didn't seem to stick in anyone's memory, he just gave me an odd look and said that he did what a writer does: He wrote more

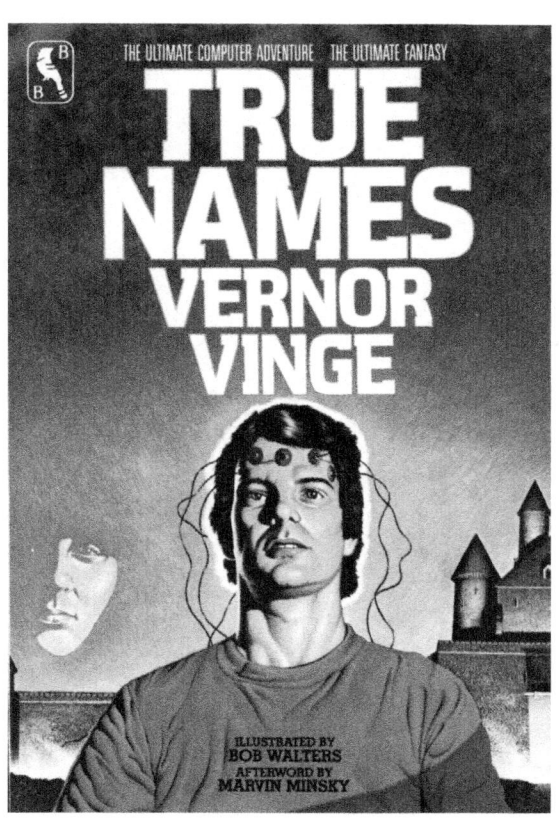

Two brilliant books which I found very influential, creating false hope that there was still an audience for individual near-future novels that were not part of series.

novels. He also made them longer, or conceived them as series—and he set them farther in the future, because he could see where the market was heading. I once heard him at an SFWA meeting giving a little lecture to his fellow writers along the lines, "Pay attention to what's happening in the market, or you may end up being unpublishable."

Vernor Vinge once wrote a wonderful novel titled *True Names*, which I admired as being savvy and visionary. Vernor explored the concept of "cyberspace" with great authority, before *Neuromancer*. The book was nominated for a Hugo Award and a Nebula Award—but didn't win, and didn't stay in print over the long term. If Vernor couldn't make a book like that work, why should I think that I could? He ended up changing his whole approach, much like Greg Bear. Instead of continuing to write individual novels of average length, he wrote a series of long interconnected novels set in the far future. They did well for him.

I wasn't sure that I could emulate either Vernor Vinge or Greg Bear, even if I was an equally good writer and had equally good ideas (which I probably didn't). Trying it would be a big gamble, and would require a commitment lasting for years, which I was not willing to make, at the age of 45. And so, having finally proved that I could write science fiction, and having been published under a good imprint, and having received a review in *The New York Times* that was enviable—I stopped.

It didn't matter. The dotcom revolution spawned *Wired* magazine, and as soon as I saw it, I knew immediately that it was where I should be. My first feature article in *Wired* was more than 10,000 words in length, and some smaller features were postponed to make room. Eventually I became one of their three senior writers. I was encouraged to write almost any of the ideas that I wanted to write, and I used a style that came naturally to me, and I was well paid.

Wired was a source of great joy—but my association with the magazine did not begin until 1993.

This volume of my reminiscences ends in 1990.

Are They Still There?

When I look back at the 1980s, I feel fortunate that almost all of my work was published, one way or another, and I met so many writers and editors who became friends. Alas, many have died now, but the writers treated me as an equal, and were generous with their time and ideas, while the editors were kind to me, often accepting books that they must have known would not sell a lot of copies.

Without being too pretentious about it, I think my fellow travelers in science fiction shared a common dream. We believed in the importance of thinking beyond everyday reality and using stories and novels to explore those possibilities. This was seldom talked about, because we didn't need to talk about it. We shared it as an implicit subtext during social events where people might express their nonconformity by behaving badly, but were always forgiven.

Within our small community, everyone loved books, everyone cared about imaginative fiction, and we felt a bond which people outside the field might not understand. As Brian Aldiss once said to me, "If you found yourself in some far-flung location, like Tokyo or Shanghai, all you'd have to do would be to find the nearest science-fiction fan. They'd take care of you."

He was right—so long as those hardcore fans existed.

I wonder if they still do.

—Charles Platt, Northern Arizona, October, 2021.

Printed in Great Britain
by Amazon